HD
6955
I85
2010

D1543893

The Good Work Guide

In memory of my father,
Roger William Isles.

The Good Work Guide

How to Make Organizations Fairer and More Effective

NICK ISLES

LIBRARY
NSCC, KINGSTEC CAMPUS
238 BELCHER ST.
KENTVILLE, NS B4N 0A6 CANADA

publishing for a sustainable future

London • Washington, DC

First published in 2010 by Earthscan

Copyright © Nick Isles, 2010

The moral right of the author has been asserted.

All rights reserved. No part of this publication may be reproduced, stored in a retrieval system, or transmitted, in any form or by any means, electronic, mechanical, photocopying, recording or otherwise, except as expressly permitted by law, without the prior, written permission of the publisher.

Earthscan Ltd, Dunstan House, 14a St Cross Street, London EC1N 8XA, UK
Earthscan LLC, 1616 P Street, NW, Washington, DC 20036, USA
Earthscan publishes in association with the International Institute for Environment and Development

For more information on Earthscan publications, see www.earthscan.co.uk or write to earthinfo@earthscan.co.uk

ISBN: 978–1-84407–557–7 hardback

Typeset by Saxon Graphics Ltd, Derby
Cover design by Clifford Hayes

A catalogue record for this book is available from the British Library

Library of Congress Cataloging-in-Publication Data

Isles, Nick.
    The good work guide : how to make organizations fairer and more effective / Nick Isles.
        p. cm.
    Includes bibliographical references and index.
    ISBN 978-1-84407-557-7 (hardback)
    1. Quality of work life. 2. Work environment. 3. Personnel management. 4. Organizational effectiveness.
I. Title.
    HD6955.

At Earthscan we strive to minimize our environmental impacts and carbon footprint through reducing waste, recycling and offsetting our CO_2 emissions, including those created through publication of this book. For more details of our environmental policy, see www.earthscan.co.uk.

Printed and bound in the UK by TJ International, an ISO 14001 accredited company. The paper used is FSC certified and the inks are vegetable based.

FSC
Mixed Sources
Product group from well-managed
forests and other controlled sources

Cert no. SGS-COC-2482
www.fsc.org
© 1996 Forest Stewardship Council

Contents

List of Figures, Tables and Boxes

Figures

Tables

Boxes

List of Acronyms and Abbreviations

BTPS	British Telecommunications Pension Scheme
CDP	crew development programme
CEO	chief executive officer
CO_2	carbon dioxide
CR	corporate responsibility
CSOP	company share option plan
CSR	corporate social responsibility
CTQ	critical to quality
DPO	defect per opportunity
EAP	employee assistance programme
EMI	enterprise management incentive
EOA	Employee Ownership Association
EOI	Employee Ownership Index
EU	European Union
FDI	foreign direct investment
FMCG	fast-moving consumer goods
GDP	gross domestic product
GE	General Electric
GVA	gross value added
HMRC	Her Majesty's Revenue and Customs
HPWS	high-performance work system
HR	human resources
HRM	human resource management
ICT	information and communication technology
IES	Institute for Employment Studies

ILO	International Labour Organization
IT	information technology
IWP	Institute of Work Psychology
LBS	London School of Business
MBA	master of business administration
MIT	Massachusetts Institute of Technology
NESTA	National Endowment for Science, Technology and the Arts
NVQ	national vocational qualification
OCL	observation check list
OECD	Organisation for Economic Co-operation and Development
OED	*Oxford English Dictionary*
ONS	Office for National Statistics
PCS	Public and Commercial Services Union
PE	private equity
PPP	purchasing power parity
PRP	performance-related pay
PwC	Price Waterhouse Coopers
ROI	return on investment
SIP	share incentive plan
TUC	Trades Union Congress
UNICEF	United Nations Children's Fund
WERS	Workplace Employment Relations Survey

Acknowledgements

This book could not have been written without the hard work and dedication of many of my former colleagues at The Work Foundation. In particular the work of Will Hutton, David Coats, Steve Overell, Alexandra Jones, Steve Bevan and Ian Brinkley has been heavily drawn upon throughout the book. Other former Work Foundation colleagues whose work I have liberally used and probably abused include Andy Westwood, Richard Reeves, John Knell, Natalie Turner, Aine O'Keeffe and Laura Williams. Maggie Smith and Harriet Langton are also owed a debt of gratitude for their support.

I also want to thank Dr Matt Davies for his invaluable help and insights when constructing the chapter on leadership. My wife Katty has offered me great support and had to put up with me during the writing of this book for which I am deeply grateful. As have my four daughters Emma, Laura, Carlotta and Rosa. Finally a big thank you to my editor Michael Fell and the team at Earthscan who have been both patient and professional in their support and guidance. It goes without saying that all errors and omissions are entirely mine.

Foreword

John Philpott, chief economic advisor, Chartered Institute of Personnel and Development

The first three entries in the *Oxford English Dictionary* definition of the word 'good' state its meaning as: '1 to be desired or approved of; 2 having the required qualities, of a high standard; 3 morally right, virtuous'. On this definition, Nick Isles has written a good book on a good and critically important subject affecting us all.

Books on work usually fall into one of a number of categories. Some are historical accounts of how work has changed over time. Others are, at one extreme, economic, sociological or management-based studies of the determinants and organization of work or, at the other, reflections on the everyday joys or horrors of work. However, the 'goodness' of work is seldom the starting point. There is universal agreement that lack of work is a bad thing. But work itself – leastways paid employment – is most often seen as primarily a means to an end rather than inherently good. Heaven, after all, is the realm of eternal rest – Hell's the place of unending toil.

Good work is thus a counter-cultural notion – which makes this book so important, especially for a post-credit crunch era in which societies are looking for ways to combine the dynamic power of capitalism with economic, human and environmental sustainability.

In the emerging era, quality of working life has to be good if organizations – private, public or not-for-profit – are to be fully successful. If not, employers find it difficult to secure the engagement and commitment they need from those they employ in order to 'go the extra mile' at work. It is of course arguable that the need of business to foster shared interest with employees is no more than a cosmetic gloss on the fundamental power inequality that always exists within capitalism. Indeed, some critical depictions of objectively good workplaces –

such as those in lists of 'best companies to work for' – portray these as little more than a con designed to seduce employees into committing their discretionary effort to the business. Yet even this view has to acknowledge that organizations are having to promise good work on one or more dimensions in order to persuade employees to commit and engage their energies.

As a result, even in the midst of the current global macroeconomic crisis, the underlying forces of structural change remain conducive to better quality work and, as Nick Isles shows in this book, there is plenty of evidence upon which to rest a positive narrative of progress towards good work. However, as Isles also shows, progress is neither smooth nor universal across or within industrial sectors, regions and nations.

The operation of simple cost-based business models that treat workers as a disposable commodity remain widespread, even in the richest of developed economies. This explains some less positive developments in working life – notably high levels of work-related stress – and the continued existence of too many poor-quality jobs. Moreover, good work is not only about the material quality of jobs. Workplace relations and trust are just as important, which is why Isles has much to say about the evident lack of fairness at work and widening pay inequalities between top executives and most working people, as well as the values organizations abide by.

With so much to be done to promote and foster good work, Isles's book is thus a practical call to arms – showing the road that needs to be travelled and illuminating the path. Having read this excellent book, you will want to join him on the journey.

Introduction

Here, you see, are two kinds of work – one good, the other bad; one not far removed from a blessing, a lightening of life; the other a mere curse, a burden to life. What is the difference between them, then? This one has hope in it, the other has not ... hope of rest, hope of product, hope of pleasure in the work itself ... pleasure enough for all of us to be conscious of it while we are at work; not a mere habit, the loss of which we shall feel as a fidgety man feels the loss of the bit of string he fidgets with.

William Morris, *Useful Work versus Useless Toil*[1]

This is a book about work. More specifically it is about an idea – good work. There are many thousands of books on work and many more on aspects of work such as management and leadership, so why another? The impetus to write the book comes from three sources. First, the world has been living through the deepest recession since the 1930s and such exogenous shocks create bow-waves of change. The established order is thrown into disarray. The intellectual landscape is profoundly disrupted. The dominant philosophy comes under renewed attack. Opportunities present themselves for change. And this change can be good, bad or distinctly indifferent depending on a range of factors. *The Good Work Guide* is, in part, my modest contribution to that debate. Second, it is my profound belief, after studying aspects of the economy for the past 20 years, that the economies of the developed world are going through such a profound change that our societies are only now beginning to wake up to what that change means for our lives. Such change is affecting the world of work as much as in any other sphere of life. Good work is a way of responding to that economic change in a way that will benefit most protagonists. Third, there is a view of human relationships, which is based on enlightenment principles,[2] that affects the workplace as much as any other sphere of human activity. Too often, people cross the thresholds of work and the normal rules of living, behaviour and civility can become suspended. This is not, I believe, due to any fundamental cause connected to work per se, but more to do with the fact that people's thinking about work is too often misaligned with other aspects of their lives.

Good work is a response to those drivers and an answer. Good work is a way of looking at work as a fully human activity. Good work does not suppose that normal rules need to be suspended whatever the form of ownership of the organization. Good work is a way of looking at work that allows both sides of capitalism – both capital and labour – to chart a mutually beneficial course for their collective endeavour. Good work, in short, allows both efficiency and profitability to lay side-by-side with ideas such as fairness and voice. Having described what good work is, the book goes on to look at how executives and others can ensure that their organizations become good work organizations. It is intended to explain and describe the route to good work as well as argue the case for good work.

So why is good work necessary? Work has always been a source of debate and sometimes a battleground both of ideas and in a more literal sense. Work is a source of power and empowerment and enables people to change both their standing in the world and material situation, or not, as the case may be. Throughout the centuries work has been about blood, sweat and tears.[3]

For, until very recently, work meant one thing – back-breaking physical labour. It was not bounded by time in any particular sense as people worked to the rhythm of the day and the season. Tasks were determined largely by the time of year and most people worked on the land for someone else. The advent of the Industrial Revolution in the late 18th century and early 19th century in England changed everything. Now time mattered and work began to intensify.

The clock ruled the lives of workers and the people who owned or managed workforces had some new measure by which they could understand productivity. Workers were worked harder when at work. Trades unions grew up as a countervailing source of influence and power. At first this was to counter the savage excesses of mill owners and others who went too far in their pursuit of profits by winning rights for workforces to work in slightly different ways. The main victories for the trades unions, throughout the 19th century and the first part of the 20th century, were to do with reducing the amount of time workers could be forced to spend working, down to a standard 40-hour week and in improving health and safety in some of the more dangerous occupations such as mining, heavy industries and manufacturing.[4]

Improvements were made to the way man and machine interlocked and productivity rose steadily until the First World War in both the US and the UK.

Even during these times some entrepreneurs understood the benefits of aspects of good work. Consulting and communicating with the workforce and looking after their well-being as Cadbury did in the mid 19th century benefited the organization as well as the people who worked for it.[5] But however well-meaning, philanthropy is one thing, whereas the systematic introduction of good work and what it means for ways of working is something else.

Arguably, until the last decade of the past century and this century there was no proven business need for good work. There were certainly good arguments from a social and ethical perspective, and I personally believe that there has always been a good business case locked away under a misunderstanding about the ways in which people like to collaborate and share rather than merely compete and maximize returns to themselves.

But the past 20 years has seen the rise of a new, general purpose technology – digitalization – which is changing the ways in which we live, think and interact.[6] Digitalization, along with the increase in global trade flows, has given birth to the knowledge economy, where human knowledge combines with the power of computers to create value. This economy does not observe the old rules of engagement very well. For example, encouraging people to work at their optimum level is a more difficult task now than it was when most work required people to turn up, switch on the machine and work at its pace. Now, *most* value-adding work in many more workplaces is discretionary. The place where people have most control is over what is going on in their heads – yet it is this that most organizations want to drag from them and apply to creating value.

Good work thus argues that to get more from knowledge workers you have to give more in return and understand what it is people require from work. After all, it is a place where they act upon the world in a rather unique way. How many people do you meet, who when asked what they do, reply 'I am a Dad' or 'I am a Mum'? Yet ask them to name the most important facet of their life and they will reply 'being a parent'.

For it is through paid work that we largely define ourselves. It is a source of pride and, for some, legacy. People want to do a good job (with very few exceptions). They want to make their mark upon the world and they generally do that best when they have an environment that allows them more control and ownership of what they do and when they do it. Good work enables, rather than disables, such instincts and behaviours and this is the subject of this book.

So the book begins by explaining in Chapter 1 the reasons for the credit crunch and the following deep recession. In Chapter 2, the rise of the knowledge economy is examined in more detail and good work as a concept is explained whereby efficiency, fairness and representation can combine to create better work for all and more profitability for the owners of the organization. Chapter 3 describes the good work organization and gives examples of good work in practice and the elements from research that indicate what makes for good work. Chapter 4 describes the central concept underpinning this author's view of good work, namely ownership and its different dimensions. Chapter 5 looks at examples of the five dimensions of ownership and how they work in practice. Chapter 6 concentrates on the role of leaders and leadership in delivering good work. And finally, Chapter 7 outlines the 10 steps to good work, a handy concluding guide for any executive who wants to create a good work environment for themselves, their co-workers and their organization.

What should be stressed is that good work is, in many senses, a contingent strategy. If the basic idea that lies at the heart of the organization is wrong, misguided, muddled or out-of-date then even the best good-work environment will be able to do little to help, unless fundamental change to the business's core business is made. If a steel maker is out-competed by steel mills in China, it is likely to close. If a cobbler finds herself unable to compete with equally good shoes imported from Italy, she will find her business withering. If a publican cannot sell enough beer to be profitable, his pub will inevitably close. Context is thus everything.

It is also everything in terms of ideas that prove influential. Ideas may be around for some time before anyone acts upon them and realizes their potential. I believe the context is now right for an exponential increase in good work – both due to the context for the future economy and the context for ideas. It goes without saying that this book has been written during extraordinary times. Despite some early signs of recovery in the second half of 2009 and early 2010, there is much ground to make up. Between 2008 and the second quarter of 2009, the UK economy had already shrunk by more than 5 per cent and the US economy by nearly 4 per cent:[7] the biggest peacetime slump ever recorded. Millions of people have been thrown out of work across the developed economies and many more in the developing world. The near 30-year hegemony of neo-liberal economic orthodoxy reached its apotheosis in 2006. Yet only two years later, it had met its nemesis. By the autumn of 2007, the largely deregulated global financial markets had begun to unravel. Very few predicted the scale of the turmoil. Even fewer predicted the extent of the crash.

For many, the decade of the noughties has proved an enriching one. The rich became super-rich and the merely well-off became rich. The top 0.1 per cent of income earners in the US and the UK have seen their wealth multiply in a quite stratospheric manner. These people earn 4 per cent of all personal earnings in the UK and a quite staggering 6 per cent of personal earnings in the US. In France, the figure is only 2 per cent. The top 1 per cent in the US take 21.2 per cent of all earnings.[8]

So any discussion of good work needs to be mindful of these extraordinary circumstances: circumstances that have shaken the foundations of current economic orthodoxy. And circumstances that have made the establishment of good work in more UK and US organizations harder than need have been the case. And yet, despite the fact that organizations have been debt minimizing as fast as they can and record levels of unemployment have been experienced, some things have been different. Firms have been trying to hoard their more knowledgeable and experienced workers offering short-time working, extended holidays, sabbaticals and career breaks.[9] This is a new phenomenon driven by the growth of the knowledge economy and lessons learnt from previous downturns.

The credit crunch, and the coordinated global recession that has followed, is not unique. There have been other times in history when financial systems have imploded and recessions have followed. The most notable was the Great Depression of 1929–1933. A downturn that the US arguably did not recover from until the 1940s.[10] What is unusual about the downturn that began in 2007 is the extent, depth and global reach of the economic hardship. Never before, not even in the period from 1890 to 1914 and the eve of the First World War (when the world last enjoyed an unbroken period of expanding international trade) has the world been so interdependent, has globalization affected so many economies. Nor should globalization be seen as anything other than a potential force for good. Becoming part of the global trading system is the quickest way for developing economies to develop. But something went badly wrong and not just with one element of the system. The whole system has failed.

To understand the need for good work, it is important to understand the reasons why such a deep and savage recession has happened. It is not the case that the credit crunch came out of a vacuum. It was the result of system thinking that was simply too shallow to understand the changes to the economy wrought by new technology, the rise of affluence and new trading patterns. Neo-liberalism as a way of understanding how economies work created the ideological foundations for the global economic system. It allowed governments to argue for lighter regulation; it enabled some people to enrich themselves quickly; it speeded up the reduction of barriers to trade (not quickly enough it may be argued) and it was given a massive impetus by the political developments that followed the fall of the Berlin Wall in 1989 and the collapse of European Communism. Understanding this story better is the subject of the first chapter.

Notes

1   Morris, W. (1884) *Useful Work versus Useless Toil*, originally a lecture. It is reproduced in full at this website: www.marxists.org/archive/morris/works/1884/useful.htm
2   For a good discussion of the Enlightenment and enlightenment principles see: http://history-world.org/age_of_enlightenment.htm
3   Donkin, R. (2001) *Blood Sweat & Tears*, Texere, London.
4   Foster, W. Z. (1956) *Outline History of the World Trade Union Movement*, International Publishers, New York.
5   www.cadbury.com.au/About-Cadbury/The-Story-of-Cadbury.aspx
6   See for example: Leadbetter, C. (2008) *We-Think*, Profile Books, London.
7   See: www.statistics.gov.uk/cci/nugget.asp?id=192 and www.bea.gov/newsreleases/national/gdp/gdpnewsrelease.htm
8   Peston, R. (2008) *Who Runs Britain?*, Hodder and Stoughton, London, p8.
9   See: www.telegraph.co.uk/finance/financetopics/recession/6005956/Do-you-dare-take-a-sabbatical.html, accessed 11 August 2009, for a typical news piece on labour hoarding.
10 See for example: Rothbard, M. N. (2000) *America's Great Depression*, 5th edn, The Ludwig Von Mises Institute, Auburn.

Chapter 1

A New Capitalism?

The roots of the credit crunch and subsequent deep recession were set down during the birth of the new capitalism in the 1970s. Corporatism had had its day. The idea that economies worked best when managed, or guided, by an activist state – indeed when both sides of industry sat down together and agreed a way forward, creating the so-called 'mixed economy' – was severely criticized by Nobel prizewinning economists such as Milton Friedman of the University of Chicago.[1] Such thinkers argued that the best way to achieve higher trend rates of growth, through encouraging entrepreneurship and investment, was to diminish the power and role of the state and free the market from as many external controls as possible.

On 11 September 1973, President Allende of Chile was overthrown by a military coup led by General Augusto Pinochet. The pogrom that followed against the supporters of Allende has been well documented.[2] Many innocent people were killed, tortured and imprisoned either because they were members of alternative political groups, or because they belonged to trade unions or academic circles the new junta disliked. Some were arrested simply because they had been denounced by people who sought to curry favour in such circumstances from the new authorities.

What is less well known is what Pinochet then did to the Chilean economy. Like-minded economists, many former Chilean students of Friedman at the University of Chicago, were brought in to run the new administration's economic policy. The so-called Chicago Boys privatized state industries, cut public spending and within a year had ensured that 50 per cent of the Chilean working age population were unemployed.[3] This was the beginning of the rise of the private sector over the public as the key economic agent – at least in ideological terms. In the Cold War battle of ideologies this made eminent sense. The free market was a western, American and democratic idea. Statist-driven economic policy was socialist, totalitarian and Russian.

In 1979, Margaret Thatcher came to power in the UK and in 1980 Ronald Reagan was elected as President of the US. Both leaders were fervent believers in the need to move towards a more free market, liberal economic agenda that had at its heart the idea of markets freed from state control. At that time, many markets in commodities, agricultural products, manufacturing and other industries were subject to tariffs, price controls and uncompetitive market environments. Dismantling this paraphernalia of state control would take time. But there was not such a problem with freeing capital. Getting rid of fixed exchange rates and allowing exchange rates to float, as happened in 1979, was the first major step on the journey. By freeing capital, capitalist activity could and would increase. Previously banks had been required to hold a cash reserve – often placed with the Bank of England in the case of the UK. Then when a downturn occurred this cash could be released back into the system to stimulate a quick economic recovery. In 1980, Thatcher symbolically abolished such reserve requirements. By the late 1980s, she had taken away nearly every control and regulation on lending and created a free market in financial services.[4]

Wall Street and the City of London soon became the epicentres of a new form of deal-based and faster-moving capitalism. Despite major recessions in the early 1980s and 1990s, the emergence of casino capitalism, led by a powerful financial services sector, increased the supply chain of smart people flooding into investment banking, commercial law and Wall Street trading houses. A young graduate from an Ivy League university in the US or Oxbridge or another Russell Group university in the UK, could become richer than their wildest dreams before they were 30. Philip Cook and Robert Frank in their book, *The Winner-Take-All Society*, argued that intense competition among able people for top financial service jobs had the effect of costing the rest of the economy by decreasing the pool of talent going into teaching, engineering and other useful occupations. They calculated that an increase in lawyers depressed real gross domestic product (GDP), whereas the same number of graduates going into engineering would increase GDP.[5]

Gordon Gekko, the fictional über trader of the 1987 film, *Wall Street*, was right to state that in this kind of world greed is good. Yet greed is not a rational emotion. Greed distorts perspectives. It leads to perverse risk-taking and it is fundamentally antipathetic to the types of collective action that underpin the best types of endeavour (on which more later). Moreover, it goes against the idea that economic man is above all else rational. And the 1980s offered only an apprenticeship compared with the rewards on offer to people in financial services during the noughties.

It is worth understanding the flaws in the neo-liberal economic argument in more detail. Free market theorists believed, and still do believe, that the mixed economy had got the balance between state and market fundamentally wrong. Markets work but states do not. The problems of inflation, low productivity and low levels of growth were due to the fact that the balance between state and market was wrong. The state should only intervene occasionally to temporarily correct market failures. The free market view is based on a number of assumptions that can be found in the 'first fundamental theorem of welfare economics'. In essence, free market disciples believe that as long as markets are well populated with new entrants and everyone has access to the same information, then unbounded competition will result and this will lead to the most efficient allocation of resources.

The critique of this view is that it treats the free market as a static ideal. Basically, the argument is that markets should work and when they don't, it is a breakdown in the engineering rather than a fundamental design flaw. In reality, as the evidence of the past 200 years shows, markets are a bit like theories of the universe – many and several. Market failure is endemic to markets that thus need to be consistently remodelled and rebalanced. And it is the task of the state (i.e. us) to undertake this work. So in today's knowledge economy (on which more later), innovation is more important to markets' overall terms of success than say it might have been 100 years ago. Innovation is a component of a market economy but its relevant value does not stay static over time.

For a free market model to work several conditions need to be fulfilled. Failure to do so will most likely lead to a market failure. Information must be transparent and equally available to all market participants at roughly the same time. Even with the advent of the internet, is there anyone who really contrasts and compares all the prices of each and every good and service they purchase? If information really were the core element it is argued to be, why do we have brands?

Next, prices in an efficiently working market should reflect all economic costs. There should be no 'externalities' that impose either costs or benefits on others that is not captured by the transaction. Do we, for example, capture the entire costs of producing, shipping and selling any given traded good? Costs such as the pollution from carbon dioxide (CO_2) emissions when the good is transported, for example? In free market theory, people are entirely rational. They are capable of exercising restraint today for gains tomorrow. They can defer gratification. They can weigh up the time and quantity involved to gain the optimum outcome for themselves in each and every case.

However, this belief flies in the face of the evidence. People are irrational and short-sighted. They don't defer gratification or weigh up options. This is why we have phrases such as 'impulse buy'. This is why people rack up credit card debts, fail to save for retirement or don't bother to invest in their education and training. Individuals will accept bias through ignorance, laziness, not having enough time or whatever else gets in the way of calm rational decision making. Governments need to consistently manage the fallout and calibrate the incentives to encourage people to behave more in their longer-term interests.[6]

Moreover people are very good at what is called 'gaming' the system. For example, a typical worker may want to maximize their reward by encouraging the manager (who is less knowledgeable than they are about their work and job) to set easy performance targets in order to be paid more. This is why individual performance-related pay on the whole rarely delivers the performance boost it is designed to do; and it is why average finance sector workers were paid alpha rates of pay. Far from being rational, many people behave instinctively, emotionally and irrationally much of the time.

Whatever the flaws in the thinking, the US and UK moved away from a mixed economy to a neo-liberal free market form of capitalism that emerged throughout the 1970s and 1980s.[7] For businesses this meant putting 'the deal' rather than 'the enterprise' at its heart. By so doing, the task of building sustainable businesses was mislaid. The chief executive officers (CEOs) of major companies around the world knew that they had little time to grow a business. Private equity funds, hedge funds and private investors such as Philip Green were ever-ready to pounce on any firm that showed a less than optimum return to investors.[8] Meanwhile, these investors, from individuals to the far larger and more potent pension funds managed by professional investment firms, looked on passively. So passively in fact that one shareholder activist, Robert Monks in the US, has described the process of management returning ever-greater shares of corporate wealth to themselves as the capture of the productive capital of these firms by the management not the investors.[9]

By the early 2000s, it was apparent that trader-driven, deal-based capitalism was driving a new, more vigorous, form of financial services innovation. This was based on two factors. The ability of private equity to borrow vast sums of money to finance the purchase of companies and the need for banks to continue to grow returns to their investors through 'hedging' their risks by inventing new forms of financial products. Both processes were driven by cheap money. Capital became ever more available and its cost dwindled at the same time. The laws of supply and demand were working well.[10]

Private equity (PE) companies tapped resources from a growing pool of international investors and by borrowing from banks. Typically, PE firms reverse the debt/equity ratio. Where a firm may be carrying one-third debt to two-thirds equity, PE companies will reverse that ratio. The assets the company formerly held, such as property, will have been sold off and often then leased back. In many cases these lean, mean firms are then sold on with an overhang of enormous debt. The knock-on effect of such deal making reverberated across the 'real economy'.[11] Boards and CEOs felt renewed pressure to cut costs and return higher levels of dividend to investors. Performance cycles grew shorter and shorter. The important thing to note is the psychological and cultural impact private equity had on companies beyond their reach. What mattered was the deal not the business.

Private equity partners at largely no, or little, risk to themselves, were able to generate returns of hundreds of millions of pounds in a very short time. This was the privatizing of wealth on a grand scale. At no other time in history has speculation offered so much gain to so few.[12] And standing on the sidelines watching were governments, regulators and us. We fiddled while Rome burned and watched the system fail.

However, private equity was merely the minor symptom of the disease. The global banking system, but particularly banks in the US and UK, were the real engines of the new capitalism. For it became apparent to the boards and senior executives running banks way back in the late 1980s that money could be worked harder. Rather than just be a bank, taking in deposits and offering loans to customers, they could become the objects of speculation themselves. By bringing together their retail banking operations and their investment banking operations they could gain access to more capital and equity.[13] The repeal of the Glass-Steagall Act by President Clinton in 1999 opened the floodgates to such activity in the US.[14]

The banks encouraged the brightest and the best minds in maths and science to work for them, inventing new forms of financial products. These products, usually labelled derivatives, bundled different types of risk together in packages that could then be rated by ratings agencies and sold on to other investors. The Wall Street banks were literally hiring rocket scientists from Pasadena to develop such products.[15] Anything could be turned into a derivative from insurance risks on weather to mortgages.

Of course not every bank followed such strategies. For every Lehman Brothers, Royal Bank of Scotland and Bear Stearns, there were other financial institutions such as some of the more venerable mutual societies, such as the Co-operative Bank or the Liverpool Victoria Friendly Society, which carried on doing business along more cautious lines. These institutions were driven by different capitalist values. Not for them the get-rich-quick approaches adopted by casino capitalists. They understood one of the fundamental points about capitalism. A point little understood by the recent so-called 'captains of industry'. It is also one of the fundamental building blocks for understanding the premise of 'good work'. Even the great Karl Marx misunderstood its potency and power to bring together both sides of industry over time. It is that capitalism at its best is about the long term. It is about doing something so well, so consistently that people sustain their interest in what you do and what you have to offer over time. This approach requires a deeper commitment to people and standards and a more cautious approach to managing risks. It often goes hand-in-glove with an understanding that a firm is part of something bigger and wider.

From their first beginnings private firms were granted the right to trade by the state. Capitalist institutions were seen as a way and means of furthering the interests of the state as much as the individuals who bore the risk of the endeavour. They were collective institutions designed to add value to the public weal as well as the private purse.

Travel back 400 years to the founding of the first recognizable companies – the Dutch East India Company for example – one finds that their documents of incorporation are explicit about the wider public benefits that must accrue from their private activities. For the Dutch East India Company this was to regulate the existing trade to maximize returns to the Dutch republics and also to fight the enemies of the Dutch republics and prevent other European nations entering the East India trade.[16]

The same principle holds for the founding of the great US and British corporations in the 19th and early 20th centuries. For example, John Cadbury, through his lifelong involvement with the Temperance Society, believed that in founding his company to provide tea, coffee, cocoa and chocolate as an alternative to alcohol, he was helping poor people alleviate their poverty since alcohol consumption was believed to be a direct cause of poverty and deprivation.[17] At heart, such corporations have always focused on more than simply maximizing profits and returns to shareholders. Great companies understand their 'reason to be'; their place in the greater scheme of things.

The financial services-led carousel of short-term returns, leveraged by excessive and risky levels of debt, is a far cry from that vision of what business is, and arguably should be, about. This is not to say that businesses should not maximize their profits. They should. But the context, rules, timescales, values and integrity with which they pursue their activities must be bounded. It is society that business should serve, not just those who own and manage the business.

In understanding why economic affairs have come to the current pass, I believe there are three fundamental drivers that have caused the credit crunch and the recession that has followed. These can be summarized as ideological, social and psychological. All, of course, are interlinked. A key determinant has been the belief that increasing GDP and the trend level of growth in an economy is overall a very good thing. This, in and of itself, is not a wrong or necessarily bad prescription. Growing affluence allows a society to do many things such as increase its spending on health and education and thus provide its citizens with better quality, longer and more enjoyable lives. But as Avner Offer says in his book, *The Challenge of Affluence*, 'affluence makes us impatient and impatience makes us unhappy'.[18] A new science of behavioural economics has been gathering evidence to support that statement. Broadly speaking, reported levels of happiness in western societies (with some notable exceptions) have not improved but stayed broadly the same, or indeed have reduced, since the 1950s.[19] It is clear that merely increasing GDP does not increase happiness whatever it may allow, or enable, in terms of improved infrastructure, public services, private wealth and increased consumption.

In the 1970s very few people questioned the basic assumption that GDP growth was the ultimate goal of public policy. The question was how to achieve it. I have briefly discussed above the rise of neo-liberalism. Corporatism in the UK and US had become a symbol of economic decline. Trying to manage an economy from the centre was something only communist states did. Only by giving the market its head could the economy grow at its true rate. By reducing the role of the state and liberalizing labour and product markets, growth at higher and higher rates would follow. This economic credo was accompanied by a political one that put the rights of the individual above the rights of the collective. This was nothing new to the US but it was a less comfortable concept to European nations including the UK.[20] But whereas Europe has never truly 'liberalized', the UK under Thatcher followed the US's lead. A form of Anglo Saxon economics emerged with a bastardized British dream mirroring the real deal over the other side of the Atlantic.

What was important was to achieve a reduction in the influence of the state, to trust the private sector above the public sector, and to cut taxes, especially for the entrepreneurial classes and middle classes in order to allow the individual the right to choose how they spent the money they earned. It was also to open up 'clear blue water' between the owners of capital and the workers. Thus today, the trade union movement has been effectively sidelined in the private sector.[21]

In delivering the dream, Thatcher's governments slashed taxes on the top earners from 80 per cent in 1979 to 40 per cent by 1988.[22] State-owned businesses from British Leyland to British Rail were privatized, allowing the public servants that had previously managed the businesses to become rich overnight. 'Inefficient' industries such as coal mining were allowed to wither and decay. By the time these reforms had been completed, and at the height of the early 1980s recession, over 3 million British workers (largely breadwinning males) had been thrown onto the scrapheap of unemployment. Whole communities were thus to be blighted by multi-generational worklessness.[23]

However, from some perspectives, the prescription achieved some very positive outcomes. Post-privatization per person productivity gains over time in some industries were of the order of more than 100 per cent and in one industry of more than 500 per cent. Productivity gains in gas, electricity and steel amounted to 70 per cent, 100 per cent and 102 per cent respectively, and BT gained increases of more than 180 per cent. Companies such as Rolls Royce and BAA gained 100 per cent and 114 per cent, respectively. Job cuts after privatization ranged from more than 75 per cent in the case of British Steel, to job increases of 15 per cent in the case of BAA. However, the job cuts that fuelled these productivity gains – and yielded short-term dividends for shareholders – were in many cases badly managed and with devastating consequences for many local communities.[24]

However, and this may have been due to the costs of restructuring the UK economy from a manufacturing base to a services base, average GDP growth between 1979 and 1997 was only 2.04 per cent including two deep recessions. This compares with average growth during the period 1961–1979 of 2.68 per cent and between 1997 and 2008 of 2.69 per cent.[25]

During the period 1979–1997, unemployment hit heights not seen since the 1930s. More than 3 million workers lost their jobs and many never returned to the labour market. On the other hand, many people certainly gained from the change of political emphasis. Those on higher earnings benefited hugely from the tax changes. Britain became a country in which overseas companies wanted to invest, ranging from the Japanese in the 1970s and 1980s to the Indian companies such as Tata in the 1990s and 2000s. Foreign direct investment (FDI) was encouraged by access to capital through the growth of the City of London as the centre of European, if not world, finance, and the UK's proximity to the continental-sized developed economy of Europe. The growing importance of the European Union was also a major factor in attracting overseas cash to the UK's permissive big business-friendly shores.

Inside the workplace, a complementary revolution was occurring. The story of UK labour relations up to the 1980s was a story of industrial strife. The relationships between bosses and workers were largely adversarial. The UK lost 29.5 million days to strikes in 1979. By 1995, this figure was down to just 415,000.[26] It seemed as though conflict was disappearing. The growing change from firms employing industrial relations experts and personnel managers to a far more sophisticated form of human resource management (HRM) seemed to be delivering more peaceful and productive workplaces. The GDP growth figures seemed to imply this was not actually the case, but the lack of strike activity seemed to indicate the opposite. Of course, the crushing of trade union power was achieved through a series of regulations and parliamentary acts during the 1980s that banned secondary picketing and made sure that a union would need to ballot its members before any strike could go ahead.[27] The power of the union activists was thus neutered. Politically this was popular. The general population had grown to dislike the level of union activity. The brutal treatment of 'scabs' was generally reviled.

But conflict had not disappeared – far from it. During the same period, the UK's industrial tribunal system began to strain at the seams. Between the late 1980s and 2000–2001, with its peak of 130,000 cases, the case load more than trebled.[28] Conflict seemed to have moved from the collective to the individual under the new forms of working environment. Productivity (as the figures above show) was not improving, nor was the overall trend rate of growth. Average earnings growth was good rather than spectacular. The people who clearly did the best out of the new orthodoxy were existing high earners and people who ran businesses. If this had been the sum total of change that the new politics of neoliberalism had wrought during the last 30 years of the 20th century it would not have lasted quite so long.

What Mrs Thatcher was so successful in doing was borrowing ideas from the US economic and political Right and making them the new orthodoxy for the UK. She created the British Dream. The Blair/Brown governments have arguably not moved away from this orthodoxy, although they have mixed in policies aimed at redistribution and social justice.

One Thatcher policy above all others stands out – the right of council tenants and others to buy their homes at relatively knock-down prices. The policy was first introduced in 1980 and then extended to leaseholders. In 1980, around 50 per cent of people owned their own homes. By the end of the 1980s that figure had increased to 66 per cent and had risen to 70 per cent by 2008.[29] At a stroke, the population of the UK was turned into a highly indebted but home-owning democracy. Average earnings were not that high but many people now felt richer as a result of rising asset prices, especially the homes in which they lived. A house was not just a home. In effect, as was to become apparent between 1990 and 2007, people were in possession of their own bank. In 1984, mortgage equity withdrawal in the UK stood at around £10 billion. By 2006, it was up to £50 billion.[30]

The effect of these policies was to drive a 'me first' culture in business and wider society. Business men and women were seen as the *fons et origo* of wisdom and knowledge. Their expertise was seen as invaluable to the process of governing. Gone were the days of 'beer and sandwiches' when representatives of the trade unions horse-traded over incomes policies with successive Prime Ministers. Now the new type of business leaders, from Lord Hanson in the 1980s to Fred Goodwin in the 2000s, were welcomed through the door of No 10 Downing Street. These men were deal makers. For them, doing business was about doing deals, not making things or supporting businesses to grow. A new culture emerged that was supposedly based on incentivizing people to perform through performance-related pay, share options, annual bonuses and other perks. A salary was no longer what mattered. What became the norm was to talk of the 'package'. Thus the psychology and culture of 'winner takes all' took over the upper echelons of the US and UK's business elites.

Incentives drove the behaviours one would expect with higher rewards granted for greater risks taken. It is worth looking at this effect in more detail because the reasons given at the time for such high levels of reward were not really reasons at all. Most importantly, and especially with the advantage of hind-sight, the idea that such large financial incentives would not create unsustainable risk is laughable.

Risk-taking is synonymous with capitalism. Risk is the oil that helps makes the parts of an economy work more smoothly. The business of being in business is indeed risky. This is why the risk management industry is so large. Many businesses invest in risk analysts and risk management systems. When things go wrong the finger is often pointed at these systems and the people who manage them. In the March 2009 issue of the *Harvard Business Review* it was argued that many financial service companies simply mismanaged risk by looking at the wrong factors. These were enumerated as a lack of appropriate data, narrow measures of risk, overlooked risks, hidden risks, poor communication and the rate of change being too fast for the systems employed. Ultimately it is the people at the top of companies who are remunerated as recompense for their judgements about risk. When that judgement is well founded, they should be well rewarded. When it is wrong, they should not – or so goes the argument.

Of course for people at the top of private companies there are other reasons given to explain why they deserve to be so well rewarded: talent, responsibility and the global nature of the labour market they work in, for example. Moreover, reward is supposed to follow performance. However, these reasons fail to stand up to serious scrutiny. A new culture of excessive rewards to those at the top developed regardless of success or failure. A winner-take-all outlook concealed by a thicket of seemingly rigorous performance measures came to dominate. This is not to say that everyone working in FTSE100 or Fortune 500 companies was part of this culture. Most people were not. Only those who had crossed the invisible line that demarcated the winners from the also-rans were deemed to be part of the club – people so talented and deserving that they would be rewarded well whatever the business performance of their companies. Think Andy Hornby, formerly CEO of failed banking giant HBOS, now installed at the helm of Alliance-Boots.

So UK CEOs have seen their pay increase in 2008 to 76 times that of the average worker compared with a ratio of 10:1 in 1980. Admittedly, compared with the pay of US CEOs (which is more than 300 times that of the average worker) this differential is modest.[31]

For the year to summer 2006, average UK CEO remuneration packages had increased by 28 per cent against inflation of 2.8 per cent and average wage increases across the whole economy of 4 per cent. Average FTSE CEO remuneration topped £2.4 million, up from £2.1 million the year before. Performance-related pay made up 55 per cent of the total, up from 46 per cent in 2003. And this was a year of one of the lower rates of salary increases for CEOs in recent times. Given that average growth in most of these organizations over time was at, or about, the level of GDP growth, such increases seem hard to justify.[32]

But does this matter? The answer is an emphatic 'yes'. There is evidence that has shown that overpaying people at the top of the organization damages, rather than enhances, the performance of organizations through lowering morale and reducing commitment. The survey found that 96 per cent of respondents believed that overpaying top executives led to poor employee relations. Differentials seem to matter. Exceed around 14:1 between top and bottom and people feel that pay and reward is fundamentally 'unfair'.[33]

And 'felt fairness', as we shall see later in the book, matters to the health of the enterprise. The rather obvious conclusion is that people are citizens as well as employees with a well defined sense of what is fair and what is not. Rewarding people regardless of how profitable the organization may be is simply rewarding greed. People instinctively understand the difference between risk-taking entre-preneurialism and very able stewardship.

Winner-take-all effects represent a form of market failure. We need vibrant capitalist organizations. We need to encourage investment in the people who run and work in them. And these leaders deserve high levels of remuneration suitable for exceptional people doing great jobs running great companies. But this should not be at the cost of ultimately perversely damaging the prospects of long-term success for those companies.

Inequality matters. High levels of inequality in wider society act as a brake on social mobility and high levels of inequality within organizations act as a brake on performance. As Richard Wilkinson has demonstrated in his book, *The Impact of Inequality: How to Make Sick Societies Healthier,* in wider society there is a strong correlation between high inequality and low levels of trust, low social capital, higher murder rates and higher levels of hostility.[34] Overpaying people at the top in relation to others has the same effect on the firm.

Thus these three factors, the ideological, social and psychological, have between them played a collective confidence trick on people and the organiza-tions they work for. Businesses and companies are collective human institutions that innovate through collaborative effort. Yet for 30 years the rhetoric has been about heroic individual genius. Much of this rhetoric has been driven by the US tradition of the frontiersman and pioneer. The people who built America were different, cast from a different mould, refugees from the collective injustices of Old Europe. America enshrined the principle of individual property rights, the right of the individual to bear arms and, the greatest right of all, to see every individual citizen as being of equal worth and merit. These 'truths' have been evident over the past 100 years in the output of popular culture from the great Westerns that made cult heroes of actors such as Clint Eastwood to the more recent films drawn from comic books such as *Batman*.

Yet the business of doing business is a more mundane and more collectivist activity. Porras and Collins in their book, *Built to Last,* followed the fortunes of the top companies over a 100-year period during the 20th century in 20 different business sectors. They compared them with the next best companies in those sectors to try and understand what they had done differently. What emerged was utterly counter-intuitive. These top firms had done the basic things very well over time. They had promoted CEOs from outside the firm on only four occasions over the period under examination, and that in only two of the 20 firms. On all other occasions they had promoted CEOs from within. Their business strategies were incremental rather than expansionary. They focused on quality of product and service above all else.[35]

Perhaps above everything they invested heavily in their people and processes that would encourage innovation. As the economy has changed, so has the need to innovate more and faster. Processes and systems that thus encourage team-working, strong social capital within organizations, collective effort, increased discretionary effort and mutual respect have become ever more important.

Human beings are a mass of contradictions. They are collectivists, group animals that like company and easily form social groupings. Economic man on the other hand is not supposed to be influenced by such matters. He is a rational self-maximizer capable of computing data efficiently in order to make the right purchasing decision on each and every occasion. This fallacy has lain at the heart of the conservative model of how to do business. I oversimplify of course, but not much.

So to recap. From 1979 to 2008, the global economy was dominated by an economics and ideology that believed that the free market unfettered from state intervention or collaboration would produce the optimal outcomes society desired. During that period the UK alone suffered three major recessions, saw society's divisions grow wider, as the richest 1 per cent took the lion's share of the promised economic dividend. Companies became less hierarchical and more unfairly run. Individuals were encouraged to believe, like their American cousins, that they could have it all. Even 13 years of a supposedly centre-left government did not fundamentally challenge this orthodoxy.

Yet as we shall see in the next chapter, the next economy, the knowledge economy is already with us. This economic model needs to be underpinned by a different set of values and understanding from that which went before. The enterprises or organizations that operate in it are going to be driven by different impulses. Economic growth is self-evidently an interdependent activity. The world has shrunk enormously as international trade has grown. The advent of a new, general purpose technology – digitalization – has allowed transaction times to speed up putting more pressure on businesses to innovate.

Customers whether of private or public goods have become more empowered through this technology and thus more demanding. Organizations and systems are struggling to keep pace with the change. Layered into this mix is the need to decarbonize growth. The planet matters because if it doesn't function properly, not much else can function either. As Lord Stern said in his landmark report for the British government in 2006:

> The evidence shows that ignoring climate change will eventually damage economic growth. Our actions over the coming few decades could create risks of major disruption to economic and social activity, later in this century and in the next, on a scale similar to those associated with the great wars and the economic depression of the first half of the 20th century. And it will be difficult or impossible to reverse these changes. Tackling climate change is the pro-growth strategy for the longer term, and it can be done in a way that does not cap the aspirations for growth of rich or poor countries. The earlier effective action is taken, the less costly it will be. At the same time, given that climate change is happening, measures to help people adapt to it are essential. And the less mitigation we do now, the greater the difficulty of continuing to adapt in future.[36]

This message has yet to be fully internalized by most people and institutions, but across the developed world one of the responses to the credit crunch has been a promise from national governments to prioritize investment in the green sector. For organizations, the impact of climate change has been partly regulatory through taxes designed to encourage recycling, etc. but also ethical. Workers now believe they have the right to demand that their workplaces 'go green'. Most institutions will have some form of staff group designed to help 'green' their workplaces. Most offices now send out diktats to turn off computers and lights if you are the last to leave the office.

This focus on values is important to the context of 'good work'. It is an enabling cultural shift that is helpful in making the argument that workplaces are fully human institutions requiring the same attention to fairness, values and vision as in other parts of life. People remain citizens when they cross the threshold of the workplace.

Another major driver of change has been the upskilling of the workforce. Across the developed economies the change from manufacturing to services has seen a general move towards a more highly skilled workforce. The Nordic countries lead the way but the UK is slowly catching up. So, for example, in 2003 only 64 per cent of the UK workforce had qualifications at level 2 or above (equivalent to five GCSEs at grades A*–C or NVQ level 2) – Germany was at 85 per cent, France at 77 per cent and the US at 73 per cent.[37]

Yet the UK has seen rapid growth in the number of people with intermediate skills in the period from 1994 to 2003. Most of this has been achieved through an improvement in the number of young people leaving school with at least a level 2 gained in their qualifications, rather than a determined effort to boost adult learning. So, for example, 72 per cent of 19–21 year olds in the UK were at level 2+ in 2002–2003, compared with 68 per cent in Germany and 66 per cent in the US, and 84 per cent in France.[38]

The more skilled the workforce, the more demanding of voice, autonomy and reward it tends to be. This may not seem to be the case in a downturn when millions of people are losing or have lost their jobs. But this downturn has followed broadly similar patterns to other recessions with the low skilled, the young and the old bearing the brunt of the layoffs. The major difference is that with nearly half the workforce being female, many more women than in previous recessions have been losing their jobs. The dole queues are no longer reminiscent of the 1930s or 1980s – they are far more gender neutral.

The other major factor affecting the way organizations operate has been the attitudinal and demographic changes occurring across the workforces of the developed world. Diversity is now the norm not the exception in many workplaces. So-called Generation Y (people born after 1981) have different attitudes to life. Studies have shown that this generation of workers believe in having a better work–life balance than their parents enjoyed. They want to live fulfilling lives where work is in balance with other elements of their existence.[39]

These workers tend to be more highly qualified than ever before. The latest figures show that 44 per cent of the population are now participating in higher education compared with 6 per cent in the 1960s.[40]

They also know that the 'job for life' has gone. A study by the International Labour Organization (ILO) showed that of 17 developed economies, the UK had the second-lowest average job tenure after the US and was ranked 12th on measures of job security above Greece, Spain, Portugal, the US and Japan but below all the other major European economies. Although such change in the so-called psychological contract between employer and employee has been a shock to many older workers, for Generation Y this is all they've known. For these individuals it is about 'employability for life' rather than a job for life. Generation Y are intensely aware of the value of brands to the value of their CVs. They tend towards a form of footloose behaviour where talented younger workers look to work for certain organizations in the knowledge that it will add lustre to their career records.

Generation Y also has great expectations of what to expect from work. Training and development and early responsibility are as desirable as financial rewards. Youthful impetuosity may be a factor, but high-flyers are now in a powerful position in the labour market to tip the employment contract in their favour. If things do not come to pass they tend to leave sooner rather than later. This is especially the case if the job has been oversold and the realities of work fail to live up to the promises of the glossy recruitment literature or the sanitized corporate induction programmes.

But the biggest problem is that younger workers feel that their bosses and older colleagues do not buy into their fundamentally meritocratic perspective on how rewards and promotions should be allocated. For them it is competence rather than time served that should be the guiding principle for judging career progression.[41]

These workers value flexibility above many other facets of work. But so do older workers at the other end of working life. The other major demographic change across developed economies has been the ageing of the workforce as people have had fewer and fewer children. This, combined with the crisis in pension provision has led all governments to raise, or consider raising, the age of retirement. Older workers, like their younger counterparts, want flexibility. They do not want full-time employment but shorter periods of work with the possibility of time off for extended breaks, to see their families or for periods of rest.

By 2010, the proportion of the working population aged between 50 and 64 will be greater than at any time since the mid 1970s. Information from the Office for National Statistics (ONS) shows that the ratio between people aged 65 plus and children under 16 will increase from 81:100 in 2003 to 136:100 in 2031.[42] Furthermore, the Pensions Commission reported in 2006 that around 11.3 million people have not been saving enough for a properly funded retirement.[43] This means more older workers will want and need employment into their dotages. For employers this means that they must offer more flexible working patterns, and for workers it will mean a lifetime of upgrading and improving their skills in order to meet the new challenges of work that emerge during their lifetimes. For someone who began work in 1970 and is looking to retire in 2015, their working lives have seen the advent of a whole host of different technologies from faxes to email to mobile phones. They would also almost certainly have experienced some form of internal process re-engineering aimed at getting more performance from the workforce often driven by new quasi-scientific thinking.

Thus in conclusion, the roller-coaster ride of this latest crash should represent the death knell of neo-liberal economic thinking. Economists such as Paul Krugman, John Kay, Will Hutton, Richard Sennett, Richard Layard, Amartya Sen and Joseph Stiglitz and their ideas must form the mainstream of government policies and organizational strategies. The combined forces of globalization, the emergence of the knowledge economy, climate change and demographic change mean that the concept of good work as described in this book should have fertile ground on which to grow.

Notes

1   www.hoover.org/bios/friedman.html

2   See for example: www.chipsites.com/derechos/history_eng.html

3   http://en.wikipedia.org/wiki/Chicago_Boys

4   www.fool.co.uk/news/investing/company-comment/2006/10/24/remember-the-big-bang.aspx

5   Frank, R. and Cook, P. (1996) *The Winner-Take-All Society*, Penguin, New York.

6   For a good discussion of the above argument in more detail see: Hutton, W. and Schneider, P. (2008) *The Failure of Market Failure: Towards a 21st Century Keynesianism*, NESTA, London.

7   For a good discussion on neo-liberalism see: www.globalissues.org/article/39/a-primer-on-neoliberalism

8   Peston, R. (2008) *Who Runs Britain?*, Hodder and Stoughton, London.

9   http://ragmonks.blogspot.com/

10 Brummer, A. (2008) *The Crunch*, Random House, London.

11 Thornton, P. (2007) *Inside the Dark Box, Shedding Light on Private Equity*, The Work Foundation, London.

12 Peston, R. (2008) *Who Runs Britain?*, Hodder and Stoughton, London.

13 Ferguson, N. (2008) *The Ascent of Money: A Financial History of the World*, Allen Lane, London.

14 www.investopedia.com/articles/03/071603.asp

15 http://chronicle.uchicago.edu/050203/math-finance.shtml

16 Ferguson, N. (2008) *The Ascent of Money: A Financial History of the World*, Allen Lane, London, pp48–49 and http://en.wikipedia.org/wiki/Dutch_East_India_Company

17 www.cadbury.com.au/About-Cadbury/The-Story-of-Cadbury.aspx

18 Offer, A. (2006) *The Challenge of Affluence: Self Control and Well Being in the United States and Britain Since 1950*, Oxford University Press, London.

19 http://news.bbc.co.uk/1/hi/programmes/happiness_formula/4771908.stm

20 For a good discussion on the cultural and philosophical differences between the US and UK see: Hutton, W. (2003) *The World We're In*, Jonathan Cape, London.

21 www.worker-participation.eu/National-Industrial-Relations/Countries/United-Kingdom/trade-unions

22 http://en.wikipedia.org/wiki/Taxation_in_the_United_Kingdom

23 www.nuffield.ox.ac.uk/users/nickell/papers/Poverty&WorklessnessinBritain.pdf

24 Thornton, S. (1998) *Reforming Public Enterprises – Case Studies: United Kingdom*, OECD, Paris; Hall, D. (2000) *Impact of Electricity Privatisation on Industrial Relations*, PSIRU, University of Greenwich report; HKFD *The Privatisation of the UK Electricity Industry*, www.hkdf.org/newsarticles. asp?show=newsarticles&newsarticle=86; House of Commons Written Answers for 16 December 1998.

25 National Statistics online: www.statistics.gov.uk/hub/index.html

26 www.statistics.gov.uk/statbase/xsdataset.asp?vlnk=134&more=Y

27 www.unionhistory.info/timeline/1960_2000_Narr_Display.php?Where= NarTitle+contains+'Anti-Union+Legislation%3A+1980–2000'

28 www.niesr.ac.uk/pdf/240708_152632.pdf

29 www.timesonline.co.uk/tol/news/politics/article1567419.ece

30 www.bankofengland.co.uk/statistics/hew/2008.htm

31 Toynbee, P. and Walker, D. (2008) *Unjust Rewards*, Granta, London.

32 Isles, N. (2007) *The Risk Myth*, The Work Foundation, London.

33 Toynbee, P. and Walker, D. (2008) *Unjust Rewards*, Granta, London.

34 Wilkinson, R. (2005) *The Impact of Inequality: How to Make Sick Societies Healthier*, Routledge, Oxford.

35 Collins, J. and Porras, J. (1994) *Built to Last: Successful Habits of Visionary Companies*, Random House, London.

36 www.hm-treasury.gov.uk/stern_review_report.htm

37 Hutton, W. et al (2005), *Where are the Gaps?*, The Work Foundation, London.

38 Hutton, W. et al (2005), *Where are the Gaps?*, The Work Foundation, London and www.dcsf.gov.uk/research/data/uploadfiles/RR548.pdf

39 Horner, L. and Jones, A. (2003) *Great Expectations: Understanding the Motivations of Young Workers*, The Work Foundation, London.

40 National Statistics online: www.statistics.gov.uk/hub/index.html

41 Horner, L. and Jones, A. (2003) *Great Expectations: Understanding the Motivations of Young Workers*, The Work Foundation, London.

42 National Statistics online: www.statistics.gov.uk/hub/index.html

43 http://news.bbc.co.uk/1/shared/bsp/hi/pdfs/30_11_05_exec_summ.pdf

Chapter 2

Knowledge, Good Work and the New Economy

It has become commonplace to describe the economy pre-crash as a new form of 'knowledge economy'. Many writers in the latter part of the 1990s began to describe a new form of so-called weightless economy that described how value was increasingly being derived from the production of not very much but ideas, intellectual property, creativity and innovation.[1] The information and communication technology (ICT) revolution was enabling companies to exploit knowledge bases to give them a competitive edge. This in turn was leading to atypical forms of employment such as flexible (hours) workers, portfolio (more than one job at a time) workers and remote workers.

This new economy was growing fast and was best represented by the emergence of the new group of dot com millionaires. These were the new entrepreneurs who had founded internet-based businesses. By 2000, this bubble was about to burst as some of these businesses, yet to trade at profit, were being valued more highly than decades-old going-concerns such as major brewery chains, retailers and manufacturing companies.[2]

The battle lines were drawn between those economists who believed that any economy could only function by having a proper manufacturing base, those who believed the future would be all about knowledge, the internet and weightless production of services and those who argued that what was being described was merely the growth of the service economy.

The dot com crash of 2000 seemed to vindicate the arguments of the 'bricks and mortar' economists.[3] The whole knowledge economy idea had been nothing more than a bubble that had now burst. However, the truth was not quite that neat. Change had been, and continues to be, occurring even if definitions have been difficult.

It is worth exploring in a little more detail what has been driving the change to a knowledge-based economy. Along with all developed economies, the UK economy has undergone a powerful and profound shift over the past 30 years away from manufacturing towards the production of services as the primary source of wealth creation. The manufacturing sector has shrunk both as a proportion of total GDP and as the major creator of jobs – down from more than 8 million jobs in 1979 to 2.5 million jobs in 2009.[4] Even the US, which is the world's largest manufacturer, has seen a major fall in manufacturing employment. Manufacturing jobs fell by an average of 1.2 per cent annually between 1979 and 2007. Put another way, the US went from 19.5 million manufacturing jobs in 1979 to 13 million jobs by the end of 2008.[5] There has been a profound shift in what we produce and how we produce it.

During the 1980s and 1990s, Britain reformed and became more competitive predominantly through an ability to compete on price rather than quality. This 'low road' has long reached its own dead end. The countries of Eastern Europe and East Asia, particularly China and India, have vast pools of cheap labour. Mass-market manufacturing will increasingly happen in the East. Moreover, as described below, markets are becoming more competitive and more global.

The growth of the world economy has offered all economies more opportunities for growth and development, but has also created more intense competitive pressures.

Changes in the developed economies are being driven by three major factors: globalization, particularly as it affects trade between Organisation for Economic Co-operation and Development (OECD) countries; ICT production and use;

and for European nations, the drive for single market completion in the European Union. Complicating matters for any country in the developed world is an ageing population and shrinking working age population at a time when more, not fewer, workers are needed.

Global opportunities are increasing: since 1980, global trade flows have gone up dramatically. As a proportion of global GDP, world trade grew by 50 per cent between 1990 and 2003 to reach 30 per cent.[6] Merchandise exports from the UK between 1990 and 2000 grew by an average 6.4 per cent per annum compared with merchandise production at 2.5 per cent and GDP at purchasing power parity (PPP) at 3.4 per cent.[7]

Yet the increase in global trade brings with it significant competitive pressures. The emergence of China as a major exporter of manufactured goods is the most significant change in the international economy in decades. Like China, India has focused on liberalizing its economy, adding impetus to the Asian-led sustaining of global demand up to 2008. In India, GDP growth since 1990 has averaged 6.2 per cent per annum.[8]

China and India are rightly perceived to threaten western industries in the low value-added sectors through their far cheaper cost base. No western business can undercut typical manufacturing labour costs of US$2 per worker per day and this has led some commentators to argue, given the parallel expansion of other Asian economies, that a fundamental shift in the international division of labour is taking place that threatens the economy and trade of many developed countries. Yet this is both to overstate the threat and to understate the opportunities.

It is certainly the case that the West cannot compete with China and India on cost. However, there is an opportunity for the West to compete and grow based on innovation and quality. These economies also offer many opportunities for investment, exports and growth to others. And global demand – potentially for high-quality, innovative products – will continue to be sustained by East Asian growth once the global recession ends. Chinese growth alone has been a major driver in sustaining overall levels of global demand. The Chinese economy (now the world's fourth largest at 13 per cent of global GDP) has been growing at 8–9 per cent a year. In 2003, more Chinese subscribed to new phone lines (112 million) than the populations of Britain and France combined. A third of its exports are now in electronics. It also accounts for about one-third of the growth in global oil demand importing around US$26 billion worth of barrels of oil in 2004.[9]

At the high-value-added, research-based end of the spectrum of international trade, the US has achieved a dominant leadership position since the mid 1990s. This suggests that international trade is a positive rather than zero sum game: winners are not necessarily offset by losers. Standard theory suggests that the UK can gain from China's entry into the world economy at the bottom end, and from the US's dynamism at the top end – but benefits depend upon knowledge-driven innovation and quality.[10]

In the medium term, however, it is the case that what happens in Europe has more relative impact on the European economies than what happens in China and India and elsewhere in the world. Nearly 60 per cent of the UK's trade, for example, is with other parts of the European Union (EU). Germany's is around 64 per cent, Spain's is around 70 per cent, France's is around 64 per cent and Italy's is around 60 per cent.[11] Common rules concerning employment rights and standards, environmental protection and competitiveness help create a level playing field on which all companies compete equally. Moreover, the EU negotiates trade terms as a bloc, which helps firms competing in global marketplaces acquire better market access.[12]

ICT is the final and perhaps most important driver of change in developed economies. ICT is having several effects simultaneously:

- it is greatly reducing the marginal cost of processing, storing and transferring information, activities that are central to knowledge-intensive sectors;
- it has spawned new industries, such as internet commerce and multimedia entertainment; and
- it is increasing the relative attractions of organizational forms – such as the network – which encourage the production and dissemination of knowledge.

The digitalization of texts, symbols, instructions, patterns, visual images and music allow huge data sets to be marshalled more efficiently than in the past. It also means that many economic activities that once depended on physical proximity, and face-to-face encounters, can now be conducted at a distance.[13]

Other countries need to follow the US's lead by capitalizing more on the opportunities that ICT offers. For example, there is growing agreement that the higher whole economy productivity growth in the US over the past 10 years compared with Europe is due in large part to the US's greater exposure to, and application of, ICT. The US's ICT advantage is closely related to spatial issues and is focused particularly on ICT use in the retail and wholesale sectors where spatial factors have greater purchase than in other sectors. Europe, with its denser populations and older cities cannot compete in this regard. It is the faster productivity growth in ICT intensive services that accounts for the largest element of the productivity growth differential between the US and Europe.[14]

Six out of 56 business sectors common to both the EU and US – office equipment, semiconductors, communication services, wholesale, retail and financial services – dominate the growth story in both Europe and the US over the past 15 years and all are heavy users or producers of ICT. Despite the importance of these sectors in both the UK and the US, the US seems to apply ICT better and it also invests more, outscoring all EU economies and investing at nearly three times the rate of the UK.[15]

Knowledge is increasingly the key to making more effective use of the traditional factors of production such as physical capital and labour. Nor is knowledge restricted to ICT, as some have argued. Although information and communication technology plays a decisive role in this new corporate environment, the concept of the knowledge economy encompasses far more than ICT alone. It refers to a cluster of competences, capabilities and institutions that may largely determine the competitive potential of firms during the 21st century. Put simply, the firms and nations that rise to the challenges posed by knowledge capitalism are likely to prosper whereas those that rely on the now-dated conceptual framework of industrial capitalism will fall behind.[16]

However, the term 'knowledge economy' continues to confuse many people despite the description above. As one report has concluded:

> The science of describing, understanding, and measuring knowledge will always be an imperfect one. The knowledge identified in this forum turned out to be capricious: sometimes sticky, often slippery, rarely tangible, frequently tacit, and extremely heterogeneous.
>
> Report of CERI Washington Forum, June 1999

A number of terms that attempt to define the knowledge economy are given in Box 2.1. Perhaps the best definition is that of The Work Foundation's chief economist, Ian Brinkley: 'We can say the knowledge economy is what you get when firms bring together powerful computers and well-educated minds to create wealth.'

In reality what has been happening is a moderately rapid adjustment to a knowledge-based economy without necessarily including a very sharp break from other forms of economic models. The point about knowledge is that it is infinitely reusable and the advent of ICT technologies has enabled companies and organizations to exploit that very renewability. This has put a strain on old ways of doing business and old forms of work organization, job design, industrial relations, management and leadership. It is why good work organizations flourish more than those organizations that have failed to understand the nature of the change around them. Competitive pressure is rising in all sectors driven by changes in demand, technology and global competition. Consumers are more discerning, businesses more cost aware. New communications technologies are reducing transaction times and shrinking the time that organizations enjoy a competitive advantage in new product design. Globalization continues to intensify trade flows. Investment in intangibles continues to outpace investment in tangibles. Fashioning a competitive response in an environment where easy sources of advantage soon dry up, demands a renewed focus on people. Human effort is, if you like, the most obviously untapped resource around. But no one should pretend that persuading people to give more is akin to tightening a nut on a machine, or striking a rich new seam of minerals. This untapped resource is arguably the trickiest to mine.

The latest OECD estimates are that 48 per cent of the UK workforce by sector (for example, financial services, high-tech manufacturing, education and health and the creative industries to name a few), 42 per cent by occupation and 31 per cent by educational qualification already qualify as 'knowledge workers'.[17]

There are three common ways of defining knowledge workers: all those who work in the top three standard occupational classifications (managers, professionals, associate professionals); all those with high-level skills, indicated by degree or equivalent qualifications (national vocational qualification (NVQ) level 4); and all those who perform tasks that require expert thinking and complex communication skills with the assistance of computers.

Box 2.1　Definitions of the knowledge economy

The role of knowledge (as compared with natural resources, physical capital and low skill labour) has taken on greater importance. Although the pace may differ, all OECD economies are moving towards a knowledge-based economy.

OECD, 1996

One in which the generation and exploitation of knowledge has come to play the predominant part in the creation of wealth. It is not simply about pushing back the frontiers of knowledge; it is also about the most effective use and exploitation of all types of knowledge in all manner of economic activity.

DTI Competitiveness White Paper, 1998

The idea of the knowledge driven economy is not just a description of high tech industries. It describes a set of new sources of competitive advantage which can apply to all sectors, all companies and all regions, from agriculture and retailing to software and biotechnology.

New Measures for the New Economy, report by Charles Leadbeater, June 1999

Economic success is increasingly based on upon the effective utilisation of intangible assets such as knowledge, skills and innovative potential as the key resource for competitive advantage. The term 'knowledge economy' is used to describe this emerging economic structure.

ESRC, 2005

The knowledge society is a larger concept than just an increased commitment to R&D. It covers every aspect of the contemporary economy where knowledge is at the heart of value added – from high tech manufacturing and ICTs through knowledge intensive services to the overtly creative industries such as media and architecture.

High Level Group on the Lisbon Strategy, *Facing the Challenge: The Lisbon Strategy for Growth and Employment*, European Commission, 2004

Table 2.1 *Knowledge workers in the UK economy, 1984–2014*

	1984 (%)	1994 (%)	2004 (%)	2014 (projected) (%)
Knowledge economy jobs	30.6	35.6	41.4	45.3
Personal services and sales	10.2	12.6	15.5	17.4
Skilled and semi-skilled manual	28.2	23.3	19.3	17.7
Unskilled jobs	16.1	13.7	11.3	8.7

Note: Knowledge economy jobs are managerial, professional, associate professional standard occupational classifications. Personal services include care, recreational and some hospitality jobs. Includes employees and self-employed.
Source: *Working Futures* 2004–2014, Table 4.1

Whichever definition is used it is clear that, very shortly, knowledge workers will constitute a majority of the UK workforce. The underlying story is one of fairly stable constant structural change in the labour market decade on decade. Over the past 25 years the share of knowledge economy jobs has increased by 4–5 percentage points in each decade, while the share of unskilled jobs has fallen by about 2–3 percentage points in each decade (see Table 2.1). Non-manual jobs in personal services and sales-related occupations have also increased by about 2–3 percentage points per decade. The share of value-added output by knowledge industries across the OECD is even more startling (see Table 2.2).

Within the knowledge economy sectors described above, such as medium-high tech manufacturing, telecommunications, education and health, there has been dramatic growth. Take what has been happening in the creative and cultural sector. Software design, computer gaming and electronic publishing has increased from 1.8 per cent of gross value added (GVA) (an alternative term to GDP) in 1997 to 2.8 per cent in 2003, an annual growth rate of 11 per cent, with employment in the sector growing by around 8 per cent per annum in the period from 1997 to 2004 to more than 520,000. In total, according to the OECD definitions, up to 2008, about 40 per cent of UK GDP is accounted for by knowledge-based industries; in addition, a total of 42 per cent of all employment has been created in these knowledge economy sectors. Ireland tops the league with 48 per cent of GDP accounted for by knowledge-based industries followed by the US, Germany and Sweden all with 42–43 per cent.

Table 2.2 *Knowledge-based industries as a share of gross value added, 2002*

Market-based industries (%)		All knowledge-based industries(%)	
Ireland	37.7	Ireland	47.8
Germany	32.1	US	43.1
US	30.5	Germany	42.8
Korea	31.2	Sweden	42.1
UK	28.7	Belgium	41.6
Belgium	28.1	UK	40.7
France	28.0	France	39.8
Netherlands	26.2	Korea	39.5
Sweden	26.1	Netherlands	38.9
Hungary	26.0	Denmark	37.4
Japan	25.6	Finland	37.3
Australia	25.4	Australia	36.7
Italy	24.8	Hungary	36.3
Austria	24.3	Canada	34.7
Finland	24.3	Italy	34.6
Canada	23.8	Austria	34.3
Denmark	21.6	Portugal	32.0
New Zealand	20.8	New Zealand	30.2
Spain	19.9	Spain	30.1
Mexico	19.0	Norway	29.3
Portugal	18.7	Mexico	29.1
Norway	15.6	Greece	23.8
Greece	13.5		

Note: Market-based are high- to medium-tech manufacturing; finance; telecommunications; business services. All knowledge-based includes education and health. Estimates for Japan available only for market-based knowledge industries.

Source: OECD science and technology scoreboard, 2005

Sceptics continue to argue that knowledge capitalism is not a real departure. The ability to invent and innovate – that is to embody new ideas in products and processes – has always played a central role in economic development. Since the Industrial Revolution, entrepreneurs have exploited a succession of scientific advances, in the process 'creatively destroying' existing industries and boosting productivity. The term 'creative destruction', coined by Joseph Schumpeter, a pioneer in knowledge economics, is itself 100 years old.[18] Of course, techno-logical development is not a smooth, continuous process: the successive evolution of water, coal and oil as energy sources each represented a wave of economic and social possibilities. At a minimum, the knowledge economy repre-sents another such wave of innovation.

Yet the shift towards a knowledge economy represents a change that is *qualita-tively* different from those associated with previous technologies. The processes associated with digitalization, together with other aspects of the burgeoning knowledge economy, such as nanotechnology and biotechnology, bring together many formerly unconnected capabilities and raise the potential of others – and do so from a new level of scientific complexity and sophistication. Societies that will fully exploit these new opportunities will need to consider more flexible and collaborative forms of wealth creation and develop regulatory, educational, research and welfare policies that are supportive of knowledge capitalism. So too firms and organizations.

The knowledge economy is multifaceted and is transforming the way that we live and work. A market system that arose primarily to coordinate the production and exchange of private goods must adapt to a world in which knowledge, the ultimate 'public good', plays a pivotal role. This adaptation will involve changes in the composition of economic output, in business organization, in factor inputs, in the structure of labour markets and in public regulation. At the same time there are new strains on the welfare state as individuals face greater uncer-tainty and firms are less capable of providing pensions and other benefits for a longer-living population. As people become more aware of the need for lifelong learning, and as the boundaries between work and learning begin to blur, schools, universities and research institutions will also need to redefine their missions.

Since basic material needs are increasingly satisfied in advanced economies, consumers are spending relatively more on knowledge-intensive goods and services – in the public as well as the private sectors. The knowledge economy is as much about healthcare and education (lifelong learning) as about the digitalized entertainment industry, biotechnology and consumer electronics. It has to do not just with artefacts in which knowledge is embedded but with any human activities involving the use of symbols.

These changes in demand are among the forces driving the ICT revolution. As firms focus more clearly on knowledge as a factor of production, they are organizing themselves in new ways. Business networks and collaborative structures are substituting for competition between large integrated firms, partly because firms are increasingly reliant on external as opposed to internal knowledge sources. Indeed, some argue that we are approaching a tipping point: the superior efficiency of the 'network', underpinned by ICT, could trigger a new round of creative destruction, and produce unexpected changes in the corporate pecking order.

Sweeping changes are also occurring in the organization of research and development and in the structure of labour markets. The complexity of the changes under way is evident in the explosive growth in the issue of patents, representing the attempted privatization of commercially relevant knowledge, and in the simultaneous advance of the 'open-source' movement, which advocates free access within cooperative 'knowledge communities'.

Meanwhile, the boundaries between the firm and the market are shifting as companies increasingly opt to buy people's knowledge and skills on the open market through outsourcing and short-term contracts, rather than hire employees for the long haul. More firms are also creating internal network dynamics allowing many more staff to work flexibly – in touch but out of sight. Smaller organizations are increasingly reliant on maintaining relationships and effective supply chains in order to understand and deliver to their customer.[19]

Firms must get the internal offer to employees right and improve the quality of work they offer. Command-and-control management styles no longer deliver the right results. Competitive pressures are growing and demand and supply need to be re-understood. Companies need to invest in knowledge more systematically than in the past, which will involve putting more emphasis on innovation. As economist William Baumol has argued, innovation rather than price competition is what drives the market process.[20]

Companies must innovate to survive. This means in the future they will need to collaborate more with universities and research institutes, pay more attention to the skills of their workforce, and participate more in the business networks through which knowledge is increasingly diffused. Providers of equity and loan capital have to devise new instruments that take better account of the needs of enterprises, whether start-ups or mature businesses, whose principal assets are intangible knowledge rather than plant and machinery or real estate.

In principle, knowledge capitalism should make work more enjoyable: it will be good for producers as well as consumers. However, unless individuals, firms and government adopt new attitudes and strategies, there could be many losers as well as winners.

Partly in response to more intense competition (reflecting deregulation and globalization), firms are focusing more clearly on knowledge as a factor of production. They are recognizing that what they have always needed is knowledge and skills rather than labour per se. The traditional employment contract is thus under pressure because firms can satisfy many of their knowledge and skill requirements without making a long-term commitment to employees. And this is shifting the boundary between the firm and the market because much work previously done inside companies by employees is now outsourced in various ways – by means of short-term contracts, the use of agency staff and the hiring of consultants. Recessions merely exacerbate such pressures.

Ownership and financial structures that grew up to support industrial capi-talism in the 19th and 20th centuries are unlikely to be well adapted to the knowledge economy. Knowledge companies have intellectual rather than physical capital to offer as collateral. Payback periods are long and uncertain. This implies the need for suppliers of financial capital that are capable of making sophisticated assessments of credit-worthiness and that have unusually long time-horizons. Knowledge companies are also unusually dependent on their core employees, those that have not been 'externalized' because their knowledge and skills are crucial to their firm's success. The knowledge capital of such firms is largely embodied in such employees. Co-ownership, after all, is often the favoured corporate structure in knowledge-intensive service sectors, such as law, accountancy and consultancy – on which more later.[21]

The knowledge economy is here to stay. The growth of knowledge-intensive firms is not going to go into reverse, whatever happens to globalization in the short term. Digitalization is a general-purpose set of technologies that are arguably still in their infancy or at least young adulthood. Productivity gains will be considerable once firms and organizations align their processes, systems and thinking to maximize those gains. After all, it took around 50 years from the invention of electricity before some bright spark worked out the most effective form of factory design to accommodate the new source of energy and power.[22]

Although it has been important to focus attention on changes in the nature and shape of the economy it does not mean that good work is only applicable for knowledge businesses: far from it. As discussed in the introductory chapters, the story of good work aligns the economic and productive with a more values-based approach to doing business. They are two sides of the same coin. An efficiency-based view of good work is only a partial story. Good work has both extrinsic and intrinsic value. It provides advantages to both sides at work in a capitalist organization – both the 'owners' of capital and the providers of 'labour'. Without such dualism, good work would be either just a worthwhile thing to have because workers feel better about their work, or a description of how to maximize productivity in the 21st century. Good work only works if it delivers benefits at all levels of operation – the economic, the social and the individual.[23]

Nor is good work merely a continuation of the human resource management school of analysis. This rather unitarist view believes that what really matters inside organizations is the relationship that individual workers hold with their managers and the organization. The so-called psychological contract is the key building block for improving productivity, performance and reducing workplace conflict (if such should emerge).

On the other hand, the more industrial relations view of work, which believes that only through collective action can labour rebalance its interests against the interests of capital, overly ignores the role of the individual and work. This world view believes that conflict is inevitable and therefore institutional mechanisms are required to deal with such conflict. Neither view is comprehensive enough to capture the full subtleties of the modern workplace.[24]

This is why 'good work' as a concept encapsulates the latest thinking and practice on combining high performance with fairness, voice and ownership.

Indeed in any economy, let alone a modern knowledge economy, it is only through ensuring fairness, voice and ownership that high performance can be achieved.

The history of good work as an idea is a long and honourable one. From St Augustine's time in the late 4th and early 5th centuries, Christian writers promulgated the idea that individuals should do 'good work'.[25] Modern impulses to charitable activity are the direct descendants of this tradition. But in the modern sense, the first time good work emerges as a concept was when the Swedish Metalworkers' Union launched 'good work' as a catch-all set of policies in the mid 1980s.[26] They believed that good work described an infrastructure for health, welfare and gender equality. Their conception of good work included nine dimensions:

- job security;
- equal and fair share of production results;
- worker co-determination;
- collaborative forms of work organization;
- skills and competence development at all levels of activity within the organization;
- recurring education throughout life;
- flexible working hours;
- workplace equality and social inclusion;
- a healthy and risk-reducing work environment.

Some may see this collection of ideas as being too weighted towards the interests of the workforce, but all of the main elements of the ideas that underpin good work are present.

In 2000, the European Union's Lisbon Strategy argued that European economies should seek not just more jobs but better jobs. Such improved working environments should include, 'equal opportunities for the disabled, gender equality, good and flexible work organization permitting better reconciliation of working and personal life, lifelong learning, health and safety at work, employee involvement and diversity in working life'.[27]

The European Foundation for the Improvement of Living and Working Conditions based in Dublin then developed in 2001 a new analytic framework that described four dimensions required for the promotion of good work. These were: ensuring career and employment security; maintaining and promoting the health and well-being of workers; developing skills and competences; and reconciling working and non-working life.[28]

Finally, in 2003, the ILO promoted the notion of decent work that was framed from an industrial relations and human rights perspective. The ILO described decent work thus:

> Decent work means productive work in which rights are protected, which generates an adequate income, with adequate social protection. It also means sufficient work, in the sense that all should have full access to income earning opportunities. It marks the high road to economic and social development, a road in which employment, income and social protection can be achieved without compromising workers' rights and social standards.[29]

Many of these prescription-based attempts to describe the conditions for good work focus on the intrinsic elements of work. They pay little attention to the extrinsic elements such as the need for organizations to survive the exogenous shocks that buffet them on a regular basis whether from the wider economy (downturns, recessions, exchange rate volatility, etc.), competitors new and old, or changes to the regulatory environment such as new taxes. This requires the people who manage organizations to focus much of their attention on the external environment in order to produce efficient outcomes for the owners of the enterprise. For private sector organizations these will be the shareholders or actual owner/managers. For public and voluntary sector organizations these will be the citizen consumers who use their services.

Perhaps the most useful source of insight into what defines good work is derived from the work of John Budd. In his book, *Employment with a Human Face*, Budd describes the conditions for good work by looking at the interface of what he calls efficiency, equity and voice from a democratic rights-based perspective.[30] Budd believes that work is a 'fully human' activity. That it is, and should be, bounded by the sort of democratic norms found in other walks of life. He does not believe that work is some form of 'separate' existence where democratic ideas of justice, due process, equity, fairness and 'rights' disappear. He argues that given the importance of work to our sense of self, our dignity and our self worth it is critical to see work as the place where equity and voice do exist. Work is in essence a public domain as opposed to a private one. This does give rise to conflict especially where many people believe that the owners of capital are the final arbiters over decisions within the workplace.

It is worth spending a little time understanding exactly what Budd meant by efficiency, equity and voice, given their central importance to the whole concept of 'good work'. As he says, the standard economic definition of efficiency is Pareto optimality.[31] In this state no one can become wealthier without making someone else worse off. If that were the case, then resources have clearly not been used efficiently enough. For businesses this means maximizing profits. Consequently, neoclassical economic theory is based on Pareto optimality and its underlying concepts. These include such concepts as rational economic man, open competitive markets and complete transparency and accessibility of the information required to make decisions in such an environment. Much of our legal framework is believed to support such a view from property rights to the law of contract.

In this worldview, often described as laissez faire, economic agents always act in a rational self-maximizing manner due to the fact that price signals and relative scarcity of resources are freely signalled and equally well understood by all agents. Market failures occur when we interfere with the workings of the free market through regulation or other interventions that knock the market off course. However, as I argued in the first chapter, there is another view, that markets *always* tend to failure, that given the impossibility of achieving Pareto optimality (just think of the thousands or even millions of price signals an adult individual has to absorb and understand each year), the social and psychological elements of efficiency are just as important as the purely economic. Indeed, people show as much interest in acts of altruism or the generation of public goods as they do in rational acts that maximize the returns to them.

In Rugby Union, for example, the needs of the team overwhelm the needs of the individual. That is why this author believes it is a superior sport to say fishing. It provides a richer, more complex arena for individuals to sublimate their own selves for the good of the team. After all, getting kicked or stamped on at the bottom of a ruck is hardly an efficient outcome for the individual. Yet that act of selflessness in falling over the ball to protect it, in order for a teammate to retrieve it and keep the move going, is the essence of the game.

So-called externalities or spillovers are continually interfering with the operation of the free market because human beings like creating public goods. We like to benefit others and do things that are not purely selfish. So if a market were allowed to develop that does not include a broader understanding of efficiency – an understanding that enables all actors in a community to benefit from the outcomes of that market – it will invariably lead to harm for some, even if it benefits many others. If a market drives down wages so far that people cannot earn enough to survive, that will create a burden for the wider society in which those people live. If a market degrades the environment by extracting minerals or natural resources in a clumsy manner such that people and animals can no longer live there, then that creates a set of broader problems.

As Budd argues, the Wagner Act of 1937 following the Great Depression, encouraged the formation of trade unions and increased workers' bargaining positions because the lowering of wages and the increase in strike action depressed aggregate purchasing power at a time when the US needed people to be buying products and services to get it out of recession.[32] This has some direct parallels for developed economies handling today's recession. More generous welfare provision for those forced into short-term unemployment, combined with aggressive job-search activity and training helps keep levels of economic activity more buoyant. Impoverishing people achieves little: offering them decent support achieves much.

What Budd argues for is a concept of efficiency that recognizes the limits of market efficiency and helps put a floor under the social and psychological dimensions of worker's expectations. He thus argues for minimum standards for workers around pay, time, health and safety, redundancy and family leave. He believes that maintaining income through insurances and pensions is a good thing for efficiency as is industrial peace through increased labour bargaining power. Workplaces need public goods, equality of opportunity and employee representation and participation.

Equity also helps drive efficiency. In the early 20th century, work was still long, arduous and dangerous. Setting and campaigning for safe minimums became the way to tackle the lack of equity in the employment relationship. Alongside such minimum standards came distributive justice (am I paid fairly for the work I do?) and procedural justice (will I be treated fairly?). As Budd describes equity it is '...fairness in the employment relationship such that employees receive the treatment they deserve including both minimum conditions worthy of any free human being and fair conditions based on objective standards of performance'.[33]

By definition, equity is underpinned by a set of rights and expectations. Writers from Kant to Pope John Paul II have described equity as an end as well as a means. People deserve as a function of their humanity to be treated with dignity. Not paying someone well or sacking them summarily reduces them to the role of a cog in the machine and offends against this core idea of human dignity. In *Centesimus Annus*, Pope John Paul II argues from this principle that markets must be controlled by broader society and work for their benefits. He argues that moral and spiritual fulfilment can be obtained only if material standards are fairly set and people at work are fairly treated. This is light years away from the view of markets expressed through the formulas of free market economists. Pope Benedict XVI in his encyclical *Caritas in Veritate*, published in 2009, echoes Pope John Paul II's sentiments by stressing the need for business managers to look after the interests of all stakeholders not just the proprietors. Indeed, echoes of Pope John Paul II's and Pope Benedict XVI's views can be found explicitly expressed in Jewish, Islamic and non-Catholic Christian traditions.[34]

Political theory also argues for procedural and distributive justice. In *A Theory of Justice*,[35] John Rawls posited the argument that workplace equity is part of a broader insistence that everyone is entitled to a minimum share of resources and equality of opportunity to engage their skills and abilities in competing for those resources. Social and economic inequalities can be tolerated only if the outcome of those inequalities benefit the worst off and all have opportunities available to them. Political democracy can function properly only if its citizens are free and equal. Lack of a material share in that society's outputs harms democracy and disenfranchises those parts of the demos so discriminated against. There is a basic level of well-being that enables people to participate fully in a democracy. It is the role of work, in part, to enable that to happen. And that cannot happen in the workplace without a degree of equity.

Budd argues that equity is a societal objective of the employment relationship. It is fairness in administration and distribution based on a perception of the sanctity and innate dignity of human beings. For it to be fully developed and deployed, however, it requires properly functioning mechanisms that enable and encourage employee voice.

Budd defines voice as 'the ability to have meaningful input into decisions'. It is not the same as democracy, although for voice to function there needs to be some level of functioning industrial democracy within the organization. 'Meaningfulness' in this context requires those institutional mechanisms designed to enable voice to be based on some form of democratic principles. In practice this means the ability of workers to express dissent as well as agreement; have access to fair dispute resolution procedures when disagreements arise; and be able to participate directly or indirectly through representatives in workplace decision making. As we shall see later, this latter element of voice, when combined with the principles of equity outlined above and an urgency for organizations to become efficient, can quickly develop into a form of 'ownership' sometimes physical, sometimes psychological and sometimes both.

Interestingly, Budd believes strongly that the voice element of 'good work' is ultimately about democracy. He argues that it is not right that democracy should stop when people cross the thresholds of their workplaces. For him the division between political democracy and economic autocracy is stark. The two are antipathetic. Democracy cannot truly flourish if most adults spend much of their time in fundamentally anti-democratic institutions. Without employee voice there can be no genuine political freedom.

Voice is also part of employee decision making. Again the argument is based on the central role of self-determination and autonomy in underpinning human dignity. This is why workplaces that entrench task and time sovereignty tend to have better economic outcomes over time. It corresponds to the old Chinese proverb, 'give a man a fish and you will feed him for a day. Teach him to fish and you will feed him for life.'[36] The great philosopher Immanuel Kant also adds weight to this view, since he believed that human dignity is based on autonomy and self-governance.[37] Participation in workplace decision making is thus morally right as well as being economically sensible – increasingly so in today's growing knowledge economy.

The final element of voice that Budd describes is the stakeholder perspective, which is underpinned by property rights. Such rights in the workplace are plural because narrower definitions may cause unwarranted harm to others. The narrow view of the firm with a simple split between beneficial owners (shareholders) and management has no place in today's economic reality. It is now the case that society at large, which includes workers and owners, has realized that too many companies have created too many negative externalities. These include an over-concentration of wealth in the hands of those who already own or earn most, and pollution of the planet so that the Earth's very bio-systems are at risk. People are aware that such inequities can be remedied only if people have a right to 'voice'. This creates a moral imperative for organizations to act more like democracies and less like autocracies. As Budd argues: 'For reasons stemming from political theory, religious thought, human dignity and elsewhere, extending voice into the workplace is a "moral imperative".'

However, it goes beyond even the realm of the moral. In advanced knowledge businesses, efficiency and effectiveness cannot be truly harnessed to optimum effect without voice; for voice underpins the very autonomies that release the discretionary effort so beloved of HRM theorists. Perhaps most importantly, good work as conceived by Budd and other writers such as David Coats argue for a plural view of the workplace rather than a unitarist view of the workplace.[38] The economic dimension supports this position. Knowledge businesses with their increasing emphasis on innovation through collaboration need high levels of industrial democracy to resolve issues quickly as they arise. The combination of measures that thus entrench efficiency, fairness and voice increasingly will deliver economic, social and psychological benefits.

From an entirely different starting point, good work has been examined in depth by Professor Howard Gardner and his colleagues from the School of Education at Harvard University. The GoodWork Project that began in 1995 has looked at good work from a largely psychological and ethical rather than economic perspective.[39] It has attempted to understand the role of individual responsibility in delivering work and how professionals strive to maintain high standards while not being blown off course by systems and cultures that militate against such ethical reasonableness.

In terms of the GoodWork research programme, good work is defined as 'work that is of excellent technical quality, work that is ethically pursued and socially responsible and work that is engaging, enjoyable, and feels good'.

It has four constituent parts:

- the individual worker and their belief systems, motivations and cultural baggage;
- the culture of the workplace;
- the influences on that culture (gatekeepers in the project's language) that determine the ebb and flow of influences on the workplace; and finally
- the reward system of wider society.

In this take on good work, it is increasingly difficult for the individual worker and individual organization to fight the forces of the market. The market economy is putting such pressure on many of the professions that traditionally upheld values and responsibilities in the workplace that such values are under consistent attack. As we have seen the traditional values of the banker have been ridden over roughshod by a new wave of 'get-rich-quick' chief executives and boards incentivized by knowingly perverse reward schemes. Parliamentarians in the UK have been found out. For many years they indulged in treating an expenses scheme as an invitation to increase their total remuneration, no questions asked. Given the UK has always prided itself on having the 'mother of parliaments' (a claim surely better made for the Ancient Greek 'demos'), this is not a minor scandal but a major indictment on how the 'market' has infected the culture of 'work' and workplaces everywhere.

Journalism is another profession under threat. Its power to investigate and inform reduced by the responsibility placed on it by the market to entertain, titillate and undermine. Take the debate over the BBC and its licence fee. Critics ultimately do not understand the wider purpose of the BBC. It quickly became a great institution not just because it was the first entrant into a new market – television. It became a great institution because it had a core mission to inform and educate not just entertain. It existed to train the best television producers and directors and sustain the UK's acting talent. It was committed to producing the very best programmes, not just programmes that would maximize advertising revenue. But now the BBC, responding to the need to marketize its operations, has become a world-class exporter of television programmes and also a provider of commercial output while at the same time training fewer people and arguably making poorer programmes. As it bows to the demands of the market, so it loses its sense of purpose and core role. The journalists, producers and directors that work in it are thus thwarted from engaging in the good work they believe their training requires them to do.[40]

Even in the Nordic countries, the market is eroding the principles and responsibilities involved in underpinning good work. The Nordic countries have been the lodestar for progressive thinkers and politicians alike. Their economic performance and levels of social justice make them world leaders on most performance scales whether economic or social. They consistently combine high levels of economic performance with flatter, more socially inclusive societies. Indeed, Denmark is unique among developed economies for having increased the reported levels of happiness across its society in the past 50 years.[41] Nordic countries have been able to balance freedom, equality, economic dynamism, and redistribution through high taxes and high welfare spending. The Danes have the highest level of social equality in the world, according to the Gini index. But according to Hans Henrik Knoop, associate professor at the School of Education, Aarhus University and director of the University Research Lab, the high standards of leadership enjoyed by Danish institutions are under increasing threat from globalizing market forces. Political and institutional decisions are being made increasingly at the international level. This means that individuals become more confused about what they are responsible for and whose values and beliefs they follow.[42]

In a similar vein of thinking, Richard Sennett in his book, *The Craftsman*, argues for an intrinsic view of good work.[43] The book is the first of three looking at what Sennett describes as technique. In his words, 'technique considered as a cultural issue'. In essence, Sennett believes that work encompasses the notion of craftsmanship, where people are motivated to do a job well for its own sake. Yet too often, social and economic conditions, values and practices get in the way. This view of work fits well within the sort of good work framework delineated above. It acknowledges that work has intrinsic value that can be done well or ill. It acknowledges the primacy of values in human endeavour, what Sennett describes as the age-old battle between hand and head. And it shows how, again, social and economic values can undermine the intrinsic values of good work.

The final area that impinges on a discussion of 'What is good work?' is what is commonly called corporate social responsibility (CSR) or corporate responsibility (CR). Let me be clear, CSR is not the same as good work. There are overlaps and areas of mutual interest but they are not the same. So what is CSR? According to the campaigning group Business in the Community, CSR covers the following:

- community – includes both community-linked activity and community investment;
- environment – includes climate change and global warming, recycling, use of hazardous materials, water consumption and biodiversity;
- workplace – covers prospective and current employees (both of a permanent and temporary nature and subcontractors);
- marketplace – covers suppliers and clients or customers.[44]

As can be seen, CSR activity can cover most areas of business activity. However, its relationship in most organizations is as periphery to core. CSR is still a largely 'voluntary' activity rather than a driver of business performance. It often acts as a shield for corporations against attempts to hold them to account or as a burnisher of corporate reputation. It includes additional sets of activities rather than activities that are essential in ensuring the organization is profitable and effective. Despite the efforts of the business lobbies it is largely a smokescreen for marginally better behaviour, a stamping or badging of activities already undertaken and, latterly, a complying with increasing statutory requirements based on the principle of polluter pays. As Robert Reich argues in his 2007 book *Supercapitalism*, if we want to make corporations behave responsibly then we must legislate for them to do so.[45] In and of themselves they will not automatically, or necessarily, behave in the ways society may wish. Stefan Stern, the *Financial Times* columnist, put it thus: 'CSR as glorified corporate do-gooding is compromised and flawed. Motives are mixed. Even within the same organization, for every convincing and substantial project being under-taken, there seems to be another more dubious one going on elsewhere.'[46]

Having said that it is clear that some, indeed many, organizations want to behave ethically and fairly. Organizations are made up of individuals and those individuals are, on the whole, ethical. They go to work, as Sennett argues in his work cited above, in order to bring their unique skills, aptitudes and experience to the task in hand. Reflecting this fact, organizational value statements abound. These are important. Some may see them as window dressing but they are what aligns any organization to a wider purpose and helps locate a wider set of objectives in the minds of stakeholders.

But being 'ethical' is not the same as good work. As has been argued, good work is rooted and based on ethical assumptions about human dignity that are universal. As such they are intrinsic. CSR is by definition usually extrinsic. Obviously CSR has been a major weapon in the armoury of the reformist environmental movement, especially around corporate reporting. Yet the impact has been largely marginal. This is because reducing harm to the environment, although important, is not the same as innovating from a carbon to decarbonized economy. Good work will help achieve the latter; CSR gets organizations doing more recycling and offering shared bike schemes.

Typically, CSR offers a set of largely benign processes that complement an organization's existing activities.[47] The drivers of CSR have been many and varied ranging from corporate misgovernance – and even malfeasance – to globalization. In particular, the global environmental movement has made regulators place the 'polluter pays' principle at the heart of new waves of legislation designed to change corporate behaviour – and corporations have responded. The FTSE4Good index was established in 2001. Independently audited by EIRIS and established in partnership with the United Nations Children's Fund (UNICEF), this index asks companies to pass a set of benchmarks and make a modest one-off donation to charity of at least £50,000. The criteria cover the major areas of CSR and the purveyors of the index claim credit for changing many corporations' policies. However, the evidence is mixed as to the effectiveness of such mechanisms in exerting sustained change.

In terms of the areas of good work, CSR offers some alternative options for activities under 'voice' and 'fairness'. These activities in themselves may well be part of the mechanism for delivering good work. Typically they fall into the following areas:

- internal processes and systems that increase levels of commitment;
- activities that engage staff and align with the set of expressed values and thus enhance the employer's brand;
- interaction with customers, markets and other stakeholders.

For example, a positive employer 'brand' can be a way of differentiating one organization from another. It helps to create a strong and distinctive identity aligned to the organizations' values and the values of the individuals. It covers most aspects of human resources (HR) processes and systems, for example, including pay and reward, benefits, holiday policies, parental leave, sickness absence, performance management, recruitment and selection. And the evidence is there for all to see. Organizations such as BP, Shell and other carbon-intensive companies have gone to great lengths with their recruitment literature to let potential employees know they are ethical. Take this example:

> It is also about our people: using their expertise, creativity and skill to compete successfully and help meet the energy challenge. This requires a mindset – or a different way of thinking about our day-to-day business – that includes balancing our short and long-term interests, and integrating social and environmental concerns into our decision-making. It's how we do business and, since 1997, has been embedded in our business principles.
>
> Shell website[48]

And on the whole it seems to be working – a least in part. The Work Foundation and the Future Foundation conducted a study to examine the impact of CSR on the employer 'brand' – *The Ethical Employee*. It was aimed at testing whether an organization's standing in the field of business ethics and CSR could tangibly affect its reputation as an employer.[49] So what did they find?

Roughly 20 per cent of employees found employers with a positive socially responsible image more attractive. These were largely younger people (18–24) and older workers over 45. Not a bad result but it still leaves around 80 per cent who are not that moved and it is this larger number that employers are aware of. It is great to have 20 per cent of one's employees being ethically aligned, but that is not an overwhelming vote for major change. The study also found that employers that matched the organization's values with those of its employees increased retention. Retention was equally affected by the extent to which promises at the point of recruitment were kept.

Since this study was completed it is probable that the 20 per cent may have increased. During the long period of growth that came to a shuddering halt in

2008, employees became more confident of their worth, more demanding of their employers and more ethically minded. There is less deference to institutional norms; more transparency through the ubiquity of digital communications; and greater awareness of self, place and planet.

Employers are going to be increasingly influenced by potential employees' attitudes to society. This is evident in Figure 2.1, which shows the attitude of respondents towards 30 leading British companies. There is a strong positive correlation between companies that are seen to take their responsibilities towards society seriously and those seen as a good employer to work for.

In 2006, international consultants KPMG reckoned that around 80–90 per cent of its 3000 graduate interviewees a year asked about its charitable donations

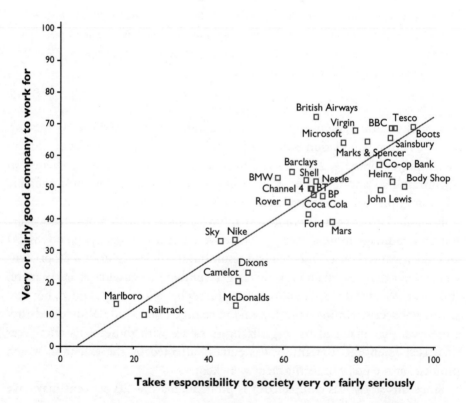

Figure 2.1 Customer and Employee Perceptions of Companies' CSR stance

and ethical policies, up from 20–30 per cent 5 years before. Cynics may say that during the peak years of the boom, why wouldn't they?[50]

A second study by The Work Foundation, *Marks and Start*, looked at the impact of two Marks & Spencer schemes to offer work placements to homeless people.[51] Using a selection of stores across the country, M&S offered placements to homeless people that included training and other support. A Work Foundation evaluation study found that more than 20 per cent of participants ended the scheme with a job either at M&S or with other employers. An important by-product of this initiative was the positive brand benefits that the business gained with both existing employees (who are used as 'buddies' and mentors) and with customers. As one HR manager said:

> It's about feeling involved in something that's really worthwhile, a feeling of satisfaction at being involved in something special. And it really improves staff's perceptions of Marks & Spencer and the kind of company it is.

Like many major companies, M&S widely communicates its CSR activities so that the brand is seen as ethical, cuddly and worthwhile, although it is clearly not enough to sustain the brand given M&S's travails of recent years – and that is the point. CSR is a 'nice to have' not an integral element, whatever the corporate literature purports to claim.

In the *Marks and Start* survey, the majority of customer-respondents felt that they wouldn't actually change their purchasing behaviour because of a company's policies. Twenty-one per cent stated they would and 18 per cent indicated they had boycotted some products.

When companies want to become serious about CSR then they call on the human resources teams for help. After all, HR has a head start in developing unitarist responses to the need for increased performance from people. One of the central tenets of HRM, for example, is that a highly engaged workforce can contribute significantly to improved business performance. Mark Huselid, the US academic, argues that HR must increase the skills and abilities of employees and enable them to use those skills and abilities.[52] The organization must thus motivate the employees to want to do that. So far, so true. Clearly organizations that just sweat their assets will not be as effective in using their human capital as those that invest more. But this does not mean they won't be successful firms. Relying on the so-called 'business case', as CSR initiatives often do, fails to really understand the underpinning ethical and 'human' dimensions to what they are striving to achieve. Treating people properly is not something that is a 'business case'; it is a fundamental right.

Still one of the best studies in the area of people's motivation within the organization is the so-called Sheffield study from 1998.[53] A team of researchers at the Institute of Work Psychology (IWP) over a 10-year period set out to answer four questions. These were:

- Is there any relationship between employee attitudes (job satisfaction and commitment to their organization) and the performance of their companies?
- Can organizational culture predict its subsequent performance?
- Do HR management practices make a difference to company performance and, if so, which ones?
- How do other managerial practices, such as competitive strategies, an emphasis on quality, investment in research and development, and investment in technology, compare with HR practices in terms of their influence upon company performance?

This study showed that 19 per cent of the variability in profitability could be explained by the existence of a reasonably narrow range of HR policies and practices. Most of these policies, as a subsequent Sheffield study found, can loosely be described as the empowerment of teams and the individuals within those teams, mediated by the organization's culture and broader attitudes from wider society.

Another study, *From People to Profits*, conducted by the Institute for Employment Studies (IES) in 1999 demonstrated a positive correlation between employee satisfaction, customer satisfaction and revenue.[54] Its approach was based on that conducted in the US at department store Sears, which showed that retaining existing customers was much more cost-effective than acquiring new ones, and that the 'service climate' created by committed employees was a central driver of success.

The researchers were able to establish a strong correlation between the perceived quality of line management, corporate culture, employee commitment, customer retention and sales volume.

Their attitudes were correlated against a wide range of business performance measures:

- cash sales;
- absence;
- staff turnover;
- customer complaints (service related);
- regional location;
- working patterns;
- staff demographics.

The model illustrated in Figure 2.2 shows the strength and direction of the relationships found by the study.

The study argued that it was critical to measure commitment, rather than satisfaction. In other studies, 60–80 per cent of customers who had defected to competitors claimed to be 'satisfied' or 'very satisfied' in surveys taken prior to

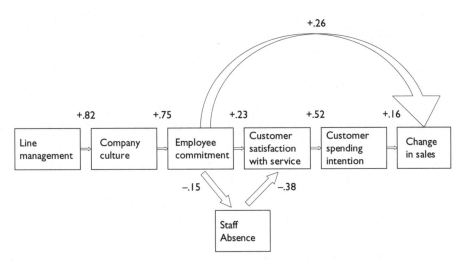

From People to Profits – The Attitude Chain

Figure 2.2 The Relationship Between Staff Commitment
and Customer Satisfaction

moving. But the main conclusion was that employee commitment impacts directly on sales through higher customer service satisfaction and thus a reduction in employee absenteeism.

This admittedly brief discussion of CSR has hopefully shown how it differs in several fundamental aspects from an understanding of good work. It may in many areas complement an organization's decision to become a good work employer but CSR practices in, and of themselves, will not inexorably lead to the organization becoming a good work organization. A spot of recycling, a badging exercise run by HR and friendly, engaged managers does not make for good work. Good work is harder edged. It drives to the heart of how organizations need to be framed and conceptualized. It tackles head on the questions around workplace conflict that reside in all organizations that are not fully democratic. It addresses the fact that people are fully human in every aspect of their lives, not just some.

Indeed as the developed economies of Europe, North America and Asia continue to evolve, good work becomes more important, not less. Creating a more genuine shareholder capitalism as long advocated by my former colleague Will Hutton can only be sustained and built upon if the principles of good work are fully understood and acted upon by governments as well as business.[55] Across the world we need to frame our international economic institutions so that they encourage and entrench the democratic ideals of inclusion, voice, fairness, equity and opportunity. We need to understand that ensuring voice mechanisms in organizations is an essential way to get more from our human capital as well as being an inherently fairer way of engaging in the business of work. Being fair makes people respond fairly. Having a plurality of ends allows people to focus their means.

In the rest of the book I will discuss how high-performance organizations often demonstrate (sometimes unwittingly) good work in action. At this point in our history the battle lines for the future of capitalism are being drawn up. On one side are the forces of the status quo, who want business to go on as usual. On the other are the forces of progression, who understand that fundamental change is required to help instil a better, fairer and more effective form of capitalism. As the great emerging economies develop they will look to the West for inspiration and example. The current crop of political leaders have a mighty task on their hands to create the right sort of frameworks from which good work can grow – but grow it must.

Notes

1 Writers such as Diane Coyle, author of *The Weightless World: Strategies for Managing the Digital Economy*, Danny Quah of The London School of Economics and Charlie Leadbetter among others.

2 www.spiked-online.com/index.php/debates/article/7055/

3 www.jobsletter.org.nz/jbl12310.htm

4 National Statistics online: www.statistics.gov.uk/hub/index.html

5 Bureau of Labor Statistics and http://investing.curiouscatblog.net/2008/09/29/manufacturing-employment-data-1979-to-2007/ or http://coltonspointtimes.blogspot.com/2009/01/truth-manufacturing-in-america.html

6 *World Trade Report 2004* (2005) World Trade Organization.

7 *World Trade Report 2004* (2005) World Trade Organization.

8 Bradford DeLong, J. (2001) *India Since Independence: An Analytic Growth Narrative*, University of Berkeley, California.

9 Chinese National Bureau of Statistics.

10 JPMorgan Chase Treasury Services.

11 National Statistics online: www.statistics.gov.uk/hub/index.html

12 High Level Group on the Lisbon Strategy (2004) *Facing the Challenge: The Lisbon Strategy for Growth and Employment*, European Commission, Brussels.

13 For a full argument see Turner, A. (2001) *Just Capital*, Pan, London.

14 Van Ark, B., Inklaar, R. and McGuckin, R. H. (2005) *ICT Productivity in Europe and the United States: Where Do the Differences Come From?*, The Conference Board, The Netherlands.

15 Reinhilde, V. (2003) *ICT and Productivity Growth in Europe*, DG Economic and Financial Affairs, European Commission, Brussels.

16 Baumol, W. J. (2002) *The Free-Market Innovation Machine: Analyzing the Growth Miracle of Capitalism*, Princeton University Press, New Jersey.

17 OECD science and technology scoreboard 2005.

18 http://transcriptions.english.ucsb.edu/archive/courses/liu/english25/materials/schumpeter.html

19 For a fuller discussion of these points and more detailed research see: www.theworkfoundation.com/research/keconomy.aspx

20 Baumol, W. J. (2002) *The Free-Market Innovation Machine: Analyzing the Growth Miracle of Capitalism*, Princeton University Press, New Jersey.

21 http://athens.src.uchicago.edu/jenni/klmcarn/FILES/papa/hbr8.pdf

22 http://papers.ssrn.com/sol3/papers.cfm?abstract_id=996823

23   Coats, D. (2005) *An Agenda for Work*, The Work Foundation, London.
24   Coats, D. (2005) *An Agenda for Work*, The Work Foundation, London.
25   See: www9.georgetown.edu/faculty/jod/augustine/civ.html
26   http://209.85.229.132/search?q=cache:2lK2kx7OI9YJ:rwl5.uwc.ac.za/usrfiles/
      users/99062813/documents/Johansson_Jan_30.doc+Swedish+Metalworkers+
      Union+Good+Work&cd=4&hl=en&ct=clnk&gl=uk
27   http://europa.eu/scadplus/glossary/lisbon_strategy_en.htm
28   www.eurofound.europa.eu/publications/htmlfiles/ef0212.htm
29   www.ilo.org/global/lang–en/index.htm
30   Budd, J. (2004) *Employment with a Human Face*, Cornell University Press, Ithaca.
31   www.iew.uzh.ch/study/courses/ws0405/331/downloads/kap2_2.pdf and in
      layperson's terms: http://en.wikipedia.org/wiki/Pareto_efficiency
32   www.encyclopedia.com/doc/1O119-NationalLabrRltnsctWgnrct.html
33   Budd, J. (2004) *Employment with a Human Face*, Cornell University Press, Ithaca,
      p20.
34   www.vatican.va/holy_father/john_paul_ii/encyclicals/documents/hf_jp-ii_enc_
      01051991_centesimus-annus_en.html and also more recently www.vatican.va/
      holy_father/benedict_xvi/encyclicals/documents/hf_ben-xvi_enc_20090629_
      caritas-in-veritate_en.html
35   Rawls, J. (1971) *A Theory of Justice*, Harvard, Boston.
36   www.quotationspage.com/quote/2279.html
37   Kant, I. (1979) *Lectures on Ethics*, Methuen Reprints, London.
38   Coats, D. (2005) *An Agenda for Work*, The Work Foundation, London.
39   Gardner, H. et al (2007) *Responsibility at Work*, John Wiley, San Francisco and also
      http://pzweb.harvard.edu/Research/GoodWork.htm
40   For an argument on public value and the role of the BBC see:
      http://downloads.bbc.co.uk/info/policies/pdf/bpv.pdf
41   http://trendsupdates.com/danes-are-happier/
42   Gardner, H. et al (2007) *Responsibility at Work*, John Wiley, San Francisco,
      Chapter 10.
43   Sennett, R. (2008) *The Craftsman*, Allen Lane, London.
44   www.bitc.org.uk/
45   Reich, R. (2007) *Supercapitalism: The Battle for Democracy in an Age of Big Business*,
      Alfred A Knopf, New York.
46   Stern, S. (2004) 'The perils of CSR', *RSA Journal*, January pp32–35.
47   See: Hoskins, T. (2008) *Corporate Social Responsibility Handbook*, 2nd edn, ICSA,
      London.

48 www.shell.com/home/content/responsible_energy/integrated_approach/sd_in_shell/sd_shell_08042008.html

49 www.newunionism.net/library/working%20life/Work%20Foundation%20-%20The%20Ethical%20Employee%20-%202006.pdf

50 www.ethicalcorp.com/content.asp?ContentID=4247

51 Jones, A. et al (2004) *Marks and Start: Opening the Doors to Employment*, The Work Foundation, London.

52 www.markhuselid.com/

53 Patterson, M. et al (1998) *Impact of People Management Practices on Business Performance*, CIPD, London.

54 Barber, L. et al (1999) *From People to Profits*, Report 353, Institute for Employment Studies, Brighton.

55 Hutton, W. (1995) *The State We're In*, Jonathan Cape, London.

Chapter 3

The Good Work Organization

So much for all the theory, what about the practical expression of good work? And how does good work link to high performance? For although there is not a great literature, or many case studies, that would describe themselves as good work, there is a lot of research output around the concept of high-performance organizations and high-performance working. Indeed, the high-performance workplace, at its best, can be said to combine the ideals of good work with new forms of work organization and the more creative management of people. The high-performance workplace is both a description of what happens when these things occur and a descriptor of a set of human resource practices. A related concept that emerges from this literature is the idea of the high-performance work system (HPWS). US academic Mark Huselid led the way in the mid 1990s in trying to prove the link between bundles of HR practices and organizational performance.[1]

To recap, the concept of good work includes moral, social and financial arguments that may encourage organizations to invest in their workforce. The human resources management industry, as alluded to above, has focused much of its research effort on proving that such investments create value for organizations as well; and that such investment feeds through directly to the bottom line. The problem with most of this theory and argument, however well meant, is that it is very difficult to prove in a thoroughly empirical way. Many have tried. Despite the criticism that much of the evidence is at worst tangential and at best correlational, the arguments are slowly convincing a growing number of businesses that nurturing human capital is the primary way they will create sustainable growth given the new economic realities. As argued in Chapter 2, the knowledge economy means shorter periods of market dominance, increased competitive pressures and a fundamental shift in the ratios of tangible to intangible investment. It is 'the people stupid' who make the difference.

A raft of books have been published in recent years that detail the rise of our more affluent society and its consequences. A key expression of that society is impatience. People want higher levels of customer service and they want it right here, right now. The only way to respond is through the interaction of customer-facing staff with the skills, aptitudes and resilience to deliver what is required, when it is required. Goods are expected to work, look great and imbue their owner with a reflected sense of their own status and position. What consumers increasingly want is also great service to accompany the 'good'. This doesn't come without effort and investment. For all the over-complicated noise from the HRM community it is this customer focus business driver that lies at the heart of why people have indeed become every organization's greatest asset. And as we have argued above, to get the most from this asset doesn't require just oil and grease and paint (for which read pay and reward), it requires an acknowledgement that people give of their best when they are empowered and working in an environment in which they have an ownership stake.

Before continuing it is worth quickly understanding the rise of HRM, as unitarist thinking still dominates boardrooms across the world when it comes to managing their human resources. HRM began with the work of Edith Penrose in the 1950s and went on to look at education and training in the 1960s and 1970s.[2] The point of this research was to counter the then prevalent idea that by accumulating financial and physical assets a firm could succeed. The idea that human capital could be a major factor of success was reinforced by studies of the rise of Japanese companies in the 1980s.[3] By the 1990s, authors such as Peter Senge and others were arguing strongly that it was the knowledge bases of organizations that gave them a competitive edge. This knowledge base resided in the knowledge workers within firms.[4]

Further work has developed the notion to find that successful organizations are those that don't just develop individuals' knowledge bases, as Huselid and others argued they should, but also scaled it up through the whole organization. Concomitant with this idea is the finding that those organizations that have a greater sense of social community are more likely to spread knowledge. Additionally, having a vision or big idea is becoming ever more important to aligning staff output and motivation with a 'bigger purpose'. The advantage of the 'big idea' is that it can overcome (when it works) those irritating internal divisions and rivalries that bedevil all organizations however big or small.

But perhaps the most important part of this high-performance story is that good HRM leads to that holy grail – self-actualization. For those readers unfamiliar with Maslow's hierarchy of needs do feel free to read the note.[5] For those who know all about Abraham Maslow you will understand that self-actualization is at the apex of Maslow's hierarchy of needs. This is that state in which an individual feels fulfilled and believes that their potential to act upon the world has been given full expression; that their talents are being used. In the workplace such a state will lead to greater levels of job satisfaction, easier recruitment and better retention. Or so the research seems to indicate. Thus, HRM has tried to make the case – a case won in high-performance workplaces – that people are not a cost but a source, sometimes the source, of value creation. This is a very long way from 1920s Taylorism.[6]

All of these ideas – knowledge being the driver of value creation; people being the key holders and innovators of knowledge; investment in people thus being the key to greater output – have a physical expression in the high-performance workplace. This is where 'good work' has the best chance to come into being and be sustained. In high-performance workplaces, new forms of work organization are evident and 'bundles' of human resource practices in operation. High-performance work systems describe how the high-performance workplace operates.

High-performance workplaces thus include most of the following:

- self-directed teams that control the how and where of their work;
- lots of training for all levels of staff;
- strong communications that allow employees to contribute their opinions (although this is not quite the same as 'voice' as discussed in Chapter 2);

- staff selection that is thorough, complex and utilizes psychometrics as well as formal interviews; that makes background checks and proper references;
- compensation that is market-based and also often group-based in terms of performance pay.

The areas in which these practices operate are described by Sung and Ashton in their 2005 work as: high-employee involvement practices; human resources practices, and reward practices.[7] And according to some studies this is not just tinkering at the edges. Such a system provides a real boost to the bottom line from an additional US$4000 per employee earned to 25 per cent higher profits and 24 per cent higher shareholder value. As the knowledge economy has developed, so such practices have spread – admittedly more in larger private sector organizations than smaller firms and the public sector – but spread nonetheless. The veneer, however, is much thinner than it needs to be. Too many organizations still find it hard to implement such a high-performance system. There has arguably been too much pressure for ever shorter, ever higher returns to footloose shareholders; too many 'get-rich-quick' turnarounds, deals and mergers for such investments in human capita to be considered, let alone made. And many workplaces have just picked and mixed practices with no clear strategic vision about what they are doing and why. This more than anything highlights the failure of the HR profession to truly influence the boardroom. It is arguable that during the 1990s and the 2000s, when a golden opportunity has presented itself to HR to change the discourse around human capital and affect systemic, whole economy, productivity improvements, it has bottled it. HR has preferred instead to stay knitting on the side while boards have self-immolated in an orgy of over-leveraged, short-termism.

Too many companies have remained 'low road' firms, particularly in the Anglo Saxon economies of the US and UK. Too many companies have preferred to stay rooted in a command-and-control management style and neo-Taylorist forms of work organization. And the HR community has focused on managing so-called performance, recruitment and reward systems, or been outsourced into the low value-adding administration of firms' human resources.

In 2005, The Work Foundation conducted a study into high-performance working in more than 2000 companies of all sizes in the UK.[8] It is worth reviewing these findings in a little more detail.

Examination of high-performing organizations reveals a wide number of practices that taken together create empowerment among the workforce and delegated authority by the managers. It is clear that the 'how' of high business performance is as important as the 'what'. For business leaders to derive meaningful benefits from research into high performance or good work they need the practical stories of real businesses that have, themselves, built and sustained competitive advantage. In such businesses it is the so-called 'intangible factors of production' – leadership, communication, engagement, etc. that determine whether the organization performs at a high level or not as can be seen from Figure 3.1 and its description of the Company Performance Index.

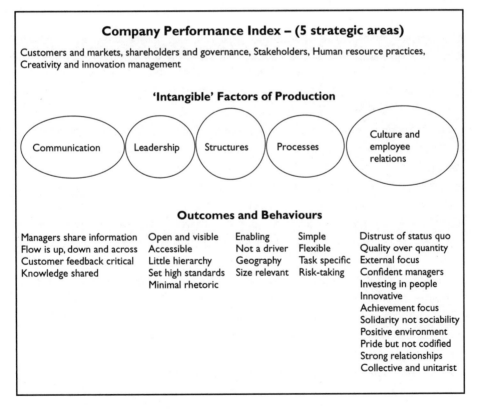

Figure 3.1 The Work Foundation's Company Performance Index

High performance is thus not a matter of defining a goal, setting a strategy and sticking to it. It is about a consistent response to the external environment with appropriate internal responses. Culture is thus as important as investment. Good work policies are as important as sales strategy. And some areas of corporate activity are far less important than many managers believe them to be. Take structure – a happy hunting ground for management consultants and chief operating officers over the years. The secret is, it doesn't really matter. The exact structure and shape used by high-performing organizations makes little difference to how they perform. There is no ideal structure. Very often organizational design appears to be more a function of size, geography and history. What matters is the culture that either empowers or disempowers expressions of ownership and the actions that flow from ownership. Form follows function. Take the case of Hermes.

Box 3.1 Case study 1: Hermes

The Hermes group was formed in 1983 from the Post Office Staff Superannuation Fund, when the fund split to become the Post Office and British Telecommunication Staff Superannuation Schemes. In 1995, the trustees of the BT Pension Scheme bought the 50 per cent holding in PosTel owned by the Post Office Scheme, and PosTel's name was changed to Hermes. Hermes was created in 1995, when it became wholly owned by the BT Pension Scheme (BTPS). As a private company it does not have shareholders. In 1997, the trustees of the scheme agreed that Hermes should begin to offer its services to third parties in both the private and public sector, as long as it: improved the overall performance of BTPS; brought enhanced scale and reduced costs; enhanced recruitment, retention and motivation of staff; and increased the value of Hermes.

Hermes' largest client remains the BTPS – worth £40 billion. As owner of Hermes, this gives Hermes' investment management an insight into the needs of other long-term investors, especially pension funds. There is a premium on keeping costs low.

Hermes has managed to weather the downturn in the market since 2000, in part, it believes, due to its corporate governance programme. This incorporates the belief that companies with interested and involved shareholders are more likely to achieve superior long-term financial performance than those without. By always voting at company meetings, Hermes aims to ensure that companies are run by managers and directors in the best long-term interests of their long-term investors. It enables them to look at how companies operate, and to build consensus with other investors to put pressure on companies to 'do something different'.

Unlike other financial institutions, Hermes does not have potential conflicts of interest, and so can 'punch above their weight' and speak out. Although it may compete on index matching with Barclays Global Investors and on corporate governance with companies such as Standard Life the organization is unique with unique offerings such as its Focus Funds. Hermes has thus taken its corporate governance programme to the next level by being the first major investment institution in the world to establish shareholder engagement funds. The Focus Funds invest in underperforming companies that are fundamentally sound but are undervalued due to a variety of strategic, financial or governance issues.

The success of Hermes depends on the astute investment of the pension contributions it manages on behalf of employees among its 200 or so clients. The focus of HR at Hermes is on improving the quality of current and future employees, particularly, although not exclusively, the quality of the fund managers. Hermes seeks those with extensive knowledge of markets, for example, expertise in retail or utilities. Performance track record, compliance and the ability to take risks are skills desired in equal measures, as many of the portfolios have a risk limit set by clients' pensions trustees and pensions advisers that require the fund managers to adhere to specific rules. For those that are not fund managers, the trade-off for lower risk jobs is a degree of job security not enjoyed by their equivalents working for Hermes' competitors. Hermes does not build up large teams when the market is buoyant, only to cut them in harder times. This engenders a culture of relative security and sensible working hours. Combined with a feeling that management is visible, accessible and tries to promote on merit, employees broadly feel they get a 'good deal'.

The top firms in The Work Foundation study were also characterized by the apparent simplicity of their processes. Again a process is no substitute for creativity and innovation. High-performance organizations thus keep processes down to a minimum but focus strongly on more communication rather than less. Too often organizations invest a lot in planning and processes, often backed up by expensive information technology (IT) systems, but ignore investment in staff, don't think through the design of their jobs and organize their workers poorly.

Process-heavy organizations love to meet, whereas high-performance organizations such as Standard Chartered don't. They are too busy getting on with the job. Decisions thus happen faster.

Box 3.2 Case study 2: Standard Chartered Bank

Standard Chartered is one of the world's leading international banks. Founded in 1853, the bank is headquartered in London and is listed on both the London and Hong Kong Stock Exchanges. The bank serves both consumer and wholesale banking customers and has the stated aim to be the 'right partner' for its customers across 56 countries. Standard Chartered employs more than 2500 people in the UK and Europe, providing products and services for multinational corporations and international banks in Europe, trading and investing across Asia, Africa and the Middle East. It survived the recent credit crunch far better than most other large banks.

Standard Chartered occupies a distinctive global footprint. Having been present in its core markets in Asia, Africa and the Middle East for more than 150 years, the bank has established strong relationships and extensive local knowledge of the markets in which it operates. The bank focuses on creating bespoke international solutions by balancing internal structures with external geographies to try to meet and exceed customers' needs.

A deep understanding of markets, institutions and clients allows Standard Chartered to be the preferred financial services partner for its customers. This combination of local knowledge and technical expertise provides the ability to utilize the bank's extensive networks. The ability to pull together the right team to create a solution tailored to meet customers' needs Standard Chartered believes gives it its key competitive advantage.

Standard Chartered also proactively communicates with its customers. For example, Standard Chartered gained the opportunity to work with Tomkins, a global engineering group, which was looking to move into the Chinese market, by offering credit rules to Tomkins within 24 hours. This required short communications lines, individual and team knowledge of products and external awareness of the market.

Five core values are the glue to benchmarking behaviour internally. The values – responsive, trustworthy, creative, international and courageous – are clearly espoused and lived, forming part of the overall strategy, 'Leading the way'. Peter Sands, the current CEO, is committed to proselytizing about sustainable banking as he believes, rightly, that Standard Chartered's methods are ones other banks should adopt.

The bank is rigorous about data putting a lot of effort into measuring employee engagement and productivity. The bank's annual tool used to measure employee and team engagement has achieved a 97 per cent voluntary participation rate. Detailed business outcome modelling has demonstrated that highly engaged teams deliver superior business performance. This includes higher revenue, profit margins and customer satisfaction as well as greater productivity.

A robust performance management system differentiates and recognizes high performance in the bank. For example, exceptional performers receive individual recognition from the chairman and group chief executive. Individual performance ratings, coupled with group and business unit performance, form the basis of reward decisions. There is a strong focus on differentiating reward according to individual performance contribution.

Finally, Standard Chartered believes good governance goes hand in hand with financial success. The bank's corporate responsibility aspiration and dedication to making a difference, ensures participation in the local communities in which, and with which, they do business. This strong tradition of supporting local communities ensures business is strongly linked to the needs of the communities. This allows the bank to better understand how their skills, products and services can be used in the course of normal business.

Communication is also a core feature of high-performance organizations. This includes communication between people as well as down and across the organization. Managers are willing to share strategic information with staff and representative bodies such as trade unions and works councils. And people value the high levels of communication. It is one of the factors most often noted in staff surveys either because it is good or because it is bad.

A related facet of communications is an organization's ability to share knowledge. This is what McKinsey, the international management consultancy, describe as 'tacit interactivity'.[9] It is the ability to absorb and capture data, information and ideas so that most people are capable of using it to innovate and deliver value to customers and other shareholders. It is *not* about simply building a knowledge management system or having a whizz-bang intranet. It is more about establishing high levels of trust, respect, reciprocity and excitement. It is about killing the idea that 'knowledge is power', that knowledge hoarding by individuals and groups is the route to success. Indeed it goes to the very heart of what makes for a good work organization. It is what a company like Rolls-Royce works very hard to encourage (see Box 3.3).

Leadership is an aspect of high-performance organizations that is much discussed and pored over. I do not intend to spend much time at this juncture discussing the topic at length given there is a whole chapter on leadership later in the book. What is clear from the literature is that in high-performance environments leadership is characterized by openness, visibility and accessibility. Leaders are not distant figures commanding and controlling the heights of strategy while everyone else toils away on the shop floor. Those days are long gone. In today's workplaces the key to successful leadership (and that is leadership that stimulates the led to give more effort and display more innovative behaviours) is authenticity and trust. People in high-performance organizations do ask the question 'why should I be led by you?' more and more often. There is little evidence of so-called 'transactional' or 'transformational' behavioural styles in high-performance workplaces. More apparent is a general lack of hierarchy accompanied by a strong focus to give people access to the resources, information and technology they need to get the job done effectively. As reflected in culture, these organizations are not particularly comfortable or even affiliative places to work and equal measures of task and people orientation are evident.

Leaders in these firms appear to set high standards and expectations of everyone around them but, at the same time, are aware of their position as role models. These leaders on the whole are stewards not visionaries.

In high-performing firms there are also some clear cultural norms. First, there is a distrust of the status quo. These organizations also value quality over

Box 3.3 Case study 3: Rolls-Royce

Rolls-Royce plc continues to operate as a world leader in four global markets – civil aerospace, defence aerospace, marine and energy. The company now has a total of 54,000 gas turbines in service worldwide.

Over the past 10 years, Rolls-Royce has developed a clear business strategy focused on financial targets, a smaller core of employees and a more trusted group of suppliers.

The Trent Engine Programme exemplifies the company's ability to exploit technology and learning gained in the civil aerospace sector, in the defence, marine and energy sectors. This transferral of technology has extended to aftermarket services, where the company has introduced capabilities such as predictive data management, which can be applied across the group.

There are several implications of this multi-stranded approach to innovation for the workforce. Manufacturing engineers have been upgraded alongside the design engineers, requiring a growth in the skill sets of the former. The designers are having to become accustomed to working in project teams with people other than designers. The development of new ICT and information systems can accelerate the product life maintenance cycle of this latter procedure. For example, designers put in information required about a component, the engineers use it and then give feedback on how this operates. Machine operators have now become multi-skilled, working within self-directed teams.

World-class performance, however, requires a culture and behaviour that embed excellence, especially in the context of reduced resources and more delegation of responsibility. This aspect is reinforced by senior managers who use site visits to ask questions on these 'soft' aspects as well as 'hard' performance, and by non-executive directors, whose role in 'asking the awkward questions' is fully recognized.

quantity, have an external as well as internal focus, and a sense of pride about their 'reason to be'. Managers seem to have a positive self-image, be concerned about their own development and expect others to think the same way too. These behavioural norms clearly underpin cultural manifestations of leadership style and internal communication.

A long-term orientation around the needs of the customer is similarly evident. Elsewhere, knowing the business, pursuing excellence and subordinating processes and structure to outcomes and delivery are evidence of a strong achievement orientation. People have some real influence over what goes on in their work unit. Allowing workers as much control as possible over when, where and how the job is done is a key feature of high-performing firms (on which much more later).

This restless curiosity and achievement focus seems to show through also in the employee relations philosophy of many of the top firms. Support, loyalty and long service aligned to the broader organizational strategies are much in evidence. A set of positive employee outcomes around pride, engagement and motivation seem more associated with a challenging, open and dynamic working environment than merely with a culture of friendliness and strong interpersonal relationships. Trust and respect are outcomes driven by belief rather than simple sociability, as is the case with welfare-to-work provider, Working Links.

Another way to examine and understand high performance is to look at what differentiates low performance. This can be summarized as follows:

- Communication and measurement: In poor-performing firms there seems to be more of a focus on a narrower range of financially driven output metrics. This contrasts with high-ranking organizations, which have a more balanced approach that treats inputs as being as important as outputs.
- Structure and process: Discussions about culture and performance are more likely to be characterized by comments about process and internal structure than they are about customer or end product. Although this may be a function of size, it is also because there is a more bureaucratic mindset in low-achieving firms.
- Culture: Poorer-performing firms do not have the same energy or passion about the business. The uneasy fear that 'it may all go pear-shaped tomorrow' is not so close to the surface as with high-performing firms and, as a consequence, there is not the same sense of restlessness with the status quo.
- Leadership: Discussions about leadership in the lower-ranking organizations focus more on 'what the numbers say' – for example, employee survey results, rather than how top managers behave and interact with others. Interactions generally are more formal, structured and 'set-piece' in format than the spontaneity and informality that characterizes higher-performing approaches.

Box 3.4 Working links

A public/private partnership between Job Centre Plus, Manpower and Cap Gemini, Working Links was set up in 2000 to deliver the government's Employment Zones in some of Britain's most disadvantaged communities. Over the past decade, Working Links has placed more than 100,000 long-term unemployed and disadvantaged people into jobs, helping them to overcome the practical barriers to finding work from arranging training or driving lessons, to paying for transport, childcare or even new clothes for an interview. Job consultants provide ongoing support to both the jobseeker and employer.

Social and economic objectives are a strong feature of Working Links, indicative of its status as a joint venture between the public and private sector. Its commercial focus is not, however, a secondary concern. Working Links uses its public/private status to develop its competitive advantage. Working with the most disadvantaged in society, Working Links aims to move people into sustainable work. It is strongly focused on partnership working with employers in order to help ensure that work placements are right for both parties.

Job consultants at Working Links enjoy access to good information as they need it. Mobile ICT such as laptops and mobile phones help them to answer any questions that candidates may have about work when they ask them. Management information has also improved. Previously, performance information took 4 weeks to reach individuals; now data arrive within a few days. This is a consequence of contracts having targets on the accuracy and timeliness of data. Getting people into sustainable work, rather than 'any old job' can make the achievement of targets more difficult. Working Links seeks to manage the tension between short-term financial concerns – getting people off benefits – and longer-term social value – ensuring that job seekers and employers get the right person in the right job.

Working Links has also undergone a business transformation and job restructuring in order to instil more management discipline to deliver on increasingly complex contractual requirements. But becoming more business focused has been a major cultural challenge. Many employees lacked commercial awareness. Contracts have stricter criteria for success. So Working Links has had to improve performance, while not allowing contracts to dictate behaviours. The tension between business goals and social purpose has been managed by Working

Links' belief that 'it's not about profits, it's about saving taxpayers money'.

At a national level, other social barriers that have emerged in recent years are changing the kind of contract Working Links delivers. These contracts deal with people living in some of the most deprived areas of the country, with some intractable social and economic problems. Working Links is responding by working with partners and smaller voluntary sector organizations with experience of these problems that are able to deliver the service, but which may not have the infrastructure to deliver a programme of work or to navigate the requirements of the contract.

The HR strategy has responded to the external business drivers of increasing competition, diversity of contracts and level of contract complexity. HR has thus initiated a major management restructuring. Contract compliance managers (performance managers) are now separate from the task of working with the job consultants (delivery managers) to reflect the increasingly complex, technical task of meeting contract requirements. Team structures have also been lengthened to create space and stretch for ambitious individuals. This involved rewriting job descriptions, for example, around the different roles required to deliver voluntary or mandatory contracts, and to reflect the 'raising of the bar for the skills required to be a performance or a delivery manager'. Leadership development and coaching is provided to support mangers in these relatively new roles.

Following the restructuring and redundancies, clarity around the space to be accountable and improving the performance of those that remained were the next cultural changes to be addressed. Managers now have access to financial and business planning information that has allowed Working Links to be honest about some aspects of the business and has raised the calibre of business acumen among its managers. Although they are most in tune with the business, they very much own their local strategic direction, as they are responsible for delivering contracts, compliance and managing the job consultants.

Communication between managers and staff has improved with weekly team meetings for managers to discuss financial issues, quality and competency frameworks and 'roles and goals' as they arise. Improving knowledge of financial matters – for example with the finance director personally briefing managers around the country – is forcing managers to accept that. Working Links has to be run more like a commercial business in order to be able to deliver social outcomes.

So what should underachieving firms do to improve their performance? (see Table 3.1.) It is clear from the evidence that the so-called 'intangible' factors of production need to be applied thoughtfully and with purpose. Successful companies are resilient and offer models of work organization that allow for flexibility in the face of exogenous shocks, enabling the individual workers and teams to have the confidence to respond to what the markets, customers, new products and other opportunities allow.

But the 'how' of successful company practice is notoriously difficult to replicate because it is by definition contingent. It is dependent on a broad range of cultural factors and the positioning of that company within its own unique sectoral setting and in its relationship with the external environment. The Work Foundation study argues that by blending the elements of high performance from the areas of its performance index, sustainable high performance would inevitably result. Performance prediction would become possible.

Central to this notion of high performance is the idea that companies that succeed understand their 'reason to be' or vocation as a first principle of their licence to trade. They continually ask themselves the question 'why is it that we continue to be uniquely placed to provide this good or service to our customers?' Such firms communicate well to all stakeholders using both unitarist and *collective* mechanisms; have processes that are simple, clear and well understood by all; are led by able stewards – not necessarily great visionaries – and have a culture that is edgy but supportive, challenging but rewarding.

The sustainable high-success company that understands its 'reason to be' and then pursues it wholeheartedly, supported by a set of values that are mutually reinforcing, was not typical of organizations before the credit crunch. The Work Foundation study argued strongly that too much focus on 'shareholder value' upsets the 'blendedness' of strategy and so leads to suboptimal outcomes. Indeed, the evidence from the research suggested a lack of shareholder engagement in strategic decision making that reinforced the conclusion that in many cases there is too distant a relationship between owners (shareholders) and managers.

In the UK, it is arguable that the boards of companies have been so incentivized to increase short-term shareholder value above all else that it is more difficult than it should be for them to focus on what the company does really

Table 3.1 *Examples of typical good and low performance in the five areas of The Work Foundation's Company Performance Index*

Good performance	Low performance
Customers and markets	
• People know who their customers are and understand their role in serving customer needs. Feedback loops are well established and feed into performance improvement and innovation	• People work for others, but have little concept or interest in where their work fits into the business as a whole
Shareholders and governance	
• Investment analysts are a 'strategy soundboard' and understand the value in the business beyond returns on investment. Investors see their role in business as part of the building function – not just as compensation for risk	• Where companies are listed, the City drives the business and its long-term investment plans. For unlisted companies, lifestyle can be more important than growth – so keep the bank manager happy and all will be well
Stakeholders	
• Understand their 'reason to be' and clearly communicate that through values, sense of shared purpose and the way the supply chain is dealt with. All connected with the business, including the supply chain, are pointing in the same direction	• Little or no stakeholder engagement beyond requirements of supplying the market with a good or service. Relationships all transactional. Workers do a 'job' – no more
People	
• People are rewarded for service to customers, innovative ideas, service to their communities and citizenship, as well as for the overall performance of the business	• People's reward and recognition is not matched with the targets they are set in their personal reviews
• Measurement of management practice (e.g., employee satisfaction surveys, balance scorecard) is a diagnostic tool for improving management and plugging gaps	• Achievement of targets is both a measure of performance and a motivator for performance. Performance targets conflict with vision of company (e.g., they are sales driven rather than customer driven)
• Company attracts and retains high-skilled workforce	• Company complains of skills shortages
• HR is strategic	• HR is irrelevant

Table 3.1 *continued*

Good performance	Low performance
Creativity and innovation	
• The culture of the organization encourages creativity and innovation as a matter of course. People are encouraged to innovate, to attend conferences, seminars and classes and to network with other people outside the organization with similar tasks or interests as a means of adding value to their work. The business has a pro-risk management style that can encourage and engage the networked, autonomous and flexible employee	• People may be encouraged to train and develop their skills but have to do this in their own time. Ideas and suggestions for change or improvements don't go anywhere. Training is limited to basic firm-specific training or health and safety briefings. The odd senior manager gets major time and money invested

well – which is make, service, broker or provide something tangible. And these firms, in many cases, suffer from a lack of access to affordable capital (a situation made far more acute since the aftermath of the credit crunch).

It is also the case that the UK has a uniquely long tail of low-performing smaller firms that lack aspiration. They are lifestyle or family businesses who are very happy where they are. For these firms, growing is what other firms do. However, for lower-performing firms that want to be higher-performing, the first lesson is to go back to first principles and understand what the firm is there for and then ask themselves 'how' they want to proceed. What are the values that will effectively encapsulate their 'reason to be' and run through all that they do?

Perhaps the most influential books that underpin this 'first principles' line of argument – which suggests that before any organization can begin to implement good work it must first understand its reason to be – have been written by James C. Collins and Jerry I. Porras. *Built to Last* and *From Good to Great* (written by Collins alone) were two groundbreaking tomes in the field of management literature both for their often counter-intuitive findings and their subsequent relatively low impact on corporate performance.[10] This is not the authors' fault I hasten to add, but more a comment on the myopia of too many corporate leaders.

Collins and Porras set themselves the task of finding the common character-istics and dynamics of visionary companies and setting them into a framework. They wanted to be able to communicate this framework to the business community. They surveyed the chief executives of Fortune 500 service and manufacturing companies and asked each chief executive for their top five visionary companies. They created a list of 20 of the most frequently mentioned and then took out all those established after 1950 leaving them with 18 visionary companies. They then set about establishing a 'control group'; companies from a similar era with similar founding products and acting in similar marketplaces. They described these as silver and bronze companies, respectively. They examined all the companies throughout their entire history. They looked at everything from start to finish including the pattern of initial investment, historical events, etc. They looked for fundamental principles and patterns that could apply across eras focusing on elements that were equally as valid at the start of the company as today. Their framework was organized into nine areas thus:

- physical setting;
- social setting;
- technological;
- leadership;
- products and services;
- vision, core values, purpose and visionary goals;
- financial analysis;
- markets and environments;
- plus an overview of general and business history in the US from 1800–1900 and for each industry represented.

They then asked themselves the question: 'What separates the visionary companies from the comparison companies over the long course of history?' Their findings were simply astonishing. The visionary companies they chose through the above method were: 3M, AMEX, Boeing, Citigroup, Ford, GE, Hewlett Packard, IBM, Johnson & Johnson, Marriott, Merck, Motorola, Nordstrom, Philip Morris, Procter & Gamble, Sony, Walmart and Walt Disney.

The comparison companies were: Norton, Wells Fargo, McDonnell Douglas, Chase Manhattan, GM, Westinghouse, Texas Instruments, Burroughs, Bristol-Myers Squibb, Howard Johnson, Pfizer, Zenith, Melville, RJR Nabisco, Colgate, Kenwood, Ames and Columbia.

None of the visionary companies had lived untroubled lives through the 100-year period of investigation. But their success was indisputable. One dollar invested in these companies on 1 January 1926 was worth US$6356 by New Year's Eve 1991. This compared with a general market average of US$415 for the control group of very good companies. The visionary companies were more than six times as profitable. They defined long-termism.

The findings, in the authors' own words, 'shattered' 12 common myths. First, the visionary companies got off to worse starts than the comparison companies and often without a really specific idea. Some had early failures. Second, visionary leaders can damage a company's health. If you don't believe me, think Fred Goodwin and Royal Bank of Scotland. Porras and Collins likened the leaders of visionary companies to the founders of the US at the Constitutional Convention, they sought to be clock builders and not time tellers. Slightly dull but very reliable.

Third, the dominant driving force for the visionary companies has not been maximizing shareholder value. Visionary companies are guided as much by core values and a core ideology as by seeking to maximize profits. Indeed, maximizing profit is an outcome of the rather dull relentlessness with which these companies go about their business.

Fourth, those core values do not have to be the same in every organization. On the contrary, they can be very different. The key is the depth of belief in the ideology and how the company lives and breathes it. Fifth, visionary companies do not change their core values. In many visionary companies, the core values have remained the same for well over 100 years. It is these values that provide the foundation for everything the organization does. Take a bank. The bank that believes its purpose is to make small businesses grow or to provide finance to ordinary people at affordable rates is likely to have more sustainable success over time than the bank that believes in growth full stop.

Sixth, visionary companies are prepared to take risks on 'big, hairy, audacious goals' in order to make a big improvement to the quality of their processes of innovation and to keep them one step ahead of their competitors. Seventh, they are not always great places to work. If you do not believe in their vision and ideologies these organizations can be very uncomfortable places to be. Great organizations are all like this from the British Army to the John Lewis Partnership.

Eighth, visionary companies innovate and experiment. They do not spend a lot of time on elaborate strategic planning. They evolve rather than grow in an orderly and planned way. They invest in ideas and then see which ones bear fruit. Ninth, and perhaps most interestingly given the belief of market fundamentalists that the market works as well in the labour market as anywhere else, visionary companies rarely hire outside CEOs to stimulate change. Visionary companies prefer home-grown talent by a factor of six-to-one compared with the control group of companies and in 1700 years of combined life spans, on only four occasions in two of the 18 companies, were there examples of recruiting a CEO from outside the firm. This reinforces the finding that these companies are unique because of the way they have constructed their DNA. To run one you have to understand it, be immersed in it and internalize the vision. These organizations prove that fresh ideas can come from within.

Tenth, these companies have a refined sense of their own history and self-worth. They want to beat what they have done before as much as, or more than, beat the competitors. Penultimately, these companies do not limit themselves to 'either x or y'. They are happy to pursue both strategies. Finally, visionary companies became visionary not because they wrote a vision statement but because they created the intangible elements of an ideology and then believed in it.

A single case study will suffice to bring the above points to life (see Box 3.5).

Perhaps the most fundamental point about Porras' and Collins' research is that it explicitly links ideas to do with evolution, human biology, human psychology and sociology with the world of the organization. It tells us that far from being these clinical, rational, scientific places in which everything flows from a master strategy, implemented by drones, managed by highly trained supervisors, the organization is a dynamic, fluid set of intangible interactions and ideas. It tells us that in order to succeed, an organization needs to be more than the sum of its parts and people who work there must really believe in what the organization stands for and achieves. This is why a clear understanding of a firm's 'reason to

Box 3.5 Walmart

Sure, everyone hates Walmart because it is the world's largest retailer, indeed the world's largest company, and it is anti-trade union. The first is not really a legitimate reason to dislike the company. The second certainly is, if true.

It was founded in 1945 by a 27-year-old called Sam Walton. He acquired a franchise licence for a single-unit Ben Franklin store in a small town, Newport, Arkansas. His first year's sales were US$80,000 and by the third year US$225,000. But in 1950 he lost his lease, and the store with it, so he moved to Bentonville, Arkansas and opened a new 'five-and-dime' store called Walton's. By 1952, this had expanded to two units and by 1962 the first large-scale rural discount store had been opened.

Sam Walton's core value was set out clearly and early – an obsession with delivering low prices on everyday goods to ordinary people. This value suffuses everything Walmart does. It is the driving ideology behind all it does and every member of staff understands this. It has been described as 'reflexive frugality'. Walmart's headquarters building is not some vast sun-reaching glass and steel tower block in New York City. It is a low-slung, strip-lit utilitarian office block in downtown Bentonville.

For the trading year 2008–2009, Walmart turned over in revenue US$378.8 billion with profits of US$12.73 billion, up US$1.5 billion on the previous year. Its new CEO Mike Duke was previously its chief finance officer, having joined the company in 1995. The man he replaced, Lee Scott, had been with the company since 1979 before becoming president and CEO in 2000.

Walmart innovates continually. On a trip to France, one of its senior executives noticed a French supermarket had no storeroom. It delivered its goods to the store on the pallets that had been loaded onto the back of the delivery lorry. This saved time, floor space and staff. Walmart has taken the idea to the extreme, cutting delivery to store times exponentially and expanding available floor space accordingly.

Walmart does not play it safe. In the teeth of some ferocious criticism of its labour practices, wage rates and recruitment strategies, its previous CEO, Lee Scott, launched the world's largest corporate makeover imaginable. He committed

Walmart to 'go green'. He promised to make its vast fleet of lorries more environmentally friendly, to source products more locally, to improve the efficiency of service to customers so that less energy was used. To make each Walmart store and depot as low energy as possible. The cumulative market power of Walmart is helping to build new green businesses and bolster existing ones such as the production of solar panels.

In the UK, Walmart is known as Asda. Asda shares the same vision with its relentless focus on keeping prices low. In 2008 it launched a new indicator to illustrate the differential regional effect of the recession and downturn on consumers.

Walmart may not be popular but it is highly effective.

be' is a prerequisite to making good work happen and be successful. Most organizations have an almost fatal love affair with process re-engineering as the route to becoming more competitive and profitable. And most process re-engineering fails because organizations do not have and hold the other elements for success.

As we have discussed above, the successful organizations also tend to be the most enlightened, organic, innovative and democratic. They believe in their founding principles, sustain them over time and enable their workforces to feel a profound sense of belonging and ownership of what they do. This sense of ownership will be described more fully in the coming chapters. It should lie at the heart of the 21st-century knowledge-driven organization. If organizations want success in the future, they need to understand that setting their people free to offer greater levels of discretionary effort comes from giving those people the ownership of the means to do so. For Karl Marx, ownership of the means of production was the holy grail of communism. Depriving the bourgeoisie of their exclusive ownership rights over capital, and rights to extract an economic rent from assets and land was the goal of revolution.[11] Now, most of the working population owns some form of share in the corporations that produce wealth through membership of a pension fund, since our pension funds are the largest group of beneficial owners of our companies. Mass exclusion from control of capital has been replaced by a major extension of ownership rights, however passively they may be exercised. The revolutionary goal of the 21st century is the leadership challenge of innovation and ideas. Getting workers to give more can be achieved only by giving something up and that something is control and ownership. Voice and equity are not marginal considerations for organizational leaders. They are the drivers for considered ownership. They should be standing items at every board meeting. Marx would wryly shake his head in disbelief.

The final element to discuss in describing the good work organization is the rise of interest in the role of healthy work in the modern workplace. In many ways this is an extension of a long-standing paternalistic tradition among organizations that have had an interest in employee welfare. The great Quaker companies such as Cadbury's in the 19th century 'looked after' their workforce. They did so from a sense of Christian moral fervour and to protect the poor working souls from temptation. Nevertheless, these pioneers created early traditions and principles from which good work springs. High-quality working environments value their employees' welfare for obvious reasons. Over the course of the past 200 years, less benign employers have been managed into the undergrowth through successive waves of regulation covering health and safety, pay, working time and employee rights such as the right to strike and the right to have paid holidays. Such rights have recently been extended across the developed world as many more women have entered, and critically stayed, in the paid labour market.[12]

This legislative programme has been underpinned by growing affluence allowing people a better trade-off between work and leisure. Traditional areas of life such as parenting have come under a more forensic spotlight. People have been encouraged to conceptualize themselves as multi-dimensional – worker, parent, lover, friend. Self-absorption has grown, as has the need to self-actualize more (see above). The workplace is no longer something to be endured but something to be enjoyed. And yet recorded stress levels have increased across the developed world. So a new interest has grown in 'healthy' working[13] by creating and developing high-quality workplaces. Take British Airways headquarters at Heathrow. This is not just an office complex. It is a village, complete with its own shops, post office, hot-desking, flexible working, and company TV. The message is clear – come to work and we will make it an experience you'll want to repeat. And the evidence shows that there is a strong link between the quality of the working environment and the productivity of workers within it. For example, studies have shown that when working an 8-hour shift, productivity per hour is higher than when working a 12-hour shift. Fatigue, insecurity, poor health and safety regimes, and stress lead to lower performance and reduced levels of productivity.[14]

Fatigue impairs judgement. In some occupations, ranging from healthcare to transport, it can be fatal. But perhaps the greatest attention in recent years has been focused on alleviating stress. The rise of stress (which I hasten to add is not a medical condition) has been a feature of governmental concern.[15] The change in the nature of much work, away from manufacturing to services and the rise of new technologies has quickened the pace of many workplaces. In manufacturing plants, workers were part of a necessary, usually linear and predictable process. Work may be grindingly dull (admittedly stressful in its own way) but it was known and manageable. In 1979, more than 8 million people, from a total work-force of around 25 million, were directly employed in manufacturing in the UK.[16] Many more were indirectly employed as part of the supply chain or service sector working within manufacturing. In 2009, the figure stood at 2.5 million out of 29 million jobs.[17]

More, new jobs have been created in the service sector. Many of these roles involve direct customer contact in care, personal services, retail, education and health. The switch in the nature of employment and the demands on employees has been too often met with ineffectual workplace organization, poor design of jobs and inadequate investment in skills and training. With the demise of the trade union movement, in the private sector in particular, many workers were asked to do more with less. The result has often been rising levels of stress.

Preventing stress among employees has thus become a boom industry. Many consultancies offer stress audits, stress busting regimes and ways and means of making workplaces healthier. Employees are encouraged to join gyms at discounted rates, helped to stop smoking and reduce alcohol intake, encouraged to take up cycling to work, and one financial services company is even lobbying for employers to give time and resources to help employees with managing their personal finances. Employee assistance programmes (EAPs) are now de rigueur.

On the whole these initiatives are harmless and often helpful. Evidence shows that companies that pay attention to their employees' well-being and health tend to have higher levels of job satisfaction and reduced rates of absenteeism. Companies that don't care tend to have higher rates of absenteeism.[18]

But perhaps the strongest link between ill heath and good work is the case to be made for when organizational injustice creates ill health. Organizational justice is when employees, on balance, believe that workplace procedures (procedural justice), interactions and outcomes are basically fair. There is a distinction to be made between concerns over process (basically 'am I listened to when decisions are being made' and 'are those decisions usually ethical and accurate?') and concerns over outcomes. That is, how much reciprocity is reflected in those outcomes that balances rewards with effort. Those rewards can be financial, career and personal. They can be both profound (my promotion means I can afford a new house or car or whatever) and banal (I was thanked for my effort by my boss's boss). The impact is what is important and that impact is largely culturally and psycho-socially determined.

This epidemiology of unfairness has led to some notable findings by, among others, Professor Michael Marmot. His groundbreaking work on the Status Syndrome followed the medical histories of 10,000 Whitehall civil servants.[19] The results were stunning. Those in the middle tiers of the service were the most stressed and had the highest levels of ill health. Stuck between the proverbial rock and a hard place, these poor unfortunates had little leeway for mistakes and were often forced to work harder and harder for little extra reward. Such effort/reward imbalances led to higher levels of heart disease, depression, anxiety, high blood pressure and heart attack. In one study, workers who felt unfairly treated were at a 55 per cent higher risk of heart problems than those who felt fairly treated. Stress and unfairness at work can mean a much shorter life.

Marmot concluded that a reduced level of autonomy over task and time in the workplace is a significant predictor of additional stress and thus a significant predictor of a range of adverse pathologies. As David Coats has argued, workers who suffer dull, demeaning work with little autonomy and low status are likely to suffer more ill health and higher levels of absence.[20] Firms thus do not bear the full consequences of their poor decisions over work organization, job design and investment since the state must pick up the tab when workers go off on long-term sickness benefits.

Although the evidence exists that unfairness causes health problems, there is as yet no clear line of sight on the exact biological, behavioural and psychological mechanisms that underpin this. People are status conscious. They work best when they feel they have some sort of say in what they do and how they do it. They watch their neighbours and colleagues to make sure they are being treated as fairly as their neighbours and colleagues. And this minefield for leaders and managers is getting tougher and more dangerous as the economy shifts and workers become more demanding of their workplaces.

The UK government has recognized the links between poor work and bad jobs and health outcomes. In 2007, it commissioned Dame Carol Black to conduct a review of the health of the UK's working age population. The review reported in March 2008.[21] Among its many recommendations two stood out. First, the review officially acknowledged for the first time that keeping people in work was a better outcome than allowing them to become economically inactive. Economic inactivity has been the silent cancer blighting so many developed economies, including the UK. It is the worst status to have if it is involuntary. The thrust of government policy should henceforth be to enable people to stay in work. Therapies should be administered while the person remained employed wherever possible. Absences from work should be short term. The second recommendation was the abolition of the time-honoured sick note.

In many UK workplaces, a culture had been allowed to grow and flourish that considered throwing a 'sickie' to be an acceptable part of working life. If the illness went on for longer than a few days, a quick trip to the doctor's surgery would result in the production of a sick note entitling the individual to more time off work or justifying existing time taken. Work was clearly a 'bad thing' to be avoided whenever and wherever possible. Primary health professionals have interpreted (understandably) their responsibility to the patient as being about removing the person from the source of harm, that is, the workplace. Too often this will make the matter worse. I myself have experienced the system first hand when going in for a routine arthroscopy on an injured right knee.[22] On coming round from the 30-minute procedure, I was handed a doctor's note that prescribed 2 weeks off work. I was walking the next day and into work the day after that, not because I am some sort of masochist but because I enjoy my work and would rather experience the ego-massaging sympathy of colleagues and not fear the prospect of getting too behind with my various projects. My experience is the more normal and natural. Inactivity is a curse, a form of prison sentence in itself. The evidence is overwhelming, work is usually better for you than not working.[23]

The new 'fit note' proposed by Carol Black's Review would be electronic and enable doctors to state clearly to the employer and employee what work they believed the person could do as well as what work they could not do. The UK government in its response agreed. As from 2010, family doctors will be able to issue fit notes. Surely this is a major step forward in recognizing the importance of keeping people working.

The UK government has also promised to make sure that general practitioners are properly trained to use the system and that such doctors understand the epidemiological basis for the intervention. Occupational health services will also be greatly expanded complementing private provision and the UK government will set up a challenge fund to incentivize improvements in the take-up of such occupational provisions in small and medium-sized firms in particular.

As The Work Foundation's David Coats commented at the time:

> No-one should underestimate the scale of the ambition here. Many of Britain's workplaces have witnessed reductions in job quality over the past decade, with an intensification of work, widespread dissatisfaction with pay and a decline in the control that workers have over their jobs. Not just government but all stakeholders (including union and employers' representatives) must shoulder their share of the responsibility for improving the quality of employment.[24]

Thus the good work organization is in some senses a chimera. It shimmers just over the horizon, out of touch but in reach. It needs a clear, and clearly expressed, reason to be, understood by everyone who works there. It needs to be open, honest and transparent and create the institutional mechanisms that will allow voice to be heard and equity to flourish. Procedures must be just and outcomes fair. The health of the workers must be seen as a completely legitimate and central concern of the employer. The good work organization goes well beyond the floor of existing health and safety legislation. It invests heavily and continually in the training and development of its staff. Communication to all stakeholders is clear, consistent, passionate and frequent. Leadership is enabling, supportive and open. Leaders need to ask themselves the question, 'why should anyone be led by me?' Customers feel valued and cherished. They have great experiences when encountering products, services and people from the good work organization. Governance is transparent and effort and reward is in balance. Absence rates are low. Workers and management challenge each other and are able to resolve differences. The supply chain is encouraged and developed and high standards of behaviour are set. Colleagues enjoy each other's company but are not complacent. Challenges are continually sought and competitiveness and edginess is a feature of the culture. Those who become stressed are helped back to full fitness. All have task and time sovereignty with work being done in self-managed teams. Recruitment is never a problem and retention is assiduously worked on. Work is done flexibly but according to the highest values and standards.

Clearly such a workplace and organization does not yet exist, but some come fairly close to many of the criteria described above. The market, government and more-demanding individuals are helping to drive companies towards a good work future. But at present there are still too few of them enjoying too little help.

Notes

1   www.markhuselid.com/
2   Penrose, E. (1959) *The Theory of the Growth of the Firm*, Blackwell, Oxford.
3   http://books.google.co.uk/books?id=qxFIp9WIylgC&pg=PA20&lpg=PA20&dq=
     Japanese+management+systems+1980s&source=bl&ots=rfBK12u17X&sig=
     tpN7D6hFF8p0faruLWoP4i8ORSo&hl=en&ei=qSWYSv3bCprLjAejjb28BQ&
     sa=X&oi=book_result&ct=result&resnum=4#v=onepage&q=Japanese%
     20management%20systems%201980s&f=false
4   www.infed.org/thinkers/senge.htm
5   www.businessballs.com/maslow.htm
6   Frederick W. Taylor along with Henry Ford is credited with inventing
     management theory. He sought to use time/motion studies to work out the
     minimal effort required at each stage of the production process by human labour.
     He then set about organizing management systems to ensure that these standards
     were met each and every time. For a fuller discussion see:
     http://en.wikipedia.org/wiki/Scientific_management

7   Sung, J. and Ashton, D. N. (2005) *Achieving Best Practice in Your Business*, Department for Business, Innovation and Skills, and CIPD, London.

8   Bevan, S., Turner, N. et al (2005) *Cracking the Performance Code: How Firms Succeed*, The Work Foundation, London.

9   www.mckinsey.com/aboutus/mckinseynews/knowledge_economy.asp

10 Collins, J. and Porras, J. (1994) *Built to Last: Successful Habits of Visionary Companies*, Random House, London, and Collins, J. (2001) *From Good to Great*, Harper Collins, London.

11 Marx, K. and Engels, F. (1848) *The Communist Manifesto*, Communist League, London.

12 www.allacademic.com/meta/p_mla_apa_research_citation/0/9/9/7/5/p99753_index.html

13 See: www.theworkfoundation.com/research/health.aspx for a raft of new thinking and research into the healthy workplace.

14 www.igda.org/articles/erobinson_crunch.php

15 www.wrongdiagnosis.com/medical/general_stress.htm

16 National Statistics online: www.statistics.gov.uk/hub/index.html

17 National Statistics online: www.statistics.gov.uk/hub/index.html

18 Coats, D. and Max, C. (2005) *Healthy Work, Productive Workplaces: Why the UK Needs More Good Jobs*, The Work Foundation, London.

19 Marmot, M. (2004) *Status Syndrome*, Bloomsbury, London.

20 Coats, D. and Lekhi, R. (2008) *Good Work: Job Quality in a Changing Economy*, The Work Foundation, London.

21 www.workingforhealth.gov.uk/documents/working-for-a-healthier-tomorrow-tagged.pdf

22 The result of a pre-season 'friendly' football match.

23 See: www.ncbi.nlm.nih.gov/pubmed/7641151

24 www.theworkfoundation.com/pressmedia/news/newsarticle.aspx?oItemId=145

Chapter 4

The Ownership Question

Ownership matters. It always has. It always will. Margaret Thatcher knew this when she released the floodgates of pent-up demand for home ownership with her right-to-buy council and housing association property in the 1980s. The knockdown prices helped, of course, but we now have 70 per cent of UK residents owning their own homes.[1] 'Subprime' wouldn't be a term we all understand if people's desire for ownership had not been allowed to get the better of them.[2] Ownership rights are thus fundamental rights. Owning things conveys status, the ability to survive and thrive, the ability to change one's circumstances from poor to average, and from average to good. Ownership allows people to belong. The type of ownership matters greatly as well. Forms of collective ownership are held in high regard by some and vilified and excoriated by others. For some, private ownership is the acme of evil materialism or an expression of self-actualization.

There is neither the time nor space in this book to look at the political history of ownership, suffice to say it lies at the heart of all major political philosophies. The Ancient Greek *demos* was an expression of political participation and ownership rights. Only citizens had the right to vote, attend meetings of the government and express an opinion. Citizens were citizens through birth, membership of the city-state and social standing that enabled active participation in public life. Athens belonged to its citizens. That was how they were defined.[3] Rush forward 2000 years and the same rule applied to membership of the British Parliament. Ownership was the key to membership and participation during the 18th and 19th centuries.[4]

The modern corporation was born in the late 16th and early 17th centuries after intrepid explorers had spent the previous 100 years utilizing the three-masted sailing ship to begin the plunder of the Earth's resources. Early explorers were granted the right to steal from other peoples by their monarchs. The Spanish and Portuguese (who invented the three-masted ship – the critical technology that enabled such daring raids to be executed) were the first entrants, followed by the English, Dutch and French.[5] In order to mount these gold-digging expeditions, their leaders needed to find the capital to stock and crew, and often have built, one or more of these grand ships. The risks were high but the returns could be magnificent.

The genius of the limited liability corporation was thus created. The limited liability corporation was the engine for greater efforts at discovery and enrichment. It allowed many parties to buy a 'share' in the venture. If it all went horribly wrong, they were not liable for anything more than the resources they had invested in the enterprise. If it went well they would be able to get both a share of the profits in the form of a dividend, but also sell on their share when they wished – hopefully at a profit. To be historically accurate, it was the Dutch who invented the limited liability joint stock company in 1602 with the setting up of the Vereenigde Nederlandsche Geotroyeerde Oostindische Compagnie or United Dutch Chartered East India Company. This new company was established to hold a monopoly on all Dutch trade east of the Cape of Good Hope and west of the Straits of Magellan.[6]

Before the advent of the Dutch East India Company, Dutch efforts to control the eastern spice trade from Spain and Portugal had enabled around half a dozen East India companies to spring up. These companies certainly enabled merchants to pool resources, for travelling by sea over such long distances was very dangerous and many ships never returned. Sharing the risk made sense.

However, the companies were time limited. They were established for a period of time (the expected length of the voyage) and then disbanded and the capital repaid to the investors. They were ventures rather than corporations. Moreover, they did not have the continuing financial muscle to build the infrastructure such as forts and ports that would allow them to keep their competitors from Spain and Portugal at bay. So the state stepped in. The Dutch States-General rolled all the companies into one big one and gave it a licence to trade through the new institutional mechanism of the joint stock limited liability company. Like its predecessors it was time limited but the duration was 21 years rather than 21 months. Moreover, any resident of the United Provinces could subscribe to a share. In total, 6.45 million guilders was raised from thousands of investors over the next decade – most of them relatively small investors. Compared with the English East India Company, which had been set up in 1600, with its 219 subscribers, the Dutch East India Company was the true pathfinder for the modern corporation.

It rapidly developed as well. By 1612, the company had decided it would not be liquidated as planned but would continue indefinitely. This meant that a shareholder could get their money back only if they sold their share or shares to someone else. This decision effectively set up the first stock market. Indeed, shares in the Dutch East India Company were being traded almost from its inception. By 1607, one-third of the company had already been transferred from its original owners. Not only that but the setting up of the company in this way allowed a 'futures' market in shares to be established.

As the company's books were subject to public scrutiny at best once a month, those who wished to buy shares, but couldn't yet register them, traded with those who wanted to sell shares in the future. This activity occurred first in an outside marketplace and then in 1608 a covered Beurs was built – the first stock exchange. In 1622, the company's governance was updated, allowing directors not a lifetime's occupancy but 3-year terms. Auditors were also appointed to check the truthfulness of the accounts. The modern company had been born.[7]

The idea rapidly caught on since it defrayed the risks of such ventures by sharing them among so many individuals. The venturer thus did not 'own' the venture. His shareholders did. Ownership of corporations became collective. A defined section of the public – the shareholders – were the beneficial owners.

Those doing the hard work – the captain and his crew – were the servants of the shareholders. The captain may have been handsomely paid for his efforts but he did not 'own' the company unless he too had bought a share in the enterprise or kept a share from his original idea.

So diffusing ownership among many people brought many benefits: more cash to fund bigger ventures; more voices to steer the organization on its journey; accountability for decision-making by the executives of the organization to the mass group of owners; and arguably a break put on excessive risk. Sharing ownership also shared the fruits of success among many and not just a few. Wealth, thus spread, helped sustain other more political institutions. For the past 400 years, other ways of owning corporations have been developed but the joint stock limited liability company is essentially one of Europe's finest enlight-enment ideas.

The reason for its success is that it allows collective endeavour to flourish. It enables more people to 'belong' to the enterprise and belonging is critical to human functioning. As Seth Godin argues in his book, *Tribes: We Need You to Lead Us*, our most primitive instincts, desires and needs require us to belong.[8] We are hardwired to do so. Organizations that understand this will perform better than those who do not. And as we have seen, the knowledge economy is based on people's ability to innovate, spark ideas, utilize higher levels of knowledge, both hard and soft, in order to create value. Godin argues that we have always wanted to belong to tribes; that we organize in tribal ways and that the advent of the internet, in enabling individuals to communicate across vast distances, enables tribes to coalesce more easily. Enabling this process is a core competence of leaders and managers in good work organizations. By creating the means to own what they do it becomes easier for people to belong. In other words, people give of their best when they have a stake in what they are doing. That stake can be a 'share' or a psychological stake in the enterprise or organization. Some of the most committed workers I have ever met worked for overseas development agencies. They did not 'own' a share. They were often on lousy pay, but they owned the organization as much as those who led them.

Indeed, for many of the top managers in these organizations, such passionate ownership often creates its own problems. Such workforces need more leadership rather than less. Negotiation is not a luxury but a necessary skill for such leaders.

The usual tools at management's disposal such as performance-related pay, additional holidays, days off in lieu, are worthless baubles to be treated with contempt. When you have internalized the idea that you are saving the world, whale, dolphin or planet, what matters most is having a say in how you go about achieving that goal.

Clearly, at one end of the spectrum there is literal ownership of the enterprise. In the UK there is a lobby group, Employee Ownership Association (EOA), that campaigns for the extension of employee share ownership schemes.[9] It makes the case that such schemes lead to greater profitability and more sustainable businesses. It's also not bad for the workforces either. The EOA calculates that employee-owned businesses count for £25 billion of the £1.5 trillion worth of UK GDP.[10] This is a small proportion, but a growing one. A typical example of an employee-owned company that has switched from being a family-owned enterprise fairly recently is given in Box 4.1.

The story of Herga is a very charming one, but EOA claims such companies make more money than others. One study suggests that co-ownership should work better because communication and consultation with co-workers would improve and employees will behave and think like owners.[11] Certainly the ex-Chancellor, now current UK Prime Minister agrees. He has offered incentives for wider employee share ownership through schemes such as share incentive plans (SIPs), company share option plans (CSOPs) and enterprise management incentives (EMIs).[12]

In an EOA survey of co-owned firms, 72 per cent reported that staff worked harder, 81 per cent that they took on more responsibility, 49 per cent that competitiveness was enhanced and 44 per cent that profits were higher. As Richard Reeves states in his EOA pamphlet, *Co-Co Companies: Work, Happiness and Employee Ownership*: 'The Employee Ownership Index (EOI) has consistently outperformed the FTSE All-Share. In cash terms, an investment of £100 in the EOI in 1992 would have been worth £349 at the end of June 2003; the same amount invested in the FTSE All-Share would have been worth £161. Conyon and Freeman estimate that an All Employee Profit-Sharing Scheme boosts share values by "about 9.79 per cent".'[13]

Such returns are correlative rather than causal, but significant nonetheless. Indeed, it also seems that co-owned companies have higher levels of job satisfaction recorded by their employees than other companies. This is not to say that

Box 4.1   Herga

- Switch manufacture.
- Majority employee-owned since 2006.
- Collective ownership of shares; some individual share holdings.

Over a 40-year period, Peter Tracey has built up his family business Herga, a specialist switch manufacturer based in Suffolk. The business has grown from six employees in 1969 to around 130 today. Turnover is £5 million and Herga has twice received Queen's Awards for Enterprise. Peter Tracey has chosen to donate his 51 per cent personal shareholding in Herga to his employees, transferring the shares to an employee benefit trust in 2006. His decision is designed to secure the long-term independence and sustainability of the business to which he admits having a strong emotional attachment. Gifting, rather than selling, the shares means that Herga is not burdened by a heavy level of debt.

Peter Tracey says that the John Lewis Partnership model influenced his thinking and – as at John Lewis – the key instrument for maintaining employee ownership at Herga is a partnership trust. Unlike John Lewis, however, Herga has also made arrangements for employees to own shares in the company directly. As part of the 2006 change, Peter Tracey gifted 4 per cent of the shares to all staff who had been with Herga for at least a year. The company also operates a SIP for employees who want to buy further company shares in a tax-efficient way.

Herga shares its success. For many years, 10 per cent of the company's profits have been shared among the team. In 2009, the first partnership bonus becomes due, when a further 10 per cent of the company's profits will be paid to all Herga's employees who have taken individual shares in the business. External shareholders (in practice a Tracey family trust that holds a residual 32 per cent shareholding) will not receive dividends in line with Peter Tracey's wishes. The aim is for the company to buy out the family trust over time, so that eventually 100 per cent of Herga's shares are owned by employees, both collectively and individually.

high levels of job satisfaction and high levels of trust are exclusive features of co-owned businesses. Many traditionally owned companies have similar high levels of trust and recorded levels of job satisfaction. However, literally owning your work is unlikely to damage your self-esteem and overall levels of happiness, as much as being a wage slave with no say whatsoever in the way you work and what you do when you are at work. This form of modern slavery has been well documented. Take this story as typical of its kind. It's about the work of Liz, a bank employee:[14]

> We had a laminated sheet of barcodes representing a series of tasks on our desk, and every time we did anything we had to swipe the appropriate barcode with a laser reader pen. We had 17 minutes to get out a mortgage offer. If the phone went, we had to answer it within two rings and all the calls were recorded and monitored to check whether we were giving out accurate information and the manner with which we dealt with the call. Every time we made a call we had to swipe the pen, and every time we answered the phone we had to swipe. You had to swipe if you were going to the toilet or to get a coffee. If you wanted to talk to a colleague you had to swipe, so that all interactions with colleagues were being monitored. When we had finished for the day, we had to log in and log out. The whole thing was then downloaded to the supervisor, who could look at the log to check productivity. It was like working for Big Brother. Some of my colleagues would say it's for the greater good – trying to get profits up. The people I worked with came from very varied backgrounds. Some women who had worked in factories didn't mind it because they were used to being closely monitored. It was the younger ones who resented it, or those who came from managerial backgrounds or were college-educated: they wanted more freedom and initiative.

And that was working for a bank whose senior executives made millions of dollars each year as they developed the casino capitalism of which this worker was a part.

Such a scenario was typical of blue-collar environments over much of the past century, where factories and manufacturing enterprises developed ways and means of improving the linear productivity of their processes and the workforces who operated them. These Taylorist mechanisms have crept into white-collar workplaces too.

But even where the work itself is not so regimented, work intensity can have the same demoralizing effect. Take this story of a young female lawyer:

> As I got more senior the work began accumulating, and with no idea when the work would come in and when I would be forced to stay late, I began not to make appointments to see friends, go to plays, etc., because it became too frustrating to cancel all the time. But that ends up leaving a vacuum in life where friends and leisure should be. After long evenings at work, weekends when I wasn't working were needed to catch up on sleep, never mind the household chores.[15]

Ownership is thus both a physical and psychological state. If the worker does not enjoy some sense of ownership over when, where and how they work, that person will not be able to fulfil themselves or their obligations to their employer as well as they might be expected to. On the whole, people want to enjoy what they do at work. After all work is a major way that adults act upon the world.

So how are people doing? How much do they enjoy their work and are they satisfied with their jobs? If we have high levels of ownership (in the broadest sense of the term) we should see high recorded levels of satisfaction with work.

Table 4.1 shows measures of work satisfaction and, at first glance, people seem relatively satisfied with their jobs. More than two-thirds of respondents (67.3 per cent) felt satisfied or very satisfied with their work or job. Women were slightly more satisfied than men. Fifteen per cent of workers were dissatisfied or very

Table 4.1 *Overall satisfaction with work or job at the moment*

	% respondents		
	Total	Men	Women
Very dissatisfied	4.8	4.4	5.2
Dissatisfied	10.2	11.4	9.0
Neutral	17.7	18.3	17.2
Satisfied	45.2	44.5	45.9
Very satisfied	22.1	21.4	22.7

Note: Survey of more than 1000 adults working in the UK.

dissatisfied with their lot with 1.6 per cent fewer women than men dissatisfied or very dissatisfied. These figures seem encouraging until the numbers of dissatisfied or very dissatisfied are translated from percentages into numbers. In stark terms, this implies that 4.2 million workers in the UK economy are pretty unhappy with their work or job. That is quite some tale of dissatisfied workers. The effects of such dissatisfaction will be felt in higher rates of absence, higher rates of turnover, lower levels of customer satisfaction and, ultimately, lower levels of productivity.

Most people feel OK about what they are doing but in good work organizations that satisfaction rating would be far higher. Great companies to work for have the highest ratings because they have set their workforce free to own what they do.

The three sovereignties

Time

Everyone wants to be in charge of their own destiny but few are. Life is like this. Chance intrudes to change things. People suffer bereavements, illnesses, injuries and acts of God. These things we have to accept. It is inevitable that we do not always enjoy our own locus of control; that it is sometimes outside us. However, when that happens day-in day-out, as some of the examples quoted above have shown, it can be devastating. Good work requires that we have more control over time, task and place. That may be fine for a home-based writer who works when the muse moves them (for muse read deadline) but how can this be true for a factory worker or a bus driver?

First, time sovereignty.[16] Time has not always been so circumscribed. Nine-to-five is a fairly recent invention. Before the Industrial Revolution, work was largely home-based and very flexible. People worked on the task at hand. Change was slow and incremental. Most people still lived in the countryside and worked on the land. Nature cannot be hurried so work had a rhythm that was both driven by nature's demands and relatively slow-paced for most of the year. People had been working like this for 1000 years. When work in the fields was not required, work in the home, such as weaving, took over. The type of work people did in 1800 would have been very familiar to an Anglo Saxon peasant living in 1066.[17]

An elite, which included craftsmen and the educated few, clustered in towns and cities serviced by a growing service sector of household servants, tradesmen and transport specialists. Builders, merchants, masons, draughtsmen, iron workers and tanners congregated in the great open sewers that were then our major cities. A fantastic evocation of a 17th- and 18th-century city can be found in Patrick Suskind's novel *Perfume*.[18] On the whole people bartered as much as worked for money. Fees were paid for piece work and finished goods. Time did not really come into it. A description of the English at work from 1681 helps shed light on how we worked then:

> When the framework knitters or makers of silk stockings had a great price for their work, they have been observed seldom to go to work on Mondays or Tuesdays but to spend most of their time at the ale-house or nine-pins... The weavers 'tis common with them to be drunk on Monday, have a headache on Tuesday, and their tools out of order on a Wednesday.[19]

This all changed with the advent of the Industrial Revolution. Now time mattered. Machines didn't sleep. People did. Thus the owners of the new cotton mills needed to organize their workforces in a consistent way. It wasn't like the rural economy where everyone worked like a dog at harvest time. The new industrialists needed to organize people to work like dogs all the time. Sweating your assets was what it was about. Nor were the early 19th century captains of industry fussy about who they employed. Women and children were just as good, if not better with their more nimble fingers, as men.[20]

At the beginning of the industrial period, workers were organized to work for up to 14 hours a day. They slept on the premises or in huts owned by the mill owners. Life was grim. Workers suffered fairly short, brutish lives in many cases. Industrial injuries reached epidemic proportions until the great Victorian legislators and philanthropists stepped in.[21]

Adam Smith, the great Scottish economist and philosopher, recognized the profound nature of the change in the way people worked.[22] For the first time, people left home to go to work. So too, E. P. Thompson who in his essay on time and work stated: 'Mature industrial societies are marked by time-thrift and a clear demarcation between "work" and "life". Time is now currency: it is not passed but spent.'[23] Industrial work thus required management of time, synchronization of the workforce and control of the units of production – the workforce.

Clocks gained two hands as minutes became more important in the new factories. Workers were made to clock in and clock off. Breaks were timed. The age of the tyranny of the clock had begun. By 1770, words like punctuality had been created to describe the new orderliness.[24] The birth of industrialism happily coincided with the rise of neoclassicism. Western Europe woke up to the true glories of Ancient Greece and Rome as the wonders of Pompeii began to be more thoroughly excavated and the idle rich began to go on Grand Tours. Poets like Byron dwelt on the wonder and awe of ancient civilizations.[25]

To people at that time, the ancient civilizations spoke of power, order, grandeur and possibilities. These civilizations were driven by forces newly unleashed in the industrial age. This view of the world allowed the early industrialists to see themselves as creating a genuinely new society that would be redefined with new layers of class placed upon the existing, still largely feudal, kingdoms of Europe. Merchants became industrialists and the rise of the middle classes became inevitable as the new industrialists needed capable managers and stewards to oversee their enterprises. Civic government grew and a civil service was born complementing the existing routes that able but lower-class people could utilize to escape their accident of birth such as the military, the professions and the clergy.

So powerful have these ideas been – and particularly around time – that we are still largely locked into a late 18th century/19th century mindset. Industrial time is still what we all largely work to even though it is inefficient, wasteful and arguably harmful to the planet in today's knowledge economy. Just look at the train timetables and see how many more services are run by train companies to get people into cities by 9am and out between 5pm and 7pm.[26]

Workers of course didn't take the tyranny of organized time lying down. They organized themselves into trade unions and spent the next 120 years arguing for less time at work for higher levels of pay. Thus was born the division between 'work' and 'life'. 'A fair day's work for a fair day's pay', became the motivating slogan for the union movement. Organized labour gave in to the demands of the owners of capital and recognized the organization of time as being the best way to deliver the new manufactured goods in an efficient manner. Instead of revolution as Marx predicted, in the UK and elsewhere, we got reform.[27]

This industrial age mindset has dominated the debate about work–life balance. But most workers that toil for long hours today are highly paid, well motivated individuals who like what they do. Those who suffer do so usually not from a lack of time sovereignty but through a lack of task and place sovereignty (on which more later). And there are still some groups of workers that fit the stereotype of horribly exploited workers.

Workers in the UK and US work the longest average hours in the developed world. This average had reduced by 1 hour per week over the 5 years to 2008 in the UK through a combination of more people in work (the increased bargaining power for those in work that comes with tighter labour markets), the impact of the European Working Time Directive (despite the opt out) and increased flexible working practices, as organizations dimly recognize that today's workers are motivated by autonomy and not just pay.[28]

However, working long hours remains a problem on three levels. First, it can harm an individual's health. Second, long hours do not equate necessarily to higher overall productivity (as seen above) and third, hours as a proxy for effectiveness is increasingly irrelevant in a knowledge economy where aspects such as innovation, ideas and charisma may be as, or more, important than just time at the desk.

Table 4.2 looks at who is working what hours in the UK economy. In total, 65.3 per cent of the population are working more than 35 hours a week and 35.7

Table 4.2 *Average hours worked per week by gender*

Hours worked per week on average	Men %	Women %	Total %
Under 16	4.4	8.9	6.7
16–25	2.7	24.9	13.9
26–35	8.2	19.2	13.8
36–40	29.9	29.2	29.6
41–50	33.8	12.2	22.9
51–60	13.7	3.2	8.4
Over 60	6.6	2.2	4.4

Note: Survey of more than 1000 adults working in the UK.

per cent work more than 40 hours a week. Nearly four times as many men as women are working more than 50 hours a week (20.3 per cent compared with 5.4 per cent). The more you earn, the longer you work. Of those earning between £46,000 and £51,000 a year, nearly 70 per cent work up to 60 hours a week and 7.7 per cent work more than that. But once you earn more than £51,000 a year, the chances of working more than 60 hours a week increase to more than 20 per cent. The self-employed work the longest hours with 25 per cent working more than 50 hours per week compared with 15.5 per cent for full-time workers. However, more than 400,000 workers are earning less than £16,000 a year for working more than 60-hour weeks – and this is an area of the labour market that is more likely to be female dominated.

The reasons why people work long hours is shown in Table 4.3. Nearly 40 per cent of people agree that they work long hours for fear of losing their job. More women than men (52 per cent compared with 35 per cent) feel this way. It should be noted that many women's jobs are part time and low paid and in sectors of the economy that are less well regulated. There is also a pay differential. The lowest paid are the most likely to feel this way. Those earning less than £16,000 a year are nearly six times as likely to fear job loss if they don't put in the time as those on more than £41,000 a year.

This level of job insecurity is understandable in a major recession but may still perhaps be exaggerated – after all, job tenure has not declined that much over the past 20 years, despite perceptions to the contrary.[29] Long hours as a route to promotion, with a response rate of 60.1 per cent agreeing with the statement,

Table 4.3 Reasons for working long hours

	Disagree	Agree	Neutral
I work long hours because I am scared of losing my job	34.6	39.3	26.1
I work long hours because I won't let my colleagues down	60.1	20.2	19.7
I work long hours because of the culture of the organization	83.3	8.3	8.3
I work long hours because of the volume of work	50.4	24.8	24.8
I work long hours to speed up getting promotion	19.8	60.1	20.2

Note: Survey of more than 1000 adults working in the UK.

indicates that 'hours in' is still the best way of impressing the boss. Helping out colleagues is comparatively less important to people (20.2 per cent) in explaining why they work long hours.

Work intensification seems to be less important than some commentators have assumed. Only 24.8 per cent of people agreed that the volume of work created their long hours. Yet self-employed people were half as likely to cite this as a reason (12.8 per cent compared with 26.8 per cent for full timers and 26.6 per cent for part timers). This would seem to indicate a strong link between control over work done and the dissipation of the negative effects of working long hours.

But what about the total hours worked? Were people happy with their lot or would they like to work less? The answer seems to be a resounding 'yes' to fewer hours from men and a more equivocal 'maybe' from women. This is not surprising given the fact that far more men than women work full time. Overall, 61 per cent of people want to work fewer hours – 70 per cent of men and 52 per cent of women.[30]

The more highly paid workers are, the greater the chances of wanting to work fewer hours. Those earning more than £31,000 a year are nearly three times as likely to want to work fewer hours than those on less than £11,000 a year, and 30 per cent more likely than those earning up to £16,000 a year. The full-time workforce wants fewer hours the most (73.3 per cent), followed by the self-employed – despite the large number working more than 50 hours a week (see above) – at 61.5 per cent. Only a quarter of part timers want fewer hours. Perhaps of more interest is that more than 37 per cent of people would like to work fewer hours even if this meant earning less and of those 42 per cent were aged 16–24.[31]

The reasons why people want to work less are many and varied but the number one reason across all ages is to have more leisure time. Forty-five per cent of those wanting to work less want to spend time doing what they enjoy, whatever that may be. For men the number rises to 50 per cent compared with 40 per cent of women. Going down the pub and on the golf course is significantly more important to men than spending time with their kids (20 per cent), friends (20 per cent) or partner (22 per cent). There are also some significant differences by marital status. Married people are more likely to want to spend time with their children (29 per cent) or partner (33 per cent) as the preferred option when more time becomes available to them. In contrast, single people, divorced people and those starting out in relationships are far more likely to want to spend time on leisure (58.5 per cent, 65 per cent and 68 per cent, respectively).

Although many people want to work fewer hours, a significant number – around 22.5 per cent – want to work more hours. The highest positive response rates were from those earning less than £11,000 a year (30 per cent) and those earning between £11,000 and £21,000 (40 per cent). Beyond £36,000 a year, no one wanted to work more hours. Of those who wanted to work longer hours, a third of the part timers among the sample who said 'yes' to this question wanted more hours. For 64 per cent, money was the reason for wanting to work longer hours. However, 40 per cent wanted to work longer hours because they enjoyed the work – the largest group in this category was aged 35–44.[32]

These data show that hours and time are still a major battleground for working people, but the reasons why are more complex than the work–life debate often gives credit for. Money is a major driver – how much is ever enough? But control is the other major driver. People want to feel ownership over their time. That is why the longer working self-employed do not care about long hours as much as employees. They have no boss standing over them. Their time pressures are market or external ones. Intense, severe and pressurizing they may be, but the self-employed seem to cope with it better than other groups of workers.

A divide exists between those who have time sovereignty and those who don't. The more educated, the wealthier and the confident control their time better. They work hard because they enjoy working and want to succeed. For those at the apex of the worker pyramid, work–life integration has become the norm. They own their time. They work when they want to because the miracle of digitization frees them from the normal boundaries by which people work. Some are workaholics, some not. What matters to them is not when they work but what they do and how they do it. They have succeeded in banishing the 'job' and instead have found 'work'. This status is enjoyed by far fewer people than should enjoy it. Without time sovereignty, ownership – the key to productivity in knowledge industries – is compromised.

But back to our factory worker or shop worker or call-centre operative, what can they do to enjoy time sovereignty? After all they are trapped in an industrial age environment where time is the obvious measure of productivity. Well how about organizing shift patterns to suit the individuals more, as Argos did with its lorry drivers at its Magna Park site in the UK or John Lewis does with its supermarket staff? How about remote working for call-centre operatives so they can fire up the system from home, to fit around children, as BT have done with some of their staff? And what about the idea of the working year of 1770 hours as used by Dutton Engineering, which has abandoned set shift patterns, enabling its staff to work more flexibly? These are enlightened companies that instinctively understand the role of ownership in driving productivity.

Poor managers, however, still insist on people being present where they can see them. So insecure and inadequate are these individuals that they still subscribe to the 'if I can't see them, the bastards are skiving' school of management. Certainly in any workforce there will be a tiny minority who will stop working as soon as they can. The opposite is true for the majority. People work best when freed from industrial-age prescriptions. This is why BT reckon their home-based workers are 20 per cent more productive than their office-based workforce.[33]

Task

As Richard Sennett argues in his book on craftsmen, human beings have an innate desire to do a task well.[34] Too often in modern workplaces that desire to do well is crushed and sublimated under a prescriptive set of conditions and boundaries. This starts with the way work is organized and the way jobs are designed. People innately want to work in the way that suits them best. But this will create conflict if it is not bounded by rules and protocols and standards. Productivity would indeed collapse if people were not sufficiently skilled to do the task in hand. There would be no point, for example, in asking me to paint a picture, or indeed paint anything as I lack the skills, talent and training to do so. Yet in many modern workplaces this is exactly what happens, particularly among managers.

It works something like this. In order to keep my publisher happy that they won't be sued, the description that follows is entirely fictional but describes a scenario that will be familiar to many working people.

Joanna and Kevin have been very good salespeople for Mulcahy and Gross – shower-ring specialists – for the past 5 years. Bob and John, two managers, have just been recruited by a rival company and the sales director, Mike French, has decided (without a lot of thought) that Joanna and Kevin deserve a promotion for their exemplary sales performance. 'Well done to both of them,' we instinctively think – a sensible example of internal promotion. It will motivate others to see there is a career to be made in Mulcahy and Gross and that hard work is rewarded.

The problem comes when Joanna and Kevin start in their new roles. Their unquestioning sales abilities – drive, ambition, competitiveness, goal orientation, focus – don't translate brilliantly into the management of people. This may also be exacerbated by the fact they are managing people who were once their peers. Joanna sets a new start time for everyone to begin work (at Mulcahy and Gross's HQ on an industrial estate just outside Swindon) of 7.45am. When Angus leaves to pick up his daughter from after-school club at 5.30pm, Joanna frowns and asks him pointedly where he is going. Angus lies and says he has a doctor's appointment. The dominant culture among the team goes from amiable competitiveness to fear and a desire to please Joanna in order to keep her off their backs. Collegiality falls. Knowledge stops being shared.

Kevin, not to be outdone, begins the process of micro-managing his salesforce. He gets each salesman to begin the working week from HQ and asks them to present an hourly update on who they have seen and what they have done for the week that has just passed. Over the next six months people leave, customers leave and everyone is scratching their heads as to why this is happening. Exit interviews reveal that people cannot stand being micro-managed in this way. Under the previous management they were given more discretion to get on with their jobs.

This case study, fictional though it is, highlights that people cannot enjoy task sovereignty if they don't have the tools to do the task. Too often good technicians will be put into management roles for which they do not have the skills, training or aptitude.

A 2007 study by the Institute of Work Psychology, led by Professor Toby Wall, concluded that among more than 100 manufacturing sites studied, the only human resource practice that made any difference to productivity was the ability of teams to direct themselves.[35] Self-management created a significant jump in productivity. This is another study that builds on the evidence from the high-performance research described in Chapter 3 and shows that giving employees more task autonomy and control leads to productivity growth.

However, there is strong evidence of declining task autonomy across the UK economy. Some have suggested that the rise of more stringent performance management systems that detail, in effect, the desired outcomes required have offset any relaxing of rules around how the job should be done. This type of approach has effectively reduced task autonomy even when the organization believed it was making delivery of the task more flexible for the individual worker concerned.

In the 2004 *Workplace Employment Relations Survey*[36] (WERS), one of the most comprehensive studies into workplace conditions conducted anywhere in the world, nearly two-thirds of workers are neutral, dissatisfied or very dissatisfied with their experience of shaping their own work (see table below).

Table 4.4 shows that only 38 per cent of employees are satisfied with their level of involvement in decision making in the workplace. Such findings are contrary to the need for ownership of task, time and place that the good work organization tries to embed. At present, too few UK workers have a means of expressing their views effectively and 42 per cent of workers are unhappy with their level of job influence. This suggests that the decline of task autonomy has gone hand-in-hand with a loss of 'voice'.

Table 4.4 *Job satisfaction (% of employees)*

	Very satisfied	Satisfied	Neither	Dissatisfied	Very dissatisfied
Sense of achievement	18	52	19	8	3
Scope for using initiative	20	52	18	8	3
Job influence	12	45	28	11	3
Training	11	40	26	16	7
Pay	4	31	24	28	13
Job security	13	50	22	11	5
Work itself	17	55	19	7	3
Involvement in decision making	8	30	39	17	6

Source: WERS (2004)

This state of affairs is exactly the opposite of that required to entrench good work across the economy. Low levels of task autonomy are congruent with lower levels of whole economy productivity growth, lower levels of profitability and high performance by organizations and reduced feelings of happiness among the workforce. No wonder everyone colluded in encouraging casino capitalism among financial services. Entrenching good work from the current starting point is hard work.

WERS also explored a range of job-related well-being measures, which produced a similar picture of general satisfaction and some shocking findings about how work makes us feel. For example, nearly one in five employees reports that their job makes them feel tense all or most of the time and 47 per cent say that their job makes them worried all, most or some of the time (see Table 4.5).

Even when organizations want to create more task autonomy they often don't get things quite right.

But to return to skills: creating a culture that encourages continual learning and development is not something at which most organizations are very good. Too many workers just aren't equipped to do the best job they can. Although investment in intangibles has risen from 40 to 140 per cent of that invested in tangibles over the past 30 years, we are still not investing enough in our workers, especially those who have already received the least investment in education, training and skills.[37] Organizations will fork out thousands of pounds to help their

Table 4.5 *Job-related well-being (% of employees)*

Job makes you feel	All of the time	Most of the time	Some of the time	Occasionally	Never
Tense	4	15	42	27	12
Calm	3	30	29	27	11
Relaxed	3	23	27	29	18
Worried	2	10	35	32	21
Uneasy	2	8	28	33	29
Content	5	33	30	22	11

Source: WERS (2004)

prospective next generation of leaders obtain a master of business administration (MBA) qualification of often dubious value, but they won't invest in a few NVQs for their junior customer-facing staff. As Will Hutton said in his 2005 report to the government, *Where are the Gaps? An Analysis of UK Skills and Education Strategy in the Light of the Kok Group and European Commission Midterm Review of the Lisbon Goals*:

> The evidence suggests that skill levels are rising and the UK has a positive story to tell. Nevertheless, while the quality of labour entering the labour market has improved, much remains to be done for those already at work. Inevitably the flow of new entrants will affect the overall stock of skills as they replace older, less well-qualified workers who retire – but this is a very slow process and a more determined effort is needed to get adults learning.[38]

And this process has begun in earnest not just in the UK, but across the developed world, as people realize that the advent of new general-purpose technologies such as digitalization, nanotechnology and biotechnology needs to be matched with more educated, skilful and enabled workers.

Place

The third element of sovereignty required to entrench a sense of ownership beyond the financial is place. Where you work can be as important as how you work and what you do for work. This has been given a new environmental colouring as we realize just how much pollution is caused by people travelling to and from their place of work. Lord Stern's report of 2007 unequivocally showed that the economic costs of inaction over climate change outweighed the costs of action by a considerable ratio. As he said then:

> The evidence shows that ignoring climate change will eventually damage economic growth. Our actions over the coming few decades could create risks of major disruption to economic and social activity, later in this century and in the next, on a scale similar to those associated with the great wars and the economic depression of the first half of the 20th century. And it will be difficult or impossible to reverse these changes. Tackling climate change is the pro-growth

strategy for the longer term, and it can be done in a way that does not cap the aspirations for growth of rich or poor countries. The earlier effective action is taken, the less costly it will be. At the same time, given that climate change is happening, measures to help people adapt to it are essential. And the less mitigation we do now, the greater the difficulty of continuing to adapt in future.[39]

The trouble is that for many people 'economic growth' is merely an outcome of giving force to their aspirations. For all that people don't want to destroy their own ecosystem, they do need to express other aspects of their personalities such as innovation, adaptability and ingeniousness. Economic growth has allowed those facets of human character and behaviour to be expressed. That is why the goal must be to decarbonize growth rather than halt it. Good work can help with this goal.

As Stern himself says:

> ...the world does not need to choose between averting climate change and promoting growth and development. Changes in energy technologies and the structure of economies have reduced the responsiveness of emissions to income growth, particularly in some of the richest countries. With strong, deliberate policy choices, it is possible to 'decarbonize' both developed and developing economies on the scale required for climate stabilization while maintaining economic growth in both.[40]

More than 29 million people 'work' in the UK economy in some way or another for some period of time each week.[41] In the US it is around 140 million.[42] There are 4.42 million organizations in the UK economy and even more establishments.[43] In the US there are more than 20 million businesses, many with more than one premises.[44] There are a lot of places where people go to work from shops, to workshops, to mines, offices and car parks.

As recently as 1995, Charles Handy predicted that having a real job inside an organization would be the occupation of a minority.[45] Similarly, William Bridges announced that there would soon be no such thing as a job.[46] As my former colleagues Steve Overell, David Coats and Ian Brinkley argued in their Work Foundation provocation, *Labour under Labour,* end-of-work gurus such as those cited above got things badly wrong when they argued that everything was about to be turned upside down by the advent of new information and communication technologies.[47]

In one sense such writers were groping towards an idea that work organization should change with the advent of this new general-purpose technology – at least for many groups of workers. The missing understanding has been the role of place in creating part of the sense of ownership critical for a good work organization to flourish. Place matters to people. How they organize their working space is important. Many readers will recognize the co-worker who creates a 'home-from-home' in their small, maybe cramped, working cubicle or the person who 'nests' in the hot-desk area, bringing from home items such as photos, mugs, sometimes cuddly toys, to make their little bit of strip-lit dystopia slightly more appealing. Where we work is important to us. The office has now become a place of implicit as well as explicit hierarchy.

Previously, status was reflected in the size of cubicle afforded to the executive. In one workplace in the UK a promotion meant an exact increase in size of office and this time there was a strip of carpet on the floor.[48] With the rise of non-hierarchical structures, the de-layering of management and the increase of informality, such distinctions have withered, although not entirely. The hierarchies of leading companies still enjoy the status trappings of place. Dining with a director of a FTSE company at their headquarters will still occur in the senior executive dining room complete with silver-service waiter in some cases – and that's just for lunch.

In the rest of the economy, hierarchy still flourishes but implicitly. One story will suffice. An organization was moving from its plush Georgian terraced property that it had long rattled around in. Beneficiary of a sweetheart deal, the grand rooms and sweeping staircases did not fit the new corporate image that some on the management team were keen to promote. So the lease on the old building was assigned and a new gleaming office signed for that allowed everyone to sit together. The building was round, which was seen as a good thing. There were no corners in which people could hide. Directors sat with staff. People were given a choice of fixed desk or hot desk. Small meeting rooms could be booked. There were quiet rooms for solitary toil. Only a small amount of space was devoted to the chief executive's office and this was freely loaned out for meetings when he wasn't present. And yet one side had windows looking on to the street and the other had windows looking onto the courtyard and the walls of the next building. The latter was duly christened the 'dark side'. The interest from most staff in where they were going to sit was intense. Those desks nearest the doors were seen as the inferior seats. The desks opposite the CEO's office were seen as the best desks as the workers sitting there could catch his eye and have their work in plain evidence to the key decision maker.

Even in a circular space place mattered. Many of the people working in that organization did not need to be present to get their work done. It was literally a waste of money to have so many people arriving each day to do work they could have done in the cafe over the street, or at their desk at home with nothing more than a laptop and a wireless router and a mobile phone. For outside the workspace, everyone is equal, everyone has ownership of where they work.

The car, train, bus and plane are symbols of pollution. Many journeys are necessary. But many more are not. In his book *Happiness*, Richard Layard quotes a survey of women workers in Texas.[49] When asked to rank a series of activities in order, with the most enjoyable at the top and the least enjoyable at the bottom, sex came top and commuting came bottom. But in the UK and US we love commuting. Almost certainly due to the dominance of London, New York and Los Angeles and other major cities' labour markets, and the demand for better-quality housing outside major conurbations, people are commuting further than ever.

In the UK between 1991 and 2001, the number of people commuting more than 50km per day increased by 30 per cent.[50] The average commuter today spends 139 hours a year travelling to work and for those working in London this rises to the equivalent of one whole month a year.[51]

Of those who do commute, 72 per cent drive, spending an average of 58 minutes a day behind the wheel. The average commuting distance is 8.7 miles which is up by 6 per cent since 1997.[52] Thirteen per cent of all long-distance trips are taken by commuters, while commuting represents 19 per cent of all journeys in the UK. In addition, 3 per cent of the population spend more than 3 hours a day commuting.[53] Yet all this additional travelling time has occurred at a time when more and more UK employees are dependent on ICT in order to perform their jobs. The latest data from the ONS reveal that around 60 per cent of the workforce have access to a computer at work, while more than 60 per cent of UK households have access to the internet.[54] It is also the case that those organizations that make most use of IT are more productive. As one study has shown, for every additional 10 per cent of employees that are IT enabled, productivity increases over and beyond the mean by 2.1 per cent in manufacturing and 1.5 per cent in services.[55] As Charles Handy and others were predicting more than a decade ago, the advent of ICT should have freed workers to spend more time working from home in portfolio careers. Yet since these predictions were made, not very much has changed. Indeed, the increase in the number of workers in the period 1995–2009 (up from 23.3 million to over 28 million) has seen a concomitant rise in commuter journeys (see above).[56] People seem to be travelling to work at least as much as before.

Yet this makes no real sense when the productivity advantages offered by ICT through redesigning jobs and reorganizing work could allow people to travel less and work more. Indeed, although we should beware of a one-size-fits-all approach to work organization and job design, it is clear that there is a considerable gap between how organizations believe they are managing for performance and how they could be managing performance. For example, the Institute of Directors believes that homeworkers are a full 65 per cent more productive than office-based workers.[57] BT believes that home-based workers saves it £70 million a year.[58] While Business Link, a government advisory body, believes that homeworking improves productivity, helps with employee retention, improves employee motivation, saves on office and building costs and reduces absence rates.[59] Moreover, most people certainly feel a close ownership of their home and its spaces. Place anxiety is replaced with home comforts. So why are we not seeing an increase in the number of homeworkers? If teleworkers (as the jargon describes people who work exclusively from home) and flexible workers (who work part of the time from home) are so much more productive, why are organizations so intent on staying firmly rooted in the 20th century when it comes to work organization and job design? The ICT revolution should be creating an evolution into a more networked economy where the importance of a person's workspace diminishes.

Academics such as Manuel Castells have argued (for example in his book the *Information Society*) that internet-created networks are a new form of social and economic organization that open up new forms of co-creation of products and value. This emphasis on ICT as the mediating mechanism through which co-creation is facilitated and generated is in alignment with an agenda that does not require the physical presence of another classical factor of production – labour – to be in the same place at the same time in a growing number of organizations.[60]

Castells and others have accurately understood that networks can now be virtual and productive and have made Marshall McLuhan's 1960s vision of a 'global village' seem very prescient.[61] But current organizational custom and practice are set too firmly against realizing the potential benefits. Investment in ICT is well below sensible levels in most firms. Those firms that have invested in ICT at higher levels are on the whole higher performing.

Yet the number of people who work exclusively from home in the UK totals no more than 780,000 and a further 2.4 million use home as their base.[62] Apart from the waste of time commuting entails it is also a phenomenally polluting activity (see Table 4.6). If we exclude these 3.2 million people from the total in employment in the UK of 29 million, we get a total of 27.8 million in employment each averaging 8.7 miles per day. Of those who do commute, 72 per cent drive (see above). The remaining commuters travel by train for the most part, but a considerable number (1.5 million) cycle. Around 66 per cent of the workforce work within 5 miles of where they live, so cycling is a good green alternative to carbon-fuelled modes of transport.[63] If we reduce our sample by the 1.5 million cyclists, we have a country of just over 26 million people commuting by carbon-fuelled transport 8.7 miles a day.

Table 4.6 *Carbon dioxide emissions by transport mode per mile*

Transport mode		CO_2 grams per mile
Car	Petrol	298
	Diesel	225
	Hybrid	200
Rail		116
Air		340
Taxi		357
Coach/bus		90
Tube		171

Source: Tyndall Centre for Climate Research,
www.tyndall.ac.uk/research/info_for_researchers/emissions.shtml

Thus car commuters, taking the average car journey to work multiplied by the number of workers using cars to get to work, provide a carbon footprint of 42,500 tonnes of CO_2 per day or, based on an average working year of 200 days, 8.5 million tonnes per annum.

The vast majority of the rest of commuter journeys are by train. These journeys leave a carbon footprint of 7300 tonnes a day, or 1.46 million tonnes a year. According to the UK government, the estimated total UK output of green-house gases is 648 million tonnes a year so commuting contributes a sizeable 1.5–2 per cent of the UK's total carbon dioxide emissions.

If companies reduced commuter journeys by even a fifth some 2 million tonnes of CO_2 would be saved a year. Moreover by allowing workers to work differently, to not get stressed by the daily commute, to communicate virtually with colleagues, clients and customers and to be trusted to get on with the task in hand, organizations would gain a productivity boost as well.

Of course there would be a deadweight cost from people being at home. This would amount to around the same amount as the savings from commuting if every commuter lived alone in a home that was otherwise unoccupied and using no heat, light or other sources of energy while they were out of the house. This is clearly not the case. Indeed, if we take just those workers with non-working partners staying at home during the day, the savings would still amount to more than 500,000 tonnes of carbon emissions annually.

Organizations that encourage flexible working and encourage employees to work part of the week from home where practicable, should be able to claim a tax break from the respective government. Individuals should be able to be incentivized for investing in home offices even if they are employees. The rise of the 'knowledge shed' should be encouraged. In short, more awards and rewards could be given for those organizations that enable people to choose the place of work that works best for them.

And yet there is a perverse outcome from the rise of the knowledge economy, i.e., the rise of the city. Despite the attractions of the country more people today, for the first time in history, live in cities across the world than live in the countryside.[64] Organizations like to congregate as they always have in clusters of like-minded businesses. A cursory glance shows the London landscape, for example, as attracting clusters of businesses to different parts of its geography. Financial services towards the east of the centre, occupying the old Roman heart of London, the creative economy clustering in the centre near Oxford Street, central government offices focusing on the north bank of the Thames at the heart of the City of Westminster. In his book, Peter Ackroyd likens London to a human body, alive, vibrant, coursing with energy.[65] Other major cities such as New York, Munich, Moscow could be similarly described. Great places attract great institutions, organizations and companies. Each wants to reflect its claim to greatness by the grandness of its physical environment. Buildings matter to people and the organizations they run and work for. The trick is to encourage people to meet but just enough to be productive and not so much that their work, sense of ownership of place and productivity suffer.

Today, the value in products and services is partly in the product and partly in the intangibles that went into delivering the product or service. This could be the quality of design of the packaging, the values advertisers have managed to associate with the brand (think Guinness or Nike) or the interaction with the consumer in the delivery of the service (a good waiter). Such outputs require higher levels of application of cognitive skills, applied knowledge and communication skills. A bad waiter working longer will simply drive away business and reduce profits however good the food served may be. A great product (robust, long lasting, high technical specification, etc.) will not sell as well if it does not have a set of values attached to it by a skilful marketing team. It may be the case that the team has to burn the midnight oil to produce a great marketing campaign or it may be the case they get there in the first 10 minutes.

What should matter for productivity is the way technology is harnessed to the capabilities of human capital in an environment that is conducive to great work. And this can be anywhere for many of our growing army of knowledge workers. Put another way, what is important to the release of effective collective discretionary effort are forms of work organization that maximize autonomy to enable the release of that discretion: in other words, a good work solution.

Too many organizations believe that high performance requires individuals to eyeball each other for 8 hours a day. In high-trust organizations where people feel secure in their work, that is simply not the case. Key to establishing such high trust is not only place but culture, custom and practice. It is how poor performance is managed as much as how good performance is rewarded. If managers engineer practices and policies in anticipation of managing the worst performers, it will reduce the effectiveness of the whole operation by stunting the autonomy of the rest. Poor performance is best dealt with by engaging, investing and coaching rather than warning, punishing and firing, unless, of course, the poor performer is beyond redemption. Creating smaller places in which to work and gather and socialize will help create incentives to work more autonomously and arguably more productively.

But what else stops organizations being radical about freeing up space? Apart from the cultural issues raised above, regulation can get in the way. The Health and Safety Executive for example lays down very stringent rules for organizations seeking to set up their employees as homeworkers.[66] The reasons are rooted in commonsense: a need to avoid discrimination between different groups of workers within one organization. Yet the set-up costs for homeworking can be prohibitive. Organizations need to navigate their way through five different sets of regulations. They need to conduct a full risk assessment of the employee's home that requires them to identify any hazards, identify who might be harmed and how, assess the risk of harm, record the findings and then reassess from time to time. To do this for all workers in a concern could be prohibitively expensive. Far better for there to be some form of quick-and-easy self-assessment option for homeworkers to fill in, that places an obligation on the individual as much as the employer. This would free organizations from some of the red tape that their representative bodies so often complain about.

To conclude, ownership is the vital ingredient of good work. It has five dimensions or autonomies:

- financial;
- intellectual or craft;
- time;
- task;
- place.

If workers are fortunate they may enjoy one or two of these autonomies. Very few enjoy all. Ownership itself has a physical, practical and psychological dimension. The worker may well own part of the enterprise (impossible for the voluntary and public sector worker) and they will certainly want to have as much autonomy as possible over their intellectual or craft inputs. Time and task sovereignty allows greater productivity on the whole, as does being free to choose the best place from which to carry out the tasks and duties of the role. In each and every case, such freedoms will be constrained by the duties and obligations required by the work. A musician cannot fulfil their responsibility to themselves and their audiences without having some form of stage on which to perform. The same is true for the rest of us. Auditing the extent of the five areas of ownership is a good starting point for any organization seeking to maximize its return from its human capital. Changes made as a consequence will make the people happier too.

Notes

1   www.timesonline.co.uk/tol/news/politics/article1567419.ece
2   Subprime refers to those borrowers, in the US in particular, who had erratic, and in some cases, no income and who at the peak of the boom were able to get mortgages, despite the fact they would get into immediate difficulties if the economy turned and interest rates rose even a small amount.
3   www.mnsu.edu/emuseum/prehistory/aegean/culture/classesofathens.html
4   See the following for an interesting overview and latest research: www.histparl.ac.uk/
5   Ferguson, N. (2008) *The Ascent of Money*, Allen Lane, London.
6   Ferguson, N. (2008) *The Ascent of Money*, Allen Lane, London.
7   Ferguson, N. (2008) *The Ascent of Money*, Allen Lane, London.
8   Godin, S. (2009) *Tribes: We Need You to Lead Us*, Portfolio, London
9   www.employeeownership.co.uk/
10 www.employeeownership.co.uk/
11 Reeves, R. (2007) *CoCo Companies: Work, Happiness and Employee Ownership*, Employee Ownership Association, London.
12 www.hmrc.gov.uk/ria/ess_ria.pdf
13 Reeves, R. (2007) *CoCo Companies: Work, Happiness and Employee Ownership*, Employee Ownership Association, London.
14 Bunting, M. (2004) *Willing Slaves: How the Overwork Culture is Ruling our Lives*, Harper Collins, London, pp38–39.

15 Bunting, M. (2004) *Willing Slaves: How the Overwork Culture is Ruling our Lives*, Harper Collins, London, p201.

16 Reeves, R. (2001) *Time Out: The Case for Time Sovereignty*, Industrial Society, London.

17 www.britainexpress.com/History/Townlife.htm

18 Suskind, P. (1976) *Perfume*, Penguin, London.

19 Houghton, J. (1683) *Collection of Letters for the Improvement of Husbandry and Trade*, John Gain, London, p177.

20 www.channel4.com/history/microsites/H/history/guide19/part11.html

21 See for example: Reeves, R. (2007) *John Stuart Mill: Victorian Firebrand*, Atlantic Books, London.

22 www.econlib.org/library/Enc/bios/Smith.html

23 Thompson, E. P. (1993) *Customs in Common*, Penguin, London, Chapter 6.

24 Reeves, R. (2001) *Happy Mondays: Putting the Pleasure back into Work*, Pearson Education, London, pp138–139.

25 Bone, D. (2004) *The Cambridge Companion to Byron*, Cambridge University Press, Cambridge.

26 www.nationalrail.co.uk/times_fares/

27 www.historyandpolicy.org/papers/policy-paper-05.html

28 www.statistics.gov.uk/glance/

29 www.statistics.gov.uk/glance/

30 Isles, N. (2005) *The Joy of Work*, The Work Foundation, London.

31 Isles, N. (2005) *The Joy of Work*, The Work Foundation, London.

32 Isles, N. (2005) *The Joy of Work*, The Work Foundation, London.

33 http://bt.com/

34 Sennett, R. (2008) *The Craftsman*, Allen Lane, London.

35 Wall, T. D., Wood, S. J. et al (2008) 'The impact of human resource and operational management practices on company productivity: A longitudinal study', *Personnel Psychology (October edition)*.

36 Kersley, B., Alpin, C., Forth, J. et al (2006) *Inside the Workplace: Findings from the 2004 Workplace Employment Relations Survey*, Routledge, Oxon

37 www.theworkfoundation.com/research/publications/publicationdetail.aspx?oItemId=52

38 Hutton, W. et al (2005) *Where are the Gaps?* The Work Foundation, London.

39 www.hm-treasury.gov.uk/stern_review_report.htm

40 www.hm-treasury.gov.uk/stern_review_report.htm

41   www.statistics.gov.uk/cci/nugget.asp?id=12

42   Bureau of Labor Statistics

43   Isles, N. (2006) *Greening Work*, The Work Foundation, London.

44   http://encarta.msn.com/encyclopedia_1741500821/united_states_economy.html

45   Handy, C. (1995) *The Empty Raincoat*, Random House, London.

46   Bridges, W (2009) *Managing Transitions: Making the Most of Change Third Edition* Nicholas Brealey, London.

47   Overell, S. et al (2008) *Labour under Labour*, The Work Foundation, London.

48   A piece of anecdata passed to me in conversation with a former colleague.

49   Layard, R. (2006) *Happiness: Lessons from a New Science*, Penguin, London.

50   www.independent.co.uk/news/uk/home-news/why-commuters-are-going-the-extra-mile-for-their-daily-grind-505165.html

51   www.guardian.co.uk/uk/2006/aug/06/jamiedoward.theobserver

52   RAC Foundation, May 2007.

53   RAC Foundation, May 2007.

54   www.statistics.gov.uk/pdfdir/ecom1108.pdf

55   www.statistics.gov.uk/articles/economic_trends/ET625_farooqui.pdf

56   Labour Force Survey.

57   www.chwaraeteg.com/downloads/WLB%20Fact%20Sheet-%20Statistics.pdf

58   BT.com

59   www.businesslink.gov.uk/bdotg/action/detail?r.s=sc&r.l1=1073858787&r.lc=en&r.l3=1073931239&r.l2=1080898061&r.i=1075398836&type=RESOURCES&itemId=1073791179&r.t=CASE STUDIES

60   Castells, M. (2000 and after) *The Rise of the Network Society: The Information Age*, John Wiley, New York.

61   McLuhan, M. (1964) *Understanding Media*, MIT Press, Cambridge, MA.

62   www.publications.parliament.uk/pa/cm200506/cmhansrd/vo060323/text/60323w09.htm

63   National Cycling Strategy, Department of Transport.

64   www.unfpa.org/pds/urbanization.htm

65   Ackroyd, P. (2000) *London: The Biography*, Chatto and Windus, London.

66   www.hse.gov.uk/pubns/indg226.pdf

Chapter 5

Fusion

Good work organizations instinctively understand that ownership matters to all engaged in the venture. Getting there is the tricky part. Like an intricate diagram of electrical wiring for a major building, the systems required to entrench good work need careful planning and implementation. Each part is interdependent on the other. Pay and reward melds with performance management. Management and leadership feed through into the how of flexible working and employee development. Recruitment and retention builds or destroys diversity and the ability of the organization to create intellectual capital.

The problem with the wiring in many organizations is that there are too many over-complicated diagrams and spurs going off to who knows where. Simplicity is the key to success. Aligning the systems with the overall vision, mission and goal is a core element of great organizations. If we take the five dimensions of ownership – financial, intellectual, time, task and place – the question to be asked is what cultures, systems and processes work best in order to entrench good work? How are each of these elements underpinned and girded by a supporting matrix of policies and behaviours that ensure the sum of the parts is greater than the whole? How do effectiveness, equity and voice (to quote John Budd) become a living, breathing example of good work in action?[1] I will take each dimension in turn and look at some of the ways organizations have been able to underpin the dimension in practice.

Financial

I discussed in Chapter 4 the ways in which employees could literally own their organization. Employee share ownership schemes have been around almost as long as companies have existed. Co-ownership represents a small, yet significant, element of the whole economy. On the whole ownership in this sense applies only to those who work in the private sector. According to the Employee Ownership Association, employee ownership is a thoroughly sensible thing to do and often occurs when a private owner of a company wants to ensure the continuing success of the company they have set up. Thus employee buy-outs are one way of creating co-owned companies. Such buy-outs are usually managed through a trust that allows considerable tax advantages and the avoidance of having to divest shares on retirement. They can be more successful than management buy-outs – a form of ownership favoured by many private equity (PE) firms when they take over a company. It is perhaps not too fanciful to imagine that in future, PE firms, in their quest for high returns will consider employee buy-outs as well as the other forms of ownership they currently favour.[2]

Employee share schemes are the other form of co-ownership and by far the more common. In these cases, shares can be given to employees, or employees buy shares with their own money or buy them at a discounted rate, or employees are given share options (a promise that they can acquire shares at a future date but at today's prices, so if the shares go up in value the employee will make a margin of profit when they buy the shares at today's prices), or finally shares are owned through a trust established to hold the shares for a period or indefinitely for a group of employees.[3]

John Lewis plc is probably the best-known employee-owned company in the UK.[4]

Box 5.1   Case study: John Lewis plc

John Lewis plc is made up of four separate businesses: the John Lewis department stores, an online catalogue business, Waitrose supermarkets and Greenbee. The 69,000 permanent staff who work for the company are called partners and own a share of the company. They own 27 John Lewis department stores, 213 Waitrose supermarkets, an online and catalogue business, Greenbee – a direct services company, a production unit and a farm with a turnover of nearly £6.9 billion in 2008. Partners receive the same share in the benefits and profits of the business as a proportion of their salaries.

John Speden Lewis, who was born in 1885, set up the partnership when he took over from his father in 1928. By 1930, he had created a governance system, set out in a constitution, that was both commercial and democratic, giving every partner a voice in the business they co-owned. John Lewis was a radical innovator who understood that the well-being of his employees had a marked bearing on the profitability of his businesses. In 1951, he signed a second trust settlement, ceding ownership of the retailing empire to the partners – largely the employees. In a telling passage from a landmark speech he gave in 1957 he said this:

> Some critics of this notion (partnership) will point out that employers carry financial risk. Even if they do, why should they ask for themselves more than a definite limited reward? Why should they claim the whole or almost the whole of any profit, no matter how great it may be? But, as a matter of fact, ever since the invention of the joint-stock-company with limited liability, the function of saving and lending, that is to say the function of providing capital, has been becoming more and more separate from the function of managing, that is to say of using capital, no matter who owns it.

He went on to say in the same speech:

> The dividends of some shareholders exceed their own highest hopes, hopes that may have been much too greedy, and the incomes of the more fortunate of the captains of industry are many times as great as would have caused the

same persons to work just as hard and for just as many years if, instead of going into business, they had happened to become, say, lawyers or doctors. This is quite wrong.

Prescient words indeed.

High standards of corporate governance lie at the heart of the partnership. And the way the partnership is governed allows the management the freedom to be as entrepreneurial as any other company. The chairman, the partnership board, the divisional management boards, the group executive and the business strategy group form the management of the company. The partnership council, which elects five partnership board directors, the divisional and branch councils and the committees for communication make up the democratic bodies that give partners a voice. The partners' counsellor and system of registrars make sure the integrity of the partnership and their democratic system remain intact. The chairman, the partnership board and the partnership council make up the main governing authorities of the partnership.

Each branch has its own forum where employees elect their fellows to represent them. John Lewis and Waitrose have divisional councils with each branch electing at least one representative. The partners' council acts as the independent director and registrars act as partners' ombudsmen offering a route for conflict resolution. John Lewis's strategy is remarkably clear and straightforward: partners should gain satisfaction from their work and status; customers should be recruited for the long term and profit is essential to enable growth and returns to all.

John Lewis is an exceptional company with a fairly unique form of governance but it conforms to many of the core elements of good work. And it is highly successful commercially. In the year to 31 January 2009, its partners shared a profit worth 13 per cent of their salaries or 7 weeks' pay. The profits are shared out in percentage terms with every employee getting the same percentage. It doesn't get much fairer than that. The partners seem to agree with a high satisfaction rating at around 70 per cent or more.

John Lewis is an unusual example of financial ownership but one that clearly works. More usual forms of financial engagement are through pay and reward systems, especially variable pay. This is quite literally a minefield. Pay is almost always seen by organizational and HR researchers as a 'hygiene' factor.[5] But what a hygiene factor it is. Get it wrong and the results can be disastrous. For pay is a cipher for fairness. People ask themselves the questions, am I fairly rewarded for my effort and am I fairly rewarded in comparison with the person who sits next to me or across from me, or does a similar job to me? Clearly some organizations (although thankfully very few) have actively discriminated against groups of workers. The Fawcett Society, for example, has campaigned long and hard to get equal pay and conditions for women in the workplace.[6]

Organizations spend a lot of money having their pay systems benchmarked by organizations such as the consultants Hay Group.[7] Market arguments abound – either for paying more to some groups of workers or less to others. These arguments have the appearance of sophisticated objectivity except when the market isn't working very well. Professor Patrick Minford, of Cardiff Business School, among others, argued in 1996 that the introduction of the national minimum wage, for example, would so distort the market as to price up to half a million workers out of a job within 3 years of its establishment.[8] Following its introduction in 1999, employment rose by more than 2 million. It stopped the social consequences of the market from hitting the low-skilled and inexperienced as hard as possible. It placed a floor under wages and its overall effect seems to have been positive for the low paid and benign for the rest of the market. Most people think it a very fair measure.

At the other end of the spectrum many people resent the vast rewards those who have been running our banks, hedge funds, private equity firms and major corporations have ceded to themselves. The pay of top executives has been rising much faster than average pay and much faster than the performance of the companies they purport to steward. Between 2000 and 2007, FTSE top 100 chief executive pay grew 150 per cent, while median earnings grew by 30 per cent. Total average earnings rose to £3.2 million in 2007 for the FTSE 100's 'golden gang' when bonuses, pensions and share options (see above) were added in. In the US, the average CEO went from earning 42 times average earnings in 1980, to 660 times in 2007.[9] As any benchmarking exercise will show, the market told us these were fair rewards. And from a 'winner-take-all' market perspective maybe they are. From a good work perspective they are a hideous distortion of the type of market that leads to sustainable success. Indeed between 1995 and 2000, the FTSE index doubled to 6900, then crashed, and didn't recover its former peak until 2007 from where it then crashed again to less than 4000. As Polly Toynbee and David Walker wryly note in their book, *Unjust Rewards*: 'During all this time, average boardroom remuneration went in one direction, up. The gyrations of the index had a peculiar non-relationship with boardroom pay, especially in the down phases.'[10]

For people at the top of private companies there are three main reasons offered as explanation of why they deserve to be so well rewarded:

- the risks they bear in taking the position of CEO;
- the fact that they are more talented and have more responsibility than anyone else;
- the fact that they are working in a global labour market where Adam Smith's invisible hand of market forces is at work setting pay levels and contract terms on an ever upward spiral.

None of these 'facts' are, in fact, wholly true. Rewarding people regardless of how the organization performs is simply rewarding greed. People instinctively understand the difference between risk-taking entrepreneurialism and very able stewardship.

Winner-take-all effects are a form of market failure. We need vibrant capitalist organizations. We need to encourage investment in the people who run and work in them. And these leaders deserve high levels of remuneration suitable for exceptional people doing great jobs running great companies. But this should not be at the cost of ultimately perversely damaging the prospects of long-term success for those companies, as has arguably happened with most of the world's major banks. The people who were paid such vast sums conformed to the usual agency-led mantra of being exceptional, visionary, 'talented' and every other epithet we can think of. They were all good but maybe not that good – as much beta as alpha. They were all living representatives of 'the successful' in the war for talent, taking high rewards and thus increasing inequality.

Yet high levels of inequality in wider society act as a brake on social mobility and high levels of inequality within organizations act as a brake on performance. Over-rewarding a few at the top harms the enterprise. Spreading financial ownership is fine as long as relativities such as the levels of differentials between classes of workers are also in some sort of balance. As we mentioned above, Richard Wilkinson has demonstrated in his book, *The Impact of Inequality: How to Make Sick Societies Healthier*, that in wider society there is a strong correlation between high inequality and low levels of trust, low social capital, higher murder rates and higher levels of hostility.[11] The same is true of organizations.

Now in casino companies like the investment banks, vast variable pay may well encourage the sort of risk-taking that generates large rewards. Indeed, the evidence seems to indicate that the financial collapse was partly driven by such aggressive pay practices. However, as argued earlier, such risk-taking when it backfires merely socializes the losses. In any organization, fairness usually leads to better results and so too with pay systems.

For pay reflects several intrinsic elements. It puts an absolute price on the individual's labour and it benchmarks that person against co-workers. The price of labour has several components: level of skill, level of experience, level of output. For any given input, when combined with capital, there will be a given output. In order to encourage workers to produce more, forms of variable pay have been introduced that range from the type of 'end-of-year' bonus described for John Lewis, to sales commissions to performance-related pay (PRP).

PRP has two manifestations – individual PRP and team or group PRP. The decision about when, where and how to implement PRP is a complex one as the paragraph quoted below suggests:

> We assume that the objective of the firm is to maximize profit. This requires that workers' compensation structure is such that they are willing to supply their labour time in the first instance. Given labour supply, the firm then selects the most appropriate compensation structure to maximize profits. Thus the firm maximizes net surplus given increased effort but subtracting both the fixed and variable costs of designing and implementing a PRP system. For time-rate workers, monitoring ensures that workers supply a minimum effort level, although at the level of the individual she may choose to supply more effort ($E > E_{min}$). As with firms,

we assume that workers aim to maximize their net surplus when choosing between time-rate and PRP systems. The workers' decision is then to maximize e $-$ C(e). The decision to opt for time-rates then becomes, $E_m - a - C(E_m) > E^* - (F/L +g) - C(E^*)$. Here, the left hand side of the equation relates to time-rates and the right hand side to PRP. If $E_{min} = E^*$ then the decision between time-rates and PRP is solely based upon the unit monitoring costs. This implies that the greater the divergence between the two, the greater the probability that a PRP system will be implemented, as PRP induces higher effort levels all else equal.[12]

But does PRP work? PRP is predicated on the idea that monetary bonuses will incentivize people to perform better. By achieving agreed goals and objectives, based on the organization's agreed strategic intentions, performance can be measured against a benchmark and additional pay awarded should those objectives be met. Unfortunately, except in a few cases, PRP doesn't work very well. Money is not as powerful a motivator as employers usually believe it to be. What matters more is relative pay and basic pay. People usually ask themselves the question: 'Am I being fairly paid for my levels of skills and experience and am I being paid fairly for my input compared with everyone else?' PRP was designed to address this last question – the ultimate element of the effort/reward equation.

Psychologist Frederick Herzberg defined two types of factors (motivation–hygiene factors) that contribute to motivation: one type contributes to job satisfaction and the other only to job dissatisfaction.[13] Factors contributing to a higher level of satisfaction on the job included achievement and recognition, opportunities for advancement and growth, level of responsibility and the work itself. Reasons for dissatisfaction were relationship with boss, supervision, company policies and work conditions, relationships with peers and salary. If a low salary results in dissatisfaction among workers, a high salary was not shown to have the same type of positive effect. The effect of PRP is thus blunted.

Performance-related pay is also fiendishly difficult to measure in many categories of employee. Targets can be set but how do you really know when the performance is exceptional? Too often PRP depends on the patronage and say so of the line manager. It is subjective rather than objective. The 'teacher's pet' gets the top PRP payout due to his assiduous flattery of his boss while the introverted technician receives a token payment. People are also smart. Objectives are too often deadweight costs, set so that they are easily within the expected performance parameters of the job. Additional pay is then given for achieving what would have been achieved in any case – a sort of backdoor pay hike. And organizations like PRP because it seems to be a smart way of keeping their pay bills lower but too many do not performance manage their staff well enough to make a difference.

Performance-related pay tends to work best in industries where job performance is easy to evaluate objectively and when the bonus is a major part of the salary amount. This is the case in financial services, recruitment jobs and sales positions. In these types of jobs, it is understood that the performance-related pay is part of the salary and that performance must be maintained for the pay to be received. The targets are 'hard' ones that people understand and can see.[14]

PRP can also have a distorting effect on performance. The banks failed because people were told to do a certain thing in return for which they would receive wads of cash and share options. It can thus incentivize perverse behaviours. Indeed, it can actually have the opposite effect intended as found in a recent study by the London School of Economics.[15] An analysis of 51 separate studies of financial incentives concluded that performance pay often disincentivized people from giving additional effort due to the perceptions people had of the fairness of the schemes. In the jargon it reduced their intrinsic motivations to do well through applying the sort of craft instincts we all have and hold dear. People suffer from 'hedonic habituation'.[16] They get used to good things very quickly. As a banker friend said to me in disgust about some of his people, 'they are telling me they're having to work for nothing and what's the point of turning up for work anymore'. The reason why they were saying these things? They had become habituated to the idea of receiving bonuses: curtailment of bonuses felt like a pay cut.

So what sort of pay and reward system works best? The answer is a fair one, transparent to all and without an excessive differential between different levels of employee. If the lowest paid is on £20,000, the highest paid should probably not get a differential more than 15 times that. If performance-related pay has any role to play then apply it to teams with very clear objectives that are a stretch not a jaunt. Evaluate progress towards those objectives quarterly after the initial performance review meeting and make sure that the objectives are capable of being supported by documentary evidence at the end-of-year or end-of-period review. Bonuses are a better bet for variable pay, based on financial criteria such as increased profits. Simplicity is the key.

Intellectual

Descartes said: '*Cogito ergo sum*'.[17] For most of us what we do at work is what we are. Ownership of skill, craft and intellectual property is crucial to our sense of self-worth and well-being. And more and more of us now work in areas that require high levels of skills, emotional intelligence and invested knowledge. Therefore, enabling innovation and intellectual risk-taking is important. The National Endowment for Science, Technology and the Arts (NESTA) has published several interesting studies on the innovation process. One such, *Characteristics and Behaviours of Innovative People in Organisations*, reviews the latest research in the field and distinguishes the different phases in the development of innovation.[18] For a start, innovation is not a linear activity. It is unpredictable. The report's authors have codified the process as comprising the following elements:

- problem/opportunity identification (either by individuals, group or organizations);
- initiation and idea generation;
- development and exploration;
- implementation; the process of establishing the value of the innovation;
- exnovation; where an organization discards existing practice associated with a previously implemented innovation, thereby allowing the adoption of a new innovation, where the life cycle starts again.

As the authors say, 'a key feature of this framework is that it does not assume a simple linear sequence of activities as often depicted' (see Figure 2 of the full report). They went on to explore at the individual level associations between innovation and (i) cognitive ability, (ii) personality, (iii) motivation, (iv) knowledge, (v) behaviour, (vi) emotion and mood states. The key messages included:

- Intelligence is a necessary but not sufficient condition for innovation. Although cognitive ability is related to innovation, it does not account for a large amount of the variance observed in individual innovative performance.
- The most common personality trait associated with innovation is openness to experience. Conscientiousness is not necessary to be innovative.
- Motivation is likely to be the most important predictor of innovative working. Management style significantly influences employee motivation to innovate. Innovative people are intrinsically motivated by change such that extrinsic rewards do not necessarily enhance innovation.
- Domain-specific knowledge is important for innovation in organizations.
- To encourage innovation, the work environment has to be open, supportive and encouraging.

The review found that the key factors the organization needed to have were many and varied. Ambidexterity, or a firm's ability to simultaneously pursue exploration and exploitation was a critical factor. This requires a set of organizational characteristics including enriched jobs, shared vision and culture, high levels of trust, organizational discipline, and flexible and supportive leaders. The team is an important structure for innovation to flourish. Leaders are responsible for enabling innovation to occur. Innovative leaders need to be intelligent, good at finding solutions, strong at planning and have high levels of empathetic skills and soft skills. Leaders that encourage risk-taking need to be strong communicators, participative and optimistic.

People who went outside the organization to learn and develop helped the organization become more innovative. A good example of this is the visit by senior Walmart officials to the French supermarket Carrefour.[19] It was on such a visit they noticed that Carrefour didn't bother to have a stock area but put the stock on pallets straight into the store. This saved time, space and reduced costs. Walmart implemented the innovation almost straightaway.

Interestingly, moderate levels of job demands and time pressure helped free up an individual to innovate. Breathing space at work is thus important, as is having a stimulating physical environment. But there is no real conclusion on what structure helps or hinders the innovation process. Function should always follow form.

Organizational culture is also critical. It should encourage risk-taking, the exchange of ideas, promote participation in decision making, and have clear goals and rewards for innovation. Resources need to be sufficient, but too much does not seem to make that much of a difference as opposed to too little. Intrinsic rewards such as identification with the idea that led to the innovation are as, or more, important as external rewards such as more pay.

An example of an innovative company – perhaps *the* example of an innovative company – is IDEO (see Box 5.2).[20]

The point about releasing people's intellectual ownership is that organizations are now required to innovate more than ever before. The pace of change and the speed of technology transfer, aided and abetted by ever faster information technology, is having an accelerating impact on the innovation processes inside

---

Box 5.2 Case study: IDEO

The global design company began life in California in 1991; IDEO is an innovation and design firm that puts its people at the heart of its designing and innovating. It has 550 employees all over the world working in every sector. It has been ranked as one of the most innovative companies in the world by Boston Consulting Group (2005–2007, *Business Week*) and was ranked fifth on the Fast Company's list of the Top 25 Most Innovative Companies in 2008.

IDEO describes its values as 'part mad scientist (curious, experimental), bear-tamer (gutsy, agile), reiki master (hands-on, empathetic), and midnight tax accountant (optimistic, savvy)'. The end-users of its products are involved from the start of the design process and each design team is brought together to work on a project overseen by a guide or more experienced team leader. The teams work how they like and when they like but usually to very tight deadlines. Prototypes are built and discarded throughout the process. Everyone involved is encouraged to own the whole. And the people who work there stay there. In many ways it is play transformed into work.

IDEO has been responsible for designing everything from shopping trolleys to new immunization technologies. It has been issued with more than 1000 patents since 1978 and won more than 350 awards.

organizations whether private, public or voluntary. As Zuboff and Maxmin argue in their book, *The Support Economy*, rewards will go to those organizations that create value not just from efficiently combining material inputs into outputs, but helping consumers navigate their way through complex choices, and from finding answers to consumers' questions about attaining psychological well-being.[21] Hence the rise of design as a more important part of the production and service process.

The choices created by affluence are simply amazing in their breadth and complexity. From iPhones and their 'apps' to television channels to blogs, the range of new goods and services is growing exponentially. This degree of choice reflects the sophistication of demand in richer societies. But it also reflects the deeper psychological and emotional needs of consumers. Ronald Inglehart makes a complementary point when he argues that economic growth and physical security have freed affluent societies from necessity, allowing the emergence of post-material values. The new values emphasize autonomy and heterogeneity over tradition and conformity:

> Post-modern values bring declining confidence in religious, political and even scientific authority; they also bring a growing mass desire for participation and self-expression ... today, the spiritual emphasis among mass publics is turning from security to significance; from a search for reassurance in the face of existential insecurity to a search for the significance of life.[22]

This is reflected in the quest for spirituality and happiness; but also in the quest for goods and services that exactly meet the specifications of particular consumers. Innovation is thus a critical part of the life of the organization and to be innovative requires a higher degree of intellectual ownership than many organizations realize.

The three sovereignties: time, task and place

Time

Most workers still work full time, usually defined as 35 hours a week or more, although there is no legal definition of full time. According to the Office for National Statistics, more than 80 per cent of UK workers work more than 31 hours a week. Some 20 per cent work more than 45 hours a week – the longest average hours of any European country.[23]

Many industries, such as manufacturing, still rely on set times for people to turn up to work through shift patterns, as do healthcare providers such as hospitals. Yet many organizations now offer some form of flexible working to their employees. A British Chambers of Commerce report claimed up to 89 per cent of the UK workforce enjoyed some form of flexible working.[24] Another study of Europe-wide flexible working practices showed that overall 66 per cent of European workers worked flexibly, citing 58 per cent in the UK and more than 70 per cent in France and Germany.[25] In the US, estimates indicate that less than a third of workers enjoy flexible working.[26]

There are three broad reasons why flexible working has grown apace across developed economies:

First, the shift from manufacturing to service industries (at least in developed economies). While production-line workers have to be physically present at one spot at more or less the same time, many categories of service workers are much less constrained. For example, a designer, writer or insurance broker can easily do their work outside so-called normal hours.

Second, the growing number of women in the workforce has compelled employers to be more flexible. There has been a huge rise in female employment over the past 25 years with many more women staying in employment after the birth of their first child.[27] Family management has thus forced a vigorous debate about so-called work–life balance. Some writers have described this as creating special treatment for women and the latest developments in some countries have led to governments giving parents the right to request flexible working arrangements, to which most organizations have been happy to agree. This has combined with other demographic trends, such as an ageing population and an ageing workforce, to create a momentum for change in the usual practices around working hours and working time.

Finally, technology has enabled workers to work more flexibly. The advent of cheaper telecommunications, mobile telephony and fast broadband access has made working anytime, anywhere a reality. Information technology giant IBM claims that today only 60 per cent of its employees actually work on company premises. The other 40 per cent are elsewhere.[28]

Of course 'flexible working' can mean a multitude of different things. Most small business lobby groups will tell anyone who listens that legislation on flexible working is unnecessary since small businesses work flexibly in any case. The point they miss, of course, is the critical difference between entrenching flexible working as a right or benefit, and making it a gift at the whim of the owner or boss. Indeed, working flexibly has a grim downside – working all the time. Everyone now knows a 'crackberry' – a person so addicted to their work they cannot put their email-receiving mobile phone down.

Other forms of flexible working include part-time working, job sharing, homeworking, career breaks, flexitime, 9-day fortnights, time banking, annualized hours and school term-time working.[29] Arguably, the recent recession has led to new forms of flexible working such as the extended holiday or time off on lower or no pay.

It should be noted that flexible forms of working time is not the same as labour market flexibility, a topic much debated by economists and policymakers. In short, this form of flexibility is all about how easy it is to hire and fire workers and how adaptable those workers are due to their overall levels of skills and education. Those on the right of the political spectrum like flexible labour markets. Countries such as the US and the UK tend to have more flexible labour markets than, say, major European economies such as France or Germany. Those on the left like a more regulated labour market where worker protection tends to be tougher (see Box 5.3 for a better definition).[30]

The sort of time-based flexibility that is the subject matter of this book is a key ingredient in delivering good work. When bounded by good management and strong leadership it can free and liberate, engage and enthuse the whole workforce. There is one slight problem with many countries' approach to flexible working, however. The employer lobby invariably wants a non-legislative approach and an approach that tends to favour some groups of workers more than others – usually parents. This can lead to rancour and discontent among groups of workers who feel they are thus discriminated against. This has been a particular issue in the US where single people feel that 'smug marrieds' (for which read any people with children) are getting a better deal, leaving them to work the anti-social shifts, or get in earlier and leave later to cover.[32]

Box 5.3 Defining the elements of labour market flexibility

The British government's Treasury identifies the following factors as contributing to labour market flexibility:[31]

- Relative wage flexibility: movements in wage differentials between different regions and sectors.
- Real wage flexibility: how rapidly 'real wages' (the pay of individuals adjusted for the rate of inflation) respond to 'imbalances between labour demand and labour supply'.
- Nominal wage flexibility: the extent to which 'nominal wages' (the pay of individuals excluding any adjustment for inflation) adjust, in particular when this demands potential wage cuts.
- Geographic labour mobility: the ability/willingness of workers to commute or move house to find work.
- Employment flexibility: this includes both the composition of work on offer and the degree of flexibility in working time.
- Functional flexibility: the ability to switch workers from one task to another because they have a wide range of generic and problem-solving skills.

Important institutional factors include:

- The tax and benefit system.
- Active labour market policies – where governments actively help the long-term unemployed back to work.
- Employment protection legislation, including minimum wages and working time regulations.
- Product market regulation.
- Collective bargaining institutions.

Indeed, many single people have argued strongly that their work–life balance is just as important as the parents in the workplace. Table 5.1 illustrates the changes to the UK workforce expected in the next two decades. These demographic shifts will have a profound and continuing impact on flexible working.

Table 5.1 *Britain over the next 20 years*

Ageing population	• 12 million over-65s by 2021 • 2.7 workers to every 1 non-worker by 2020 (compared with 4:1 in 1990) • 3 million more workers aged over 35 • 1.3 million fewer workers aged 25–35
Changing recruitment pool	• Only 20% of workforce made up of white, able-bodied men under 45 years in full-time work • 80% of workforce growth will be women • 8% of the workforce will be from an ethnic minority by 2030
Changing families: 2020	• 1 in 5 UK workers will be mothers • 1 in 10 children will be stepchildren • Single parent families will be 25% of all families • Average age of mother at birth of first child will be 31 • 1.8 children per family
Eldercare	• Up to 10 million people will be caring for elderly relatives

Source: *Britain in 2010*[33]

Thus applying such flexible working policies fairly is important. Some employers use a menu approach to flexible working as one of a range of benefits they offer staff, usually after a year's service.

Case study: Asda[34]

Many employers choose to focus on flexible benefits because of a need to recruit in a specific labour market. Retailers will typically want to recruit aesthetically. They want their staff to resemble their customer base. For a major supermarket such as Asda this can prove difficult, especially to recruit older workers. Its solution was to target older workers with a specific range of time-based flexible working benefits that sit alongside a broader range of benefits. It was the market leader when it introduced what came to be known as 'benidorm leave' in the late 1990s.

Asda is one of the UK's major retailers, which became part of the Walmart group in June 1999. Asda now has more than 350 stores in the UK, employing

160,000 people (called 'colleagues') and has 15 million customers. More than 90,000 of its staff own shares in the business.

It is also the UK's largest employer of people aged over 50. Asda sees a distinct benefit to employing people aged 50 and over, claiming that it makes business more efficient, more flexible and more cost-effective. Asda regards company desirability as key to attracting good people and it is therefore essential that it gets its reputation right. A key part of this is creating stores that reflect the demographics of the areas or country in which it operates.

This is also the way that Asda approaches recruitment. The initial driver for recruiting older workers was the opening of a new store in Broadstairs, Kent, in the late 1990s. To truly reflect demographics in this area meant employing a workforce where 50 per cent of workers were aged 50 or over.

Asda had worked out that some of the more common myths about older workers were wrong. Myths such as 'you can't teach an old dog new tricks' for example. It found its older workers willing and able to be trained in customer-service techniques. Morale and customer service at this Broadstairs store was improved and anecdotal evidence suggested that customers liked talking to someone like them. This should not really be a surprise. Fashionable hairdressing salons, catering for 25–40 year-olds employ people who mirror their client base. So do DVD stores and many other customer-facing businesses. People like people like them.

Asda introduced initiatives that encouraged older people, thinking of reentering the job market, to consider Asda. So it held pensioners tours, 'bring granny to work days', trial days working in a store, etc. But perhaps of most interest was the innovative way it tailored its benefits to reflect the needs of older workers. It created different categories of leave:

- Carers' leave gives colleagues up to 3 months off work to look after a dependant; it was introduced as a result of feedback from older colleagues.
- Benidorm leave was based on the idea that it is not just students who want to travel, but mature people without dependants too. Many older employees liked to take a couple of months out to travel somewhere warm during the winter.
- Grandparents' leave recognized that because couples left starting a family later and returned to work sooner, grandparents were often relied on to help with childcare.

Asda recognizes that its staff are necessarily diverse. It has constructed its flexible working benefits to reflect that diversity. For example, mothers need school holidays free, but students and older workers want to work in popular holiday times because it is too expensive for them to travel at this time. It thus launched what it calls the 'Seasonal Squad', in Christmas 2003. This initiative was looking to find 8000 permanent temps who, while on a permanent contract with Asda, work for only 10 weeks a year. This scheme was perfect for both the over-50s and students. It cut the £2.6 million annual budget for finding temporary workers, which involved much wasted effort and time.

The organizational outcomes were positive, with lower absence levels, reduced turnover and improved morale. Asda has taken a classic menu approach to the provision of flexible working, tailoring benefits to suit the needs of the different demographic groups within the organization. It is also quite keen on employee voice, despite the well-known anti-union stance of its parent company Walmart. Every three months, the headquarters team at Asda House get together for briefings and information exchange at something it calls the Early Brunch. The top executives mingle with the buyers and the office staff to pat people on the back, exchange corporate messages and get feedback. It has also set up listening groups that allow people to feedback concerns, and get feedback, and which complements their staff survey, *We're Listening*.

It gives parents 3 hours off to settle their children into school when they start school at five, allows up to 4 weeks off (unpaid) for emergencies and that can be extended to 8 weeks (unpaid) during the summer. It also has the full suite of maternity, paternity and adoption leave.

Case study: BT[35]

Another major organization that has been going through tough times recently, but which is committed to taking forward a flexible working agenda, is BT.

BT's crowning achievement is to understand the power of the home. It has, probably more than any other major organization, encouraged the spread of home-based working. It has even developed a consultancy offering to help other organizations set up their workers with home offices and acclimatize to home-based working. BT believes that its flexible working practices have been a major element of its efficiency and modernization drives of recent years. And it has the data to prove it. For example, 98 per cent of women who leave BT for maternity leave now come back, saving more than £3 million in recruitment and induction costs alone. This is because BT, like 90 per cent of all organizations, has embraced the 'right to request' flexible working legislation as it works with the grain of its existing thinking around staff retention. BT has encouraged around 11,000 of its work-force to work from home, equipping and training them to do so. BT homeworker productivity is up by 31 per cent by 2009 and BT believes their overall productivity is around 20 per cent higher than office-based workers. It has also been ruthless about stopping people from working long hours for its own sake. Its anti-presenteeism stance has led to workers working more intensely over less time through their 'self-motivated teams'. BT's way of working has allowed new flexible working products to be developed, such as the technology that facilitates working from home. This has also led to a new business for BT in selling its capability to others. Absenteeism is also down in BT as a result of its drive on flexible working. It stands at around 40 per cent of the national average of 8–9 days per worker per year.

Case study: PricewaterhouseCoopers[36]

Then there are the professional service firms, lawyers, banks and management consultancies. Notorious for demanding long hours of working, they offer a brutal form of sleep-deprived apprenticeship with the large carrot of partnership dangled before the young worker's eyes to keep him, or increasingly her, focused on the task at hand. But even here there are glimpses of change.

PricewaterhouseCoopers (PwC) is arguably the world's leading professional services organization. It employs more than 130,000 people in 126 countries. The UK firm employs 13,500 partners and staff, 50 per cent of whom are female. The firm operates from more than 30 locations. It offers a full range of management consultancy interventions including a 'greening work' offer.

PwC promotes work–life balance as a 'business critical' issue and not simply the 'right thing to do'. It says: 'The provision of leading-edge policies, systems and processes to support balance, and asking our people every quarter how they feel about their work–life balance have both now become integral to how we manage our business.'

But it has a problem due to the nature of its staff and the nature of its client-deadline-driven business. By the late 1990s, it had identified that two-thirds of its people were struggling to achieve a work–life balance. So it set about a major programme of change to create a more flexible working environment and a culture of supported self-help. The policy was driven by a single idea – everyone is different.

It audited all its human resources policies, which included flexible working (e.g. part time, job share, annual days, homeworking), career breaks, childcare vouchers, enhanced maternity leave, fully paid paternity leave, flexible leave arrangements, employee assistance programme and lifestyle management support and training.

Then it tried to get the senior managers to 'walk the talk' to build a management culture that allowed people to feel it was OK to work their hours and not feel they had to work double their hours. It encouraged interaction with the board to ensure the board gained an understanding of what was stopping people gaining a better work–life balance. It also launched PwC LifeStyle, accessed through the PwC intranet. This acts as a source of support for people seeking to address issues of balance, either as individuals or as managers of others. The portal was developed in partnership with specialists in the fields of work–life balance, pregnancy, childbirth, parenting, eldercare, relationship management, stress management and time management, nutritionists and health professionals. The intranet site provides advice, tools and support that are highly practical in order to help people juggle the balance between life and work.

What these case studies illustrate is that within their context, culture and business need, organizations are able to develop degrees of flexibility that can deliver more time sovereignty to their workforces. It may not be the complete freedom a very few enjoy to decide exactly when they work but it is a degree of flexibility that takes into consideration personal circumstances. As consumers within the workplace, employees want as much customization as they do as consumers of goods and services. Customization, difference and choice don't disappear as concepts when the threshold of the workplace is crossed. Indeed, the evidence emerging from a more educated (at least on average) and more demanding new cohort of workers is that flexibility is something they value as much as any other aspect of work.

Task

How does a worker do a job well? What are the ingredients that make delivery of the task successful and satisfying? How do workers gain task sovereignty – the

Box 5.4 Case study: Her Majesty's Revenue and Customs[37]

In the world of public service and the public sector there are many interesting stories of how organizations have tried to introduce mechanisms that enable the workforce to have more control over time.

Her Majesty's Revenue and Customs (HMRC) is responsible for the administration of direct taxes plus tax credits, child benefit, National Insurance contributions and stamp duties together with the collection of student loans and national minimum wage enforcement.

It has around 37 million customers and handles a yearly tax income of around £220 billion. The Public and Commercial Services Union (PCS) is the largest civil service union in the UK, with more than 300,000 members. The HMRC employs 50,000 people across the UK, 90 per cent of which are represented by the PCS. The HMRC needed to extend its opening hours to the public, while helping staff to retain a good balance between work and personal life, so it established the OurTime project in partnership with the PCS and with support from the Trades Union Congress (TUC). Working together, the union and management created surveys and focus groups to establish what staff wanted before matching staff and business needs. Three pilot studies were then established. An enquiry centre and telephone team pilot-tested the scope for extended opening to volunteers. The third pilot, in the risk, intelligence and analysis team, tested the mutual benefit of increased flexibility for staff where there were no external customer interfaces. They tested a variety of flexible working arrangements including variable core time, personal core time, no core time, compressed working week/fortnight and banking time.

Three training packages were commissioned from specialists and tested in the trial offices. Take-up was very good, especially once staff saw the practical benefits of flexible working enjoyed by their colleagues. According to HMRC, the project was successful both locally and nationally.

'how' and 'what' of work? (See Box 5.4) There are two ingredients for task sovereignty – motivation, which is both intrinsic and extrinsic, and skill. The first is determined by the character, practice and custom of the individual worker, their workplace and how they are managed and led, and the second the degree of education and training and development that the worker has enjoyed throughout their life and working career. The former will be touched on in more depth when leadership is examined. The latter is about training and development.

There is now little doubt that those organizations that train most, tend to keep their staff longer and have more productive workplaces. The emergence of the knowledge economy as a response to more refined customer preferences, the speeding up of international tradeflows and the rise of the general-purpose technology that is digitalization means employees can no longer simply 'learn a trade' and then go and practice. Lifelong learning is now a necessary part of work. People need to be inculcated with the habit of learning through nursery and school and take those habits into the workplace. Training is the thing. The UK government recognized this in 2006 when it published the *Leitch Review of Skills*.[38] Without more employers training more people more intensely (especially the low skilled), the UK economy would fall behind the economies of others. The US government set up One Stop Centres after the 1998 Workforce Investment Act.[39] The centres make it easier for the unemployed, as well as the employed, to gain access to the support they need in one place and thus train more or train up to get back to work.

So too the European Union. The much maligned Lisbon Strategy for Growth and Jobs had investment in people at the heart of its policy prognosis.[40] Every country is engaged in a race for the high ground of the most trained, best developed workforces, capable of producing more with less. Some are succeeding more than others with the East Asian Tiger economies of Singapore, South Korea and latterly India and China producing millions of new graduates each year.[41]

Of course the West in general has some inbuilt advantages with a stronger and longer established university system and more cash with which to fund research. Yet it is still the case that too many organizations do not invest in training their workforces. The reasons given – especially by smaller businesses – are that training will only mean their investment benefiting a competitor. The more skilled individual will seek to increase their wages by moving to another organization.[42] This myopia leads to damage. It harms the ability of the organization to compete, and it leads to ossification of the skills of the workforce and the lowering of morale. And low morale leads to lower productivity. It is a vicious circle.

Skills and investment in human capital are increasingly important elements in driving up national productivity too. This cannot be done without a good foundation. Communication, technical and academic skills are as important as each other but basic skills are a *sine qua non* for everything else. That is why initiatives such as the UK government's Train to Gain scheme is so important.[43] Demand for learning and skills acquisition is important. Career progression can be enhanced through organizations creating greater variety in the way people can learn and access learning.

It is certainly the case that employers in the UK spend money on development and training. The figure is around 3.6 per cent of their wage bill, which is high by international standards.[44] However, too much is spent on basic or firm-specific short training courses and too much is invested in expensive MBA-style training for those who already have high levels of skill. The so-called 'war for talent', beloved of the HR profession and headhunters, too often does not extend to exploring the talents within firms and organizations.

Some countries have made the training of employees compulsory. The results have been mixed. Where they have worked, the compulsory training has demonstrably helped employers, the individuals being trained have been well-motivated and the schemes have been flexible. The compulsion comes in different forms. The right to time off to train is one such form. In Denmark, around 9 per cent of eligible people take up the offer each year. The training is financed through sectoral levies, is targeted at low-skill employees who have been with the same employer for at least six months and wage reimbursement is paid to the individual.

Levies are another popular way of increasing the amount spent on training and development. The UK construction industry operates a levy system. In Malaysia, levies boosted training participation by 20 per cent, and in Australia by 23 per cent.[45] So government has a major role to play in increasing the overall training spend of businesses either through fiscal stimuli, exhortation and/or some form of compulsion.

So too individuals. Individuals must also want to learn and be trained. They must be prepared to spend more to gain better qualifications and higher levels of skills. This requires a culture of lifelong learning such as the Nordic countries, The Netherlands and Belgium (to name a few) enjoy. The UK government has instigated a range of reviews to the skills system in the UK to help embed such a learning culture in which resources are attached to the learner through some form of learner account. These accounts give financial support to those at the bottom end of the learning ladder around basic skills and NVQ levels 2 and 3 or equivalent, while higher-level students can access cheap loans and means-tested grants in order to take up university degrees.[46] Apprenticeships have been, and are being, widely expanded to include newer sectors such as the creative and cultural sectors.[47] This reflects the shift in the nature of the economy and the fact that the apprenticeship brand is still liked and respected by many people.

The people who make decisions in firms – the managers – also need to be trained and highly skilled in the functions of management. Yet some countries do vastly better than others. The US, France and Germany produce better managers than the UK. The reason is that they invest more, train more and create higher levels of task discretion.[48]

Having higher skills has other benefits too. The higher the skill level, on average, the higher the pay. Firms who invest in skills for their employees create higher levels of security among those employees. Firms like Microsoft, McDonald's, Waitrose, Rolls-Royce and Aviva understand that creating more skilled workers enables higher levels of discretion and more complex work to be done. For employers, higher-skilled workers means more value-adding work. It also usually creates other externalities such as higher levels of satisfaction with work. On the whole, knowledge workers are more satisfied with their own jobs than non-knowledge workers with lower levels of task discretion. But even in routine work, some employers stand out as investing in training and skills. Take the McDonald's fast-food chain (see Box 5.5). Its name has become associated with low-quality work – the so-called McJob, a term that made it into the *Oxford English Dictionary* (OED) in 2008. Yet McDonald's disputes this. It invests a lot in its workforce and is currently campaigning to have the term dropped from the OED.

Place

Where you work is important. Most writers prefer somewhere quiet and free of distractions. Foreign exchange traders need a bank of computer screens and telephones and the ability to check what they are doing with colleagues in close proximity to them. Actors need a stage or open space in which to perform. Travelling sales people need a vehicle to get from a to b. Pilots need a plane. Retail assistants require a shop. Butchers need somewhere to cut up meat. The

Box 5.5 Case study: McDonald's[49]

The restaurant staff (called a crew) in a typical McDonald's outlet is made up as follows:

- 55 per cent of McDonald's hourly paid staff are students, usually in further or higher education;
- many other McDonald's employees have low self-esteem and have been recently unemployed – some for a long time.

On the whole, the 'raw material' that McDonald's has coming in from the labour market is of variable quality and often interested in short periods of work. Yet McDonald's has always invested in training. The founder of McDonald's, Ray Kroc, before his restaurants even became profitable, was prepared to invest a great deal of money in training staff. Mr Kroc believed in the American Dream and that through hard work and high standards success could be achieved. America in the 1950s and 1960s was a very entrepreneurial environment and Ray Kroc proved to be one of the great American entrepreneurs.

He opened McDonald's Hamburger University in the basement of a restaurant in Elk Grove, Chicago, in 1961. It was initially aimed at Kroc's growing number of franchisees and instilled his high standards of value, service, cleanliness and quality. Kroc had certain ideas about the right training mix for his workforce. He believed that dedication, entrepreneurship and wider skills in service and quality would deliver outstanding customer service.

McDonald's has thus established a strong development culture. There are six management and crew training centres in the UK – the main one is at the East Finchley corporate headquarters, but others are in Manchester, Glasgow, Sutton Coldfield, Woking and Leeds. These make up the UK's equivalent of Hamburger University. At crew level, all are trained whether part time, full time, hourly paid staff or salaried managers undergoing their compulsory in-restaurant training. After inductions and team orientation sessions, every employee embarks on their individual training plans. There are no set timescales as there are many crew members only working for a handful of shifts each week. All the development plans stem from the same essential principles that Kroc introduced in the 1950s: quality, service and cleanliness.

Everyone follows their own crew development programme (CDP), which consists of hundreds of units and levels. These units fit as closely as possible to the NVQ framework. Much training and learning is done through 'sitting by Nelly', i.e. learning on the job from a more experienced crew member. However, units are also delivered through attending classes in the crew room or in the restaurant itself. Additionally, e-learning modules can be completed during allotted times in the crew rooms using the crew computer station and by accessing the company intranet site. Individual crew member pay is determined by their personal performance and is assessed on the whole by monitoring progress through their observation check lists (OCLs – competence assessments in the same mould as those in the NVQ programmes), as well as their performance in each of the quality, service and cleanliness elements.

Once crew members begin to progress through their development plans, new positions quickly become available; training squad, dining area supervisors, party organizers, etc. In fact, each McDonald's restaurant has its staff organized around many different layers and functions. First supervisory and management positions also become available. At 18, employees can become floor managers and at 20, they can become shift running floor managers – a midpoint in a restaurant career. From there, employees may expect to rise to a trainee manager position and then to the positions of 2nd assistant, 1st assistant and then restaurant or general manager. With that comes better pay and conditions and still more training, plus a company car for those at restaurant manager level or above.

Once in a restaurant manager position, employees continue with further intensive development. Through a combination of time in restaurants and at a UK management training centre, managers will progress through hundreds of training days. Courses and units include:

- employee relations training;
- time management;
- staff retention and discipline;
- personal leadership and effective coaching;

- employee communications;
- learning to manage shifts;
- community image;
- managing staff development;
- optimizing restaurant food cost;
- accounting and financial procedures.

General managers are now expected to complete further programmes such as a diploma in management from Nottingham Trent University. McDonald's came 74th in The Times Top 100 Graduate Employers, recruiting more graduates than Bank of America, Sky, Airbus, Pfizer, Fujitsu and the Ministry of Defence.

list of places in which people work or ply their trade is endless. The important point about place is to ask the question, how much discretion do I have or do I give my employees to choose my or their place to work?

We have seen above in the discussions on time sovereignty how much place is connected to time. Homeworking has risen sharply over the past decade, for example, as organizations have sought to free up their workers in an attempt to gain productivity benefits and, on the whole, this has been working. Commuter trains on Fridays into London and New York from the suburbs and the shires tend to be less busy than on other days of the week. This is not because people are all starting long weekends but because they are able to choose to work from home on any day of the week due to the advances in remote-working technology over the past decade. (Fridays allow that added frisson of the weekend starting when work finishes, rather than when the individual gets home after their commute on an unpleasant and usually crowded train or metro.) Indeed, the recession has increased the number of people who work exclusively from home in the UK from 2.1 per cent of the workforce to 2.5 per cent as people turn to self-employment, increasingly based from home.[50]

The business benefits from downsizing the corporate space should also not be underestimated. Increasingly, office-using organizations realize that their corporate show homes are often barely used by staff whom they have enabled to work flexibly. Downsizing is not just something that 'empty nesters' now do. Larger corporations are realizing that big overheads mean smaller profits and heating, lighting and taxing large offices doesn't make much sense. The buildings certainly look prestigious but are they that cost-effective?

For example, in the US many organizations have made considerable savings from encouraging their employees to work from home some of the time. AT&T was able to reduce its office space costs by 50 per cent. Since 1995, the company has saved US$500 million in office lease costs by promoting telecommuting. Telework, the piloting of which began in 1988, allowed IBM to drastically reduce the need for office space and save US$56 million per year across the company. After 2 years, the company negated the need for 2 million square feet of office space. Merrill Lynch reported in 2003 saving US$5000–6000 for each office space eliminated through the use of telecommuting. The Texas Workforce Commission Appeals Department reduced its requirement for office space by 1824 square feet by 2000 by having 19–22 attorneys telecommute.[51] We have even seen the rise of the 'desk hutch' during the recession, which has enabled companies to sub-let space within their downsized offices to third parties, utilizing previously 'dead' space.[52]

Apart from space reduction, space utilization is also part of place sovereignty. Work processes define the use of space as much today as they did in the days of Taylorism. But now that people are indisputably the most important factor of production in a knowledge economy, space needs to be designed to suit their work processes rather than they be required to fit into the space provided for a manufacturing process. Office space allocation has dwindled from 350 square feet per employee in the 1980s to 150 square feet today as employers have reduced costs associated with space.[53]

How space is designed and conceptualized is critical to any good work organization. Space can help or hinder performance and limit attempts to work more effectively. It can also be a matter of felt fairness and equity. There are plenty of office design companies but few that take a demographic approach to office design. Different groups of workers want different things. For example, so-called Generation Y (born between 1980 and 1992) are very happy with work benches and open plan.[54] Older generations prefer more privacy. Separate offices, rather than denoting hierarchy, can be common areas to be used for quieter working.

Meeting rooms are essential for privacy, common spaces for play. Indeed, some commentators have described work as the new home, a place where people come to socialize as much as work, to engage with peers in what they love to do and would do anyway even if they were not being paid. Most people meet their partners at work. The rise of the female workforce has meant a more mixed workplace where people flirt as well as focus on the task at hand.

Designing spaces that can accommodate such a wide variety of complex needs is difficult. Perhaps the biggest change to workspace has come from the need for people to meet more rather than less in the knowledge economy. Rather than drive people apart, knowledge work requires people to sit together and be together more. As described above, innovation is a collective act. IDEO, for example, cannot work unless people are in each other's faces, deliberately competing, joshing, testing and driving each other on. Space to do this type of work is thus increasingly important. The children's ball pit in the heart of the advertising conglomerates' offices may be funny but it serves a purpose, to help the creatives who work there feel it is OK to think beyond the usual adult boundaries. Off-site awaydays attempt to do the same thing. Get people to give more of themselves in an environment that subtly changes the rules around normal engagement.

Case studies

The Pratt Corporation, a large-format graphic design firm located in Indianapolis, combined its three locations into one building to optimize efficiency and create a better corporate culture among design, production, fulfilment and installation departments.[55]

Pratt's interior office space was renovated to reflect the company's product, which in turn reinforced the alignment with the corporate vision and mission. Exposed pipes running through the office were painted cyan, magenta, yellow and black, the colours Pratt uses in large-format printing. Senior staff workstations were equipped with coloured acrylic windows – the same material indigenous to Pratt's production work – and a hinged, sliding door that could be closed for privacy. Senior staff members were given the opportunity to select the graphic for their workspace sliding door.

Skype[56]

With most of its staff under the age of 30, Skype wanted to design its offices to reflect the concerns, interests and attitudes of its overwhelmingly youthful workforce.

It created a domestic feel, with living rooms, lounges and kitchens instead of boardrooms, cubicles and canteens. It wanted a 'living room' to work in, so a series of 'soft' spaces were created in between the open plan desks, to break up what would otherwise be a monotonous layout. A kitchen/cafe where people can hold impromptu brainstorms, seated around big, diner-style booths was also created.

The flagship office is now setting the precedent for Skype's other offices around the world.

GE Money[57]

Newcastle has a very competitive call-centre industry. Retaining staff can be very difficult. GE Money has more than 100,000ft² of office space. After wide consultation with staff, GE Money revamped its entire workspace. Simple things like more daylight and zonal breakout areas have made a huge difference. Each team now sits in its own colour zone – a feature introduced to increase team spirit and fun, and inter-team competition.

Green space

The other major driver that is changing the way we look at space is the environment and how to reduce the carbon footprint of workplaces. The fact that places do still matter to organizations, but that ICT offers an alternative to face-to-face meetings, suggests two conclusions. First, people still like to talk to each other face to face, and this has benefits for creativity and innovation. Therefore, businesses that wish to be green but also want to encourage the trust and creativity that can stem from face-to-face interaction are likely to benefit most from locating in areas to which their employees can travel easily (preferably by bike or public transport, which is greener than using cars) and that also contain other, similar businesses with whom employees are likely to meet. Often, but not all the time, that means cities. Second, businesses could still make much better use of technology to avoid too many journeys, particularly international trips.

There are, however, other innovative ways of organizing work that could affect a carbon footprint: flexible working enabling people to start and leave at different times could reduce congestion; making more use of video conferencing and telephone conferences can reduce the need for travel; support for childcare facilities nearby could reduce the number of journeys and improve retention.

Businesses can take a 21st century approach to 'place' in the way they do business. This means thinking about where they locate their offices, ensuring they think about what that means for employees' travel arrangements and for the way in which employees will interact, providing opportunities for people to work at home as well as in the office, and also making effective use of technology to reduce journeys for meetings. For example, a green approach to 'place' would be to think through the business and the green implications of locating in a business park that provided new and environmentally friendly office accommodation but which is only accessible by car, compared with locating in a city centre that has excellent public transport to a wide catchment of areas, but perhaps less environmentally sustainable offices.[58]

Businesses cluster. And they tend to cluster in cities. This happens for a wide variety of reasons from economies of scale, to proximity to supply chain, to the fact that innovation requires creative people to enjoy face time with each other. Cutting the carbon footprint of organizations will require a highly integrated approach to planning, housing development, the devolution of some work outwards and building affordable housing inwards in the hearts of the cities. It means getting public transport right to help people travel more greenly and it means more flexibility in work organization and job design.

The 21st century idea of 'green' work needs to be one that accepts that the place of work can vary and that organizations should be making green choices about where their main workplace is – connected to public transport where possible, making use of sustainable technologies – but also that employees should have some flexibility about working at home as well. This dovetails with an increasing concern among employees about the environment and the role their place of work takes in protecting the environment.[59] Many companies from Marks & Spencer[60] to Balfour Beatty make lavish promises about reducing their carbon footprint. Thinking about place is one such area to consider in making good those promises.

Place sovereignty is thus one of the key dimensions of ownership and thus good work. It can also have positive externalities such as reducing carbon footprints and retaining talented people.

The case studies cited above are obviously partial. They explain some dimensions of ownership but usually not all. Combining the five dimensions of ownership with a view of work rooted in the democratic principles of workplace citizenship outlined in Chapter 2 will create the type of environment in which good work can thrive. And good work is a principle answer to the 21st-century productivity challenge faced by most organizations. Customization, affluence, the environment, competition from overseas, faster change, innovation and financial constraints are all common pressures being felt by organizations across the globe. Good work, in part, offers a different way of handling them.

Notes

1   Budd, J. (2004) *Employment with a Human Face*, Cornell University Press, Ithaca, NY.
2   www.employeeownership.co.uk/
3   www.employeeownership.co.uk/
4   www.johnlewispartnership.co.uk/
5   http://en.wikipedia.org/wiki/Hygiene_factors
6   www.fawcettsociety.org.uk/
7   www.haygroup.com/ww/services/Index.aspx?ID=1535
8   www.res.org.uk/society/mediabriefings/conferences/conf1996.asp
9   Toynbee, P. and Walker, D. (2008) *Unjust Rewards*, Granta, London.
10 Toynbee, P. and Walker, D. (2008) *Unjust Rewards*, Granta, London.
11 Wilkinson, R. (2005) *The Impact of Inequality: How to Make Sick Societies Healthier*, Routledge, Oxford.
12 Cowling, M. (2007) *Performance Related Pay Coverage in the UK*, Institute for Employment Studies, Brighton.
13 www.businessballs.com/herzberg.htm
14 www.arrod.co.uk/archive/concept_PRP_doesnt_work.php
15 www.management-issues.com/2009/6/25/research/performance-related-pay-doesnt-encourage-performance.asp
16 http://books.google.co.uk/books?id=7YCT2Tfri70C&pg=PA205&lpg=PA205&dq=hedonic+habituation&source=bl&ots=UxI8ZRGby9&sig=

44EzHa0CKFH9Hl51djJQA_XQR3k&hl=en&ei=70-ZSvGrAc-TjAe_
m9GoBQ&sa=X&oi=book_result&ct=result&resnum=1#v=onepage&q=
hedonic%20habituation&f=false

17 http://en.wikipedia.org/wiki/Cogito_ergo_sum
18 www.nesta.org.uk/characteristics-and-behaviours-of-innovative-individuals-in-
    organisations/
19 Fishman, C. (2006) *The Wal-Mart Effect*, Penguin, New York, p66.
20 www.ideo.com/
21 Zuboff, S. and Maxmin, J. (2002) *The Support Economy: Why Corporations are
    Failing Individuals and the Next Episode of Capitalism*, Penguin, New York.
22 http://ksghome.harvard.edu/pnorris/Acrobat/Inglehart.pdf
23 www.statistics.gov.uk/statbase/product.asp?vlnk=8291
24 http://83.137.212.42/sitearchive/eoc/PDF/Transformation_timelords_report.pdf
25 www.avaya.co.uk/emea/en-us/resource/assets/premiumcontent/flexibleworking.pdf
26 www.reuters.com/article/lifestyleMolt/idUSTRE50T16S20090130
27 See: *Labour Force Survey* for trends. www.statistics.gov.uk/statbase/Source.
    asp?vlnk=358
28 www.economist.com/daily/news/displaystory.cfm?story_id=13685735
29 www.personneltoday.com/articles/2008/10/29/48157/peopleperhour.com-fuels-
    uk-rise-in-home-working.html
30 See: Adair Turner's *Just Capital* for a very good description of the different forms of
    flexibility. Turner, A. (2001) *Just Capital*, Pan, London.
31 Taken from Coats, D. (2006) *Who's Afraid of Labour Market Flexibility?*, The Work
    Foundation, London, pp4–5.
32 http://findarticles.com/p/articles/mi_m4467/is_11_54/ai_67590799/
33 www.esrcsocietytoday.ac.uk/ESRCInfoCentre/about/CI/CP/the_edge/issue2/
    britaintowards_3.aspx
34 See: Turner, N. and Williams, L. (2005) *The Ageing Workforce*, The Work
    Foundation, London, and www.asda.jobs/all-about/index.html
35 See: Jones, A. (2006) *About Time for Change*, The Work Foundation, London, p21,
    and bt.com
36 www.pwc.co.uk/ and Jones, A. (2006) *About Time for Change*, The Work
    Foundation, London, p33.
37 Jones, A. (2006) *About Time for Change*, The Work Foundation, London, p24.
38 www.hm-treasury.gov.uk/leitch_review_index.htm
39 www.dol.gov/dol/topic/training/onestop.htm
40 http://ec.europa.eu/growthandjobs/index_en.htm

41 See for example: Hutton, W. (2007) *The Writing on the Wall*, Jonathan Cape, London.

42 www.hm-treasury.gov.uk/leitch_review_index.htm

43 www.traintogain.gov.uk/

44 Extrapolated from OECD data.

45 www.hm-treasury.gov.uk/leitch_review_index.htm

46 www.hm-treasury.gov.uk/leitch_review_index.htm

47 www.ccskills.org.uk/Qualifications/CreativeApprenticeships/tabid/82/Default.aspx

48 Bloom, N. et al (2005) *Management Practices across Firms and Nations*, management paper, CEP, London School of Economics, London.

49 Westwood, A. (2003) *Are we being Served?*, The Work Foundation, London, pp20–29.

50 *Labour Force Survey.*

51 www.ivc.ca/officing/index.html

52 http://ezinearticles.com/?Saving-Office-Space-During-Tough-Financial-Times-With-a-Desk-Hutch&id=2550322

53 http://findarticles.com/p/articles/mi_qa5361/is_3_68/ai_n29003964/

54 www.internalcommshub.com/open/news/oxygenz.shtml

55 www.facilitiesnet.com/ceilingsfurniturewalls/article/Repurposing-Office-Space-for-Maximum-Impact–10832

56 www.morganlovell.co.uk/our-work/case-studies/skype/

57 www.morganlovell.co.uk/our-work/case-studies/ge-money/

58 For a very good exposition of these arguments see: www.theworkfoundation.com/research/ideopolis.aspx

59 See Isles, N. (2008) *Greening Work*, The Work Foundation, London.

60 www.guardian.co.uk/business/2007/jan/15/marksspencer.retail

Chapter 6

The Good Work Leader

More than any other management subject, leadership attracts nonsense. As John Knell and Richard Reeves note in their entertaining business book *The 80 Minute MBA*: 'Here's the bad news: five books on leadership are published on a typical day. This torrent of advice on leadership is enough to provoke an anxiety attack in the staunchest executive. Now for some good news: the majority are so bad that they can be safely ignored.'[1]

A search of the Ebsco business and management publications database reveals that in 1971 there were 136 published articles on leadership. By 1981there were 258. By 1991 there were 1105 and by 2001 the number had risen tenfold to 10,062. A search of the books section of the Amazon.com website in July 2009 revealed 351,127 results for the word 'leadership'.

Leadership is a subject that is over-exposed and little understood. Most people, for example, would have only the dimmest understanding of the difference between managing and leading. Leadership literature covers every-thing from 'living leadership' (as Reeves and Knell ask in their stage presentation of *The 80 Minute MBA*, 'what exactly is "dead" leadership when it is at home?'), to spiritual leadership (and this has nothing to do with priests), heroic leadership, primal leadership, servant leadership, followership leadership, campaigning for leadership (why exactly?), liquid leadership, transformational leadership, resonant leadership and authentic leadership.

In addition, there are as many views on what leadership is, as leadership theories to support them. Take this selection for starters:

A true leader always keeps an element of surprise up his sleeve, which others cannot grasp but which keeps his public excited and breathless. (Charles de Gaulle)

A good leader can't get too far ahead of his followers. (Franklin D. Roosevelt)

All of the great leaders have had one characteristic in common: it was the willingness to confront unequivocally the major anxiety of their people in their time. This, and not much else, is the essence of leadership. (John Kenneth Galbraith)

Forethought and prudence are the proper qualities of a leader. (Tacitus)

Nearly all men can stand adversity, but if you want to test a man's character, give him power. (Abraham Lincoln)

What you cannot enforce, do not command. (Sophocles)

Leadership is not magnetic personality – that can just as well be a glib tongue. It is not 'making friends and influencing people' – that is flattery. Leadership is lifting a person's vision to higher sights, the raising of a person's performance to a higher standard, the building of a personality beyond its normal limitations. (Peter F. Drucker)

It's vital to foster an environment in which clever people are inspired to achieve their fullest potential in a way that produces value for all the stakeholders, and this is tough because clever people do not want to be led and they have little interest in the corporate organization chart. Some very talented individuals can produce remarkable results on their own, but typically clever people need the organization as much as it needs them. Within it clever people want a high degree of protection and recognition that their ideas are important. They expect their leaders to be their intellectual equal but they do not want a leader's talent and skill to outshine their own. Great care is needed with clever people: if you try to push them you will end up driving them away. You need to be a benevolent guardian rather than a traditional boss. You need to create a safe environment for them, encourage them to experiment and play and even fail, and meanwhile quietly demonstrate your expertise and authority. You may sometimes begrudge the time you have to devote to managing them, but if you learn how to protect them while giving them the space they need to be productive you will see your clever people flourish and your organization accomplish its mission. It will make the effort worthwhile. (Rob Goffee, London Business School [LBS])

Leadership abounds with metaphors. There are war metaphors. Donald Rumsfeld, the former US Secretary of Defense, called his book *Leadership Wisdom of a Battle-hardened Maverick*. There are game and sport metaphors, leaders 'trust their swing' (golf) or 'they break all the rules' or leadership is 'like the great game of life'. There are art metaphors usually likening leaders to being the conductor of an orchestra; and machine metaphors aplenty with leadership being like an engine or having a toolbox or being made up of parts. Then there are all the spiritual and religious metaphors with all their obsessions and temptations and fables of leadership. Leaders are about spreading hope or even healing.[2] What this tells us is that leadership is everything and nothing.

In short, leadership is a subject area populated by many misguided attempts at wisdom. There is no point in writing a biography about yourself as the CEO of a great company or organization that simply says 'be me', because no one else can be you. Yet often in striving to give an example, a leader is cited, their qualities listed and the implicit message sent – copy this. In this chapter I will not try to attempt to add another stereotypical 'leader' category to those already out there, despite the chapter heading. Nor will I give an endless series of biographical descriptions of what great CEOs did in building organization X or company Y, entertaining and informative though that might be. What I will attempt to do is describe the fundamental principles that could be said to underpin the management and leadership of any good work organization. For without great leadership and management, all that has been described before in this book will come to nought.

The most important point about leadership I want to make is that leaders and their managers create cultures. Cultures are exactly that – a milieu in which the different elements of good work discussed above can flourish. For how often have you heard about the importance of culture in determining the success of an organization? High-performance cultures are not necessarily very comfortable places in which to work. They will often be guided by a strong and dominant ideology reinforced by a clear set of values. Often in commercial organizations that will be testimony to the strength of conviction and personality of the company's founding father. Some are driven by paternalistic concerns to look after their workforce such as the concerns that drove John Speden Lewis (founder of the John Lewis Partnership); some by a vision of great customer care such as drove Ray Kroc who founded McDonald's or Sam Walton who founded Walmart (see Chapters 3 and 5). Some just wanted to be the very best at what they did such as the founders of Boeing.[3] Whatever drove them, these leaders all had the same passion for success, the same inner strength of conviction, and so did the managers who carried out their orders. I will say more on how leaders navigate culture below.

However, before looking at leadership per se it is perhaps best to look at the difference between leaders and managers (see Table 6.1). In brief, management is a set of responsibilities, hopefully combined with competencies, that ensures processes are followed and tasks completed. It often helps if managers are also good leaders, but that isn't always the case. Managers are responsible for organizing, planning, directing and controlling. Leaders just lead. Leadership is an aptitude, a state of being and a state of mind. Without leadership, people will not achieve the vision – whatever it is. They also need to convince those outside their direct control to follow them and believe them.

Professor of management, Henry Mintzberg, talks about the need for managers to have five minds that enable them to synthesize insights into a comprehensible whole.[4] He argues that separating management from leadership is dangerous in that managers without leadership qualities tend to be dull administrators, and leaders without management ability tend to be disconnected and tending to the hubristic. In this view, management moves beyond the task or

Table 6.1 *Leadership and management*

	Leadership functions	Management functions
Creating an agenda	*Establishing direction:* Vision of the future, develop strategies for change to achieve goals	*Plans and budgets:* Decide action plans and timetables, allocate resources
Developing people	*Aligning people:* Communicate vision and strategy, influence creation of teams which accept validity of goals	*Organizing and staffing:* Decide structure and allocate staff, develop policies, procedures and monitoring
Execution	*Motivating and Inspiring:* Energize people to overcome obstacles, satisfy human needs	*Controlling, problem solving:* Monitor results against plan and take corrective action
Outcomes	Produces positive and sometimes dramatic change	Produces order, consistency and predictability

Source: Buchanan and Huczynski (2004) p718, based on Kotter (1990)

process and inhabits the world of the mind – like leadership. All good managers must be capable of action and reflection and collaboration. To do so requires high levels of analytical ability and a worldly outlook. Thus there are five perspectives to be examined when managing:

- managing oneself, i.e. having a reflective mindset;
- managing the organization or processes, i.e. having an analytic mindset;
- managing the context in which one operates, which reflects the ability to look outside and be worldly;
- managing relationships or the ability to collaborate;
- managing change, i.e. being able to act.

Combining these five attitudes of mind enables managers to manage. For example, as Alinsky stated, what happens to you cannot become an experience unless the person has the space and time to reflect on what has happened to them.[5] Otherwise it just becomes a series of happenings disconnected and separated by time; so, too, with the ability to analyse. Without analysis there can be no good organization. Good analysis allows a common understanding of what needs to be done and how the performance is to be measured. Good analysis combines hard with soft – the ability to understand data and the ability to interpret meaning, values and motivation.

Good managers are also able to look outside their immediate working environment and understand the world in which they operate. This may be the broader needs of the organization and not just their little bit of it, or it may be the context in which the organization is operating, from the competitive environment to the rules and regulations by which the organization must operate imposed by whichever regulatory authorities the organization is operating under. It also means experiencing what the end-user experiences. That is why retailers such as Tesco and Asda insist their senior management team spend time each year working on the shop floor. Only by doing this will they gain an insight into the customer/worker/supplier perspective.

Collaboration is also as much a mindset as anything else. Neo-liberal economic theory has tried to persuade us that people are rent-maximizing rational individualists. Yet collaboration is at the heart of all we do. Collaborative managers listen more than talk; they get out more than stay stuck behind a desk, and they control less and enable more. Collaboration requires the manager to be at the heart of the network, not apart from it.

Action also requires a different mindset to that expected. It is not simply about exhortation, diktat and goal setting. It is about understanding the route map, tackling the exogenous shocks that will come along, understanding the team's capabilities and setting a clear direction for them to follow. Change can deflect managers from this type of action into a regressive, reactive form of action that does not allow reflection or the ability to recognize that not everything in the world is changing at the same speed or time. Good management is thus a combination of these five mindsets woven together to supply the right balance for effectiveness.

Leadership is a more complex thing altogether. Leaders must manage but they must also demonstrate far more aptitudes and skills than managers. Leaders feel things, managers learn things. The point about leadership, and particularly good work leadership, is that values, vision and belief are the essential starting point.

They are the *fons et origo* from which leadership springs. Leadership starts with belief. Servant leadership is a trendy term that mis-describes the need for belief.[6] Just think Jesus, Gandhi and Martin Luther King and you will understand what is meant. Certainly for good work to flourish in an organization it helps if the work-force believe the people in charge stand for something meaningful. But a label such as servant leadership hinders, rather than helps, people understand what is meant.

The first problem with defining leadership is that it is a quite abstract phenomenon like love, freedom or happiness. The second is down to the theoretical construct that underpins how people see the role of the leader. Some see leadership as a set of untaught but intuitive traits; others see leadership as stemming from a set of social processes capable of capture and being taught. A mix of both views is probably a sensible starting point. Indeed, Northouse identified four common themes in the way leadership is perceived:[7]

- leadership is a process;
- leadership involves influence;
- leadership occurs in a group context (I suppose you could lead yourself but it would be a somewhat lonely activity);
- leadership involves attaining a goal.

Looking at the latest leadership literature (for those hardy folk who have the stamina), one strand of thinking stands out above all others – the requirement for authenticity (on which much more below).[8] This strand of leadership thinking emerges from a consensus perspective among key academics and research studies that leadership emanates from the leader. The leader acts as an energizer, visionary and catalyst with a set of communication, problem-solving, decision-making and people-managing abilities. Alongside these soft skills, leaders must also have harder skills such as problem solving, information processing, customer service and delivery as well as high levels of political acumen. They must also demonstrate innovation and creativity and entrepreneurship. These rare creatures must also never tell lies and have the ability to empathize, trust and be trusted. Leaders thus combine both hard and soft skills in equal measure. Perhaps the over-riding finding from much of the research is that leaders must be balanced individuals – partly blessed with aptitudes and the genetic raw material to

Table 6.2 *Key leadership concepts*

- **Trait versus process leadership**: the trait approach proposes that leadership is a quality that resides within specific individuals, whereas the process view sees it as a phenomenon that resides in the context and behaviours of the interacting people

- **Assigned versus emergent leadership:** assigned leadership refers to situations where the leader has been formally assigned his/her role, whereas emergent leadership is where a leader becomes visible because of the way other group members respond to her/him

- **Leadership and power**: power and leadership are related because both involve the process of influence. In organizations we can distinguish between position power (where authority is assigned by rank) and personal power (where authority is assigned by followers). True leadership tends to rely on a power that arises from relationships and a desire of followers to be 'led'

- **Leadership and coercion**: coercion is a form of power that relies on the use (or threat) of force. Classic examples of coercive leaders include Adolf Hitler, Stalin, Jim Jones and David Koresch who used power for their own aims rather than the general benefit of the group. Such methods and techniques are generally not included in models of what good leadership is about

- **Leadership and management**: leadership and management are phenomena that have a lot in common. Both involve influence, working with people, goal achievement, etc. However, it has been argued that there are some significant differences. To be successful, these two activities need to be balanced and matched to the demands of the situation

Source: Northouse (2004) p3

succeed as a leader and partly emergent, the result of the learning, influences and training they receive on their journey to leaderhood (see Table 6.2).

But do leaders really make much of a difference to the organizations they lead? The evidence is rather mixed. Porras and Collins in their seminal work, *Built to Last*, argued that it was better for the CEO leaders to be 'clockmakers rather than time tellers'.[9] By this they meant that the leaders of the outstanding companies they studied were a trifle dull. They did the basics well – kept telling the corporate story, managed the processes, had the self-belief to take risks and innovate. These leaders inspired through keeping the idea burning bright for their workforces – whatever the idea was. Whatever they were doing, it clearly worked for the outstanding firms in the Porras and Collins studies.

Yet good empirical evidence for the link between leadership and performance is in relatively short supply. I am sure the boards of Royal Bank of Scotland, Lehman Brothers and AIG all thought they had top-class leaders. The leaders of those financial institutions were certainly remunerated as though they were. The fact is that cause and effect are very difficult to unravel when so many different intangibles are interacting pretty much constantly in the typically complex environment of an organization. How does one work out what the leadership element is of good or bad planning, organizing, setting direction, aligning people to goals and motivating and inspiring them? The answer is 'with great difficulty'. The intangible factors that lead to great performance are probably greatly impacted by the quality of leadership, but proving this is the case empirically is a holy grail for leadership researchers. Most leadership research categorizes and describes rather than empirically proves anything.

What is required is that management and leadership development lead to management and leadership capability that then translates into performance. But an a priori question then springs to mind. What is performance? After all, performance has many aspects. There is the impact on the individual leader. How are they performing in their role, especially after capital investment in their development? Leadership attributes tend to be soft ones such as the ability to inspire and motivate, or the ability to communicate effectively, rather than hard technical skills, which are easier to measure.

Then there is the effect on group performance. Some of these so-called soft measures such as improved communication and motivation may translate into harder measures such as reduced absenteeism, lower staff turnover and greater engagement.

Finally, there is organizational performance. Measures here include turnover, profitability, staff turnover, wastage of resources (cost cutting), customer retention and satisfaction, raised share value and improved staff satisfaction. All of these and none of them may be due to the quality of the leadership. It may be that a good deal, where another business has been acquired, leads to a rise in the share price. That deal may have been done using huge amounts of bank borrowing, rather than an acquisition funded primarily through growth and profits. The short-term gain for the leaders of the merged organization would be shown in bonus payments and share options. The pain to shareholders and laid-off workers if the deal goes sour due to a financial crisis will be felt for a long time. Is this an example of good leadership or individual profit maximization?

Some measures of leadership show through quickly. For example, a poor communicator who becomes a better communicator will show up in staff feedback as an improved leader. However, the feed-through to organizational performance may be far slower to show. Then there is the wider societal benefit to be gained from having better leaders running our public, private and voluntary organizations. The UK government, for example, has poured money into leadership development through the Economic and Social Research Council. As Westwood and Keep argued in 2003 there was little evidence then that the current supply of leadership development was really giving the UK the skilled managers and leaders the economy needed.[10] MBA courses and other higher-education interventions do not seem to really deliver very good leaders at all. On-the-job development seems far better than off-the-job training. It is detailed, work-based activities such as giving and receiving detailed feedback, goal setting and action planning that really work.

What are also crucial are the quality of the development and the culture of the organization. Leadership capabilities do not become leadership externalities without appropriate permissions to use them. If we consider the culture created by coercive leaders, this point is easy to understand. Hitler's generals during the Russian offensive and the defence of Normandy knew what they needed to do, but the culture of the German High Command would not permit them to use their leadership capabilities to any good effect. In particular, Hitler's insistence on defending every square foot of Stalingrad, for example, lost him the Second World War more quickly (thankfully) than otherwise would have been the case if he had allowed General Paulus the discretion to do the sensible thing, which was withdraw.[11] Now Hitler may have been insane, and those around him knew he was insane, but such was the power of the dominant leader and the dominant culture that very little could be done to check the course of history by releasing the leadership potential of some very fine German military leaders. If it had, the war would have been shorter, as Field Marshal Rommel and others in the German High Command would have sued for peace in June 1944.[12]

In terms of the impact of leadership on the organization, again the evidence is fairly weak. One study of 800 Sears stores in the US does seem to indicate that the quality of line management had a direct bearing on business results, at least according to the workforce. As described in Chapter 2, a similar study of 100 stores of a major UK retailer by the Institute for Employment Studies had a similar finding (see below).

In another study, the training of managers during the early part of the 2000s saved BT £270 million over a 5-year period due to reduced errors and better handling of customer complaints. While another study found that 63 per cent of firms identified an impact on business performance from management training and development.[13]

The impact of leadership on countries' productivity and performance has long been of interest to national governments. Harvard Professor Michael Porter in his 2003 study for the UK government of the UK's productivity performance

Sainsbury's: Commitment & Performance

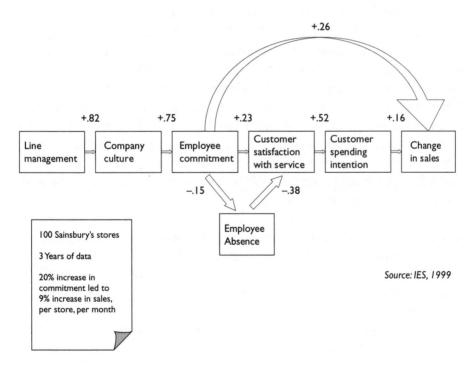

Figure 6.1 Sainsbury's: Commitment and performance

was sceptical that leadership development was a major factor in the UK's generally unenviable productivity performance.[14] At that time, the UK's productivity per hour worked was 40 per cent below the US's and 20 per cent below that of Germany and France.[15]

What tends to emerge is that some countries, the UK being one, have a historical shortfall in developing high-quality managers and leaders when compared with the US or Germany or France or the Nordic countries. One of the reasons cited for this poor track record is the role that class and conflict have played in UK workplaces. Managers and leaders have tended to be recruited from upper-middle and middle-class backgrounds. They were often university educated, drawn from the roughly 8 per cent or less of the population who went to university a generation ago. They were thus removed from understanding the people whom they led and managed. This, combined with an adversarial trade union culture, meant British managers and leaders were among the worst in the world.[16]

Although this is a slight exaggeration, it is not a completely unfair caricature. Much has changed since the mid 1980s. Nearly 40 per cent of each cohort now go on to higher education; workplaces are far less homogenous and more diverse; only 20 per cent of private sector organizations have trade union members and many of these were formerly public sector bodies that have been privatized.[17] Adversarialism is slowly giving way to partnering approaches between managements and unions.[18] Perhaps fundamentally the UK has been at the forefront of enjoying the changed benefits of the rise of the knowledge economy. Organizations have been addressing the management and leadership deficits suffered by previous generations of British workers because their markets and customers indirectly require it of them.

So in terms of the impact of leadership on performance, the evidence is not watertight. What can be concluded with some confidence is that leadership is part of a bundle of human resource practices that need to be developed together. It is not so much what you do as how you do it that seems to matter most. Second, leaders' influence on the motivations of their employees is clear cut. Good leaders motivate for performance, bad leaders do not. And finally, culture matters to the exercise of leadership. Leaders need to be encouraged, fed back to and supported. Without such an environment to work in, however skilled and able a leader you may be, it will not be enough to overcome the cultural hurdles you face. These can include risk aversion, an under-skilled workforce, a sloppy or non-existent performance management regime, and a general lack of confidence and low trust among peers, especially among the top team. Leadership is but one part of any organization's capabilities. In good work organizations, a particular brand of leadership is more likely to flourish than another (on which more later). It is also likely that the move towards greater transparency on non-financial criteria in organizations' annual reports is helping to focus a spotlight on aspects of leadership capabilities within organizations.[19]

Before considering what may be the best approach to good work leadership, it is worth looking at what happens when organizations get leadership badly wrong. This is particularly the case where 'leadership' is seen as the only answer. Clearly some leaders are bad people. Dennis Kozlowski at Tyco, Andy Fastow of Enron and Conrad Black of the Telegraph Group ended up being indicted. These individuals were so narcissistic they believed they could use the organization's resources entirely as they wished and usually for personal gain and aggrandisement. These are the exceptional cases. There are other situations where more subtle social and psychological factors undermine the principles of good leadership.

Hero leaders can actually imprison the 'led' in a belief in their own inadequacies. All decisions flow from and to the top. The followers 'believe' that the hero leader's words are the literal truth and that only the leader can offer them guidance and show them the truth. Workers de-skill themselves in this environment. They shut down their ability to think rationally and take decisions. They do not believe they are capable of inspiring or motivating or achieving. This view is particularly apparent in organizations that promulgate the inspirational leadership school of thinking. As Gemmill and Oakley said in 1992:

> When pain is coupled with an inordinate, widespread and pervasive sense of helplessness, social myths about the need for great leaders and magical leadership emerge from the primarily unconscious collective feeling that it would take a miracle or messiah to alleviate or ameliorate this painful form of existence.[20]

In turn, leaders themselves can easily lose touch with reality. These fall into three main areas. First is the area of strategic vision. Being convinced about the importance of a strong unifying vision is a strength shared by many leaders. If the vision is compelling and effective, that is a force for motivating great achievement among the workforce. However, being so committed to a particular vision such that it blinds you to alternatives that may be more effective, or keeps you from updating the vision to make it resonate with current workforce and customer requirements is a bad thing all round. A conviction that when the facts don't fit with the vision the facts are wrong is common among narcissists. Such leaders often remain unchallenged by those who realize the error being made.

The next way that leaders can lose touch with reality is that they start believing their own press. This is often the case with highly effective communicators. It isn't that communication is not generally a good thing. On the whole it is. But communicating the information well is one thing, being selective about which information to use in order to convince followers of your rightness is another. What then happens is that the leader begins to believe his or her own propaganda, deluding themselves through repetition and the often positive feedback they receive from followers that they are right. Arguably former Prime Minister of the UK, Tony Blair, was guilty of this type of leadership failing over the decision to go to war with Iraq.

In this instance, following the Al-Qaeda attacks on the US on 11 September 2001, Blair first argued that the decision to invade Iraq was in pursuit of the war on Al-Qaeda terror groups since Iraq harboured such terrorists. Many people pointed out that Saudi Arabia harboured more Al-Qaeda cells than Iraq and that in fact Iraq was not known to be the home of Al-Qaeda or any of its operatives. Indeed, it was noted at the time how much Saddam Hussein, Iraq's unpleasant, highly narcissistic and downright evil dictator, disliked Al-Qaeda. After all, Al-Qaeda did not believe Hussein ran a sufficiently tight shariah state.

Side-stepping this argument against action, Blair then argued that Hussein and Iraq had broken UN resolutions and therefore were a legitimate target for attack, as the Iraqis allegedly had weapons of mass destruction that they were supposed to have destroyed and had not. UN weapons inspectors went into Iraq and found no weapons of mass destruction despite the presentation of 'intelligence' before, and during, their visits by government advisers that such weapons did exist. The reality on the ground was that the sanctions imposed since the previous Gulf War in 1990–1991had been so effective that Saddam Hussein's regime had not been able to muster up the resources to restock their weapons of mass destruction. The previous decision to use sanctions to control, and eventually unseat, Saddam Hussein had been a good policy that was working.

Blair then went on national television and answered parliamentary questions in the House of Commons apologizing for the fact no weapons of mass destruction had been found. Ignoring this inconvenient fact, he then argued that as Saddam Hussein was thoroughly unpleasant it was a good thing anyway that Britain had gone to war to remove him from government, even though he hadn't actually been doing the things Blair had said he was doing, at the time he said he was doing them. In Blair's worldview, the war was a justifiable one whatever the reasons given, since Saddam Hussein was evil and so should be removed. The fact that going to war in such a manner may well have contravened international law, and that he had also formally misled Parliament as to the evidence that underpinned the reason for going to war was irrelevant. His belief in the rightness of his vision was the dominant factor. Those around him who had misgivings, like the then Attorney General, were sidelined or brought into line.[21]

The third way in which a leader may undermine her or his effectiveness is to have poor management practices. Often, charismatic leaders are poor in a number of areas. They may not manage sideways, upwards or downwards well, their behaviour may be highly erratic and not conform to the usual workplace norms. They may often be poor at administrative detail and implementation, and fail to plan for their succession as they often believe that no one could possibly adequately fill their shoes. Action and new initiatives crowd out the successful implementation of existing initiatives, however good they may be. Often such leaders are highly sensitive to criticism, shun close emotions, don't listen, lack empathy and are highly competitive. They also tend to think they cannot be taught anything new and place too much trust in their instincts.[22]

In Ancient Rome, commanders returning from foreign wars with their booty and slaves would often be granted a triumph. This allowed the victorious leader to parade in his chariot through the marble and gilt-clad streets of Rome showing off his prizes won in battle and conquest. On the back of the chariot stood a trusted slave whose job it was to whisper in the victorious general's ear 'Remember thou art mortal'. Some modern corporations try a similar technique by ensuring the visionary leader has a sidekick that can temper her or his narcissism. More often the board of directors or trustees have the job of keeping overpowerful CEOs and their teams in order. Sometimes, however, it just doesn't work. Boards fail to pick up the warning signs, or the board is too dependent on the patronage of the CEO who recommended them for their seats. Or the leader has too strong a personality compared with the personalities of those who sit in governance. Then trouble will inevitably follow.[23]

So what of the good work leader? How should good work organizations seek to develop their leaders in order to ensure that good work is a reality rather than a promise? The starting point, as I have set out in this book, is to understand how society and the economy has changed and moved on. The hierarchies and rules that sustained leaders in the past no longer have the same effect. Deference has well and truly died. As Dame Shirley Williams commented in 2003:

> I do think it [the death of deference] poses the most colossal issues for institutions. Whether we're politicians or whether we're church leaders, or whether we're surgeons, a great deal of professional attitudes in this country and elsewhere depend upon an assumption of deference of other people towards oneself – the surgeon who won't tell you anything about your condition, the cleric who expects to be respected because he's got a dog collar on. What's actually happened, I think, in our world – and I am very much in favour of it – is that people are increasingly judged in terms of their achievement, in terms of whether they do in fact, live by what they believe in.[24]

Networks are rapidly replacing hierarchy in most organizations. Firms contract out processes that used to be performed in-house and not only because they search for cost savings; the contractors are likely to possess more or complementary skills to those held in-house. All this leads to the contracting out of back-office services to companies like Capita and Serco, which are growing exponentially; the growth of off-shoring; the downgrading of head-office functions; and the emergence everywhere of denser supply chains and joint ventures.

Professor Manuel Castells has called this development the emergence of the network economy and society.[25] The networked firm is more porous, leaner and flexible than its conventional counterpart. This development is not confined to the private sector – many of the controversies that have plagued public sector reform over the past 10 years are only ways of opening up the public sector to the advantages of networking.

It is even more important that leaders of the networked organization have a clear conception of the organization's vocation and communicate it across the entire network that now constitutes the organization. A network needs more leadership, not less; more social capital to hold it together; more shared values; and more shared sense of its purpose. In particular, it means that leaders are compelled to distribute their leadership, empowering others to lead at the multiplicity of leadership points – leadership nodes if you will – that inevitably come with a network.

This generation of leaders has to build relationships, achieve its ends by influence rather than top-down control, maintain connections, embrace diversity, accept and manage complexity, engage with people both inside and outside the organization and facilitate rather than direct. Good leadership has always entailed these qualities but the new organizational forms require this approach more, not less. There is less social distance between leaders and the led, and leadership styles that work best in this new environment are those where leaders are open, sociable and considerate.

They are also likely to need to express more so-called feminine attributes than traditional male ones. In a society currently still fascinated by the cult of the hero leader this is quite a challenge. Female aptitudes such as the ability to empathize, communicate well, socialize easily, read contexts and adjust to cultures are all the leadership qualities increasingly in demand. The death of deference and the retreat of hierarchy make soft skills and abilities even more important than before. Organizations may plan campaigns for growth and expansion or impact or change, but it is now the case that to deliver such campaigns will require the highly sensitive attributes of the female rather than the male. Now this is not to suggest that the 21st century will be dominated by female leaders. The evidence so far is to the contrary. What it does suggest is that, regardless of gender, it is feminine attributes that will be required more than male ones.[26]

Change has also affected the way in which corporate leaders behave. There is not the time any longer to spend lots of time making decisions. Digitalization, globalization and the shift to high-value services have combined to make some attributes of leadership more powerful than others. Perhaps more than anything, people require higher levels of transparency and authenticity in their leaders. They may not go to church anymore and research their minor symptoms of illness on the internet rather than go to the doctor, but people have not changed. They still need reassurance, seek certainty and desire lives free from pain and want. Thus we have seen the rise of the new shamans from homeopaths to reflexologists, from the life coach to the personal trainer.[27] Deference may have died but we still want to believe. Perfectly rational, sane adults spend millions of pounds or dollars each year taking remedies that have no basis in any known science as palliative remedies. They believe these homeopathic pills and unguents will work and so, very often, they do. The placebo effect is very powerful indeed.

Organizations are not immune to such forces and pressures. Authority is still invested in position, but without personal authenticity the 21st century leader will not last long. Authenticity is the essential ingredient that allows trust to grow and people to be led. Good work cannot flourish without a leadership cadre that is authentic and trusted. And authenticity essentially comes from being oneself.

What this means is that it is very difficult to model oneself on anyone else. We should all be familiar with this idea when we discuss our favourite film stars. Often critics will talk about someone being the new Sophia Loren or Robert de Niro or Al Pacino. But great actors are unique. We do not like them because they are the new someone. We like them because they are authentic on screen. They imbue certain characteristics, values and meaning through the parts they play, which we respond to.

This search for authenticity has been driven by a lack of authenticity in those institutions that formerly were deemed to be authentic.[28] This has been coupled with the rise of customization and individualization – having so much choice puts pressure on individuals. The selfish gene is never far away. Yet selfishness erodes shared moral values and erodes the authentic in all of us.

In the workplace, strict hierarchies are disappearing and so too is meaning. Hierarchy and climbing up it created the meaning in work for many people before 1992. People now look to their leaders for that meaning. Put another way, in 1990 you may have had three managerial levels to rise up through before becoming a departmental head. Now there is just the departmental head and everyone else. There may be differences in salary between people but not in hierarchy. The hierarchy has gone underground; it is too often dependent on the patronage of the departmental head rather than the explicit status of a job title. In some ways this is not a bad thing. If people's status depends more on what they do and achieve than on the badge they wear at work, it is arguably more honest and will lead to higher performance than the old hierarchies where people could be promoted on a Buggins's turn basis.[29]

But in considering the good work leader, we need to consider the aspects that drive authenticity. First, good work leaders need to have a sufficient level of self-knowledge about what leadership is about, combined with a compelling sense of purpose. They must also be aware of the fact that all leadership is situational.[30] Winston Churchill was a great war leader but a lousy peacetime politician.[31] Good organizational leaders are capable of sensing the mood of the organization or the situation and adjusting appropriately. More than anything authenticity requires the leader to be consistent in doing what they say they will do. Too often leaders mean what they say when they say it, but do something completely different. Trust is built on deeds not words until the deeds persuade that the word can be trusted.[32]

The authentic leader is great at communicating the same face to everyone regardless of the need to play different roles in different circumstances. A leader will be different with a member of staff they know well, and a customer they don't, but both people should be able to feel the leader's authenticity and underlying self. To do this a leader has to be very comfortable with themself. Confidence is a key attribute of great leaders. This is not to mean they do not doubt themselves. Far from it. Doubt is a dominant emotion. What I mean is that they have the ability to make judgements and to trust those judgements. Confidence attracts and is attractive.[33]

Leadership is by nature manipulative at times. It is about getting sometimes sceptical people to follow your wishes, commands, whims and insights. To do this requires the ability to know the sort of actions and differences that help achieve one's leadership goals. Take this example from Rob Goffee and Gareth Jones's book, *Why Should Anyone be Led by You?*:

> We met and observed a cleaning supervisor in a large New York office building. Marcia is a Puerto Rican American woman who leads a team of office cleaners. She is a larger-than-life character – in every sense. She is intensely proud of her

origins and yet a subtle reader of the many cultures represented by her team. She can be brash – this is New York – but it's done in a knowing kind of way. Her language and clothes are exotic. She uses humor to devastating effect: woe betide the slovenly cleaner. Her passion is for the office workers to notice and comment favourably on the offices. With all this, members of her team know that she cares about them and about getting the job done right. In unpromising circumstances she has forged a high performance team.[34]

Or consider one of the few corporate leaders people might trust, Alan Sugar of television programme *The Apprentice*. When not on television or advising the UK government on business issues, Alan Sugar is an entrepreneur and highly successful businessman. The fact he can juggle all these different media and jobs and remain successful is because he oozes authenticity. He is able to make those situational judgement calls that mean people trust and believe him wherever he is and whatever he is doing, whether in the TV studio or in No 10 Downing Street.

Being able to respond to context is also a critical skill. Franz Humer, chairman of Diageo, picked up his skills when employed as a tour guide in his 20s. Then he worked for tips and he soon could work out which groups were likely to give him the biggest tip to an accuracy of 10 per cent.[35]

The good work leader also needs to be skilful at how they communicate. Some leaders are great platform orators such as Bill Clinton. Some are better in small groups or one-to-one such as Gordon Brown. Whatever the medium that suits you best for communicating, use it.

This book has been about good work. The elements of good work are a combination of efficiency or performance, fairness or equity and voice. The glue that binds these three elements is ownership of which I have argued there are five dimensions. It is these elements that the good work leader must keep in the front of their mind as they go about their business of leading. What is it that the people who follow me expect from my leadership that leads to a greater sense of ownership? What are the standards, behaviours and aptitudes that my followers would wish to see me demonstrate day-in, day-out?

Authenticity is, for many reasons, the key attribute that followers require in their leaders. But the evidence indicates that they also want their leaders to generate meaning, excitement and a sense of community as well. People feel more comfortable when their leaders show something of themselves. They do not like to work for automata. Many fine managers will never be leaders because they always bring their 'work heads' to work. People like to feel they understand what makes you different. The popularity of reality shows about so-called celebrities is due to the prurience and inquisitiveness about each other that does not go away once we all go to work. People are always seeking an angle to identify with their leaders. They always want to feel that this person might just understand them and their needs too.

Meaning is required because meaning enables followers to know that their contribution has been recognized. The leader must find the means and ways to recognize effort and reward it, not just formally, once a year, or quarterly through appraisals, but spontaneously. The famous CEO of General Electric (GE), Jack Welch, was well-known for sending handwritten notes thanking or encouraging people for jobs well done or effort put in.[36]

People respond to praise more than criticism. Criticism makes most people withdraw into themselves and become fearful of taking risks. Authentically praising someone is about spontaneity and the recognition by the praisee that the praise has been given despite the huge workload and strain the leader is under. Another form of delivering meaning that many leaders just ignore is responding. Those leaders who take the time to respond directly to colleagues are not just doing the day job, they are also delivering meaning.

In too many cases, leaders create hierarchies of response or fail to respond if the question is difficult or sensitive. I know of many leaders who almost always fail to respond to emails from colleagues requiring a decision. Instead of simply letting them know the message has been received, there is silence. Now the point is that it may seem very sensible and proper to consult with other people before making a response. Often the things people are writing to leaders about are not things that can be answered in a knee-jerk manner. But authentic leaders know how to respond in every situation and invariably do so quickly. In this case, a short holding note, thanking the individual for their concern/enthusiasm/initiative/persistence etc. is all that is required. The authentic leader understands the need to create meaning.

An example of this was the way in which the director of a major overseas development agency worked in the days before email. He travelled the world with his job and was often away three or four times a year for 3 weeks at a time. He met regularly with government ministers and officials and World Bank and IMF experts on development issues. His workload was enormous. Yet he made certain that any memorandum that was sent to him was responded to first thing the next morning, or as soon as he humanly could. He made sure he was always at his desk by 7.30am in order to carve out the additional time to do this work. It did not matter who had sent the memo. In the latter years of his working life at the agency, he contracted an unpleasant tropical disease but this didn't alter his way of working. In many other ways he could be quite the bureaucrat, but he certainly knew how to give meaning to his staff. He was also a fine orator. He knew that he could preach, and preach well, because he spoke about the things that mattered to him. And because they mattered to him, they mattered to those who followed him. Even those who didn't particularly like him personally admired him and thus followed him. He was authentic as a person and as a leader.[37]

The importance of generating meaning is that it can only really be achieved through a high degree of reciprocity. Reciprocity requires the led to tell the leader what things will create meaning for them. To do this requires the leader to encourage, and be happy with, mechanisms of voice whether through trade unions or other forms of collective expression. Leaders need to be comfortable dealing with and discussing issues with such bodies. Too often they are not, delegating discussions to the HR chief, or in former times, the industrial relations specialist. This is a disastrous way to encourage reciprocity. It creates an unnecessary distance between the leader and the led and is disrespectful of the very institutions established to help create better work for all.

Leaders are also responsible for setting tone. People usually want to be excited by the people who lead them. After all it is the leader's job to raise standards, encourage others to perform at a higher level and give greater discretionary effort. The root of such excitement is always values and the leader's personal commitment to those values and vision. Think of The Body Shop, Microsoft, Rolls-Royce, Apple and many others and you will know something about the leaders who founded them and why. These leaders infect everyone else – workforce, customers, shareholders – with a heightened sense of excitement and a heightened sense of the possible. If you have been fortunate enough to work with someone like this then you will know exactly what I mean. They are a source of energy rather than a drain on energy. They ask what's next rather than complain that something hasn't been done. They are full of possibilities rather than doubts. Such people are rare. If you have had the good fortune to work for them, or are working for them, enjoy it.

Nor are they necessarily loud extroverts; but they will all have a presence. I witnessed a CEO of a major education provider interacting with his global sales-force at an important event where he was announcing significant change. He had put in a lot of effort for the day. But what was most impressive was the energy he gave to the 100-plus people in the room. He wasn't raging or preaching, just speaking with a conviction that was utterly authentic.

People also need to belong. It is hardwired into us through our evolution from apes to human beings.[38] The loner, so beloved of Hollywood films, is actually a sick sociopath best avoided. Leaders must make people feel they belong. There are two sides to belonging in organizations – sociability and solidarity. Sociability describes affective relationships between people. It describes shared values and a sense of friendship held on equal terms. Solidarity describes task-focused cooperation between people. People do not need to be friends to exhibit solidarity since it comes from a shared interest. It is the necessary building block for team working for example.[39]

Highly sociable organizations tend to be more enjoyable places to work and have higher scores for innovation. People enjoy working in highly sociable organizations. They form friendships and trust each other more. Creativity is high, enthusiasm is strong, people pull for each other more. The downside is that they can become very clubby. Poor performance by 'friends' is tolerated. Cliques form and diversity suffers. For leaders this can create enormous obstacles to change.

Solidarity too can clearly benefit organizations but it has its own set of problems. The benefits solidarity brings are focus and the ability to rapidly mobilize people to achieve a given goal. The British Army operates like this with its highly refined *esprit de corps*. It is what makes it arguably the best professional army in the world. But in conforming, as solidarity encourages people to do, bad goals as well as good goals can be set and strived for. Organizations with high levels of solidarity are contemptuous of dissent and do not want people to question the path taken, even when it can lead to disaster. The Charge of the Light Brigade comes to mind. Leaders remain unquestioned and the organization dissolves into factions, each fighting their own corners. Turf wars abound.

The New Labour governments of Tony Blair and Gordon Brown have expended considerable effort and energy in trying to establish a more joined up approach to the business of government by getting Whitehall ministries to work more closely together. This has had partial success with ministries offering joint announcements and working on joint initiatives such as the emerging work on worklessness and skills. However, one thing remains. All the other departments fear and dislike the Treasury. Indeed, it is still the case that many government departments remain in too many silos bounded by their own forms of solidarity.

Goffee and Jones in their work describe four types of culture – networked, communal, fragmented and mercenary – which exhibit different levels of sociability and solidarity.[40] The type that seems to have the best mix of sociability and solidarity is communal with high levels of both. Companies such as Apple and Ben & Jerry's exhibit these characteristics. Leaders act as part of these cultures. Indeed some leaders create such cultures. Within one organization there will be different sub-cultures. I cannot think of a single organization where that is not the case. The leader's task is to navigate these cultures. They do so by being authentic but also by being able to conform to the culture just enough to get things done.

A good work leader coming into an organization that is a long way from where he or she wants it to be does not blunder in and say 'everything is wrong, we are going to change everything overnight'. A process needs to be established to move the organization to the sort of mix of sociability and solidarity that will work best with the people available and the vision of the organization. In a non-hierarchical world, leaders who fail to learn this critical lesson will usually be rejected and ejected by their workforces.

The alternative risk is that the leader conforms too much and goes native. By doing this, they will stifle their ability to change things and the organization could quickly become rudderless.

To conclude: in order to become a good work leader I have argued that being authentic is the core attribute. It is important that you are surrounded by people who will support you but also are strong enough to question you. You will be able to communicate and move people as well as instruct and tell people. You need to understand the cultures and adapt to them in order to sustain trust and authenticity. You should be seeking a dominant culture that balances sociability with solidarity. You must challenge and excite the led in a continuous way.

All of this is not easy to achieve, but achieve it you must in order for good work to flourish.

There are not many people for whom leadership is a natural calling. Most people require experience to build the necessary base from which to become a leader. Leadership is not merely a trait but an expression of values, vision and experience. It is also mundane. It is about setting an example. It is about keeping on doing the right thing even when you feel like taking some time out or doing something entirely different. You need to be able to read contexts, manage the relationships between the leader and the led, reveal enough of yourself to inspire trust, be able to conform when required, and manage the external agenda and external relationships with skill and élan. You need to welcome the voices of others, and not just those close to you, into your decision making. You must be courageous in ways you haven't thought of. For example, it is often the case that people have shelf-lives in organizations. Whatever is done they cannot rouse their enthusiasm any longer. Often these are people you may have come to rely on in all sorts of ways, but it is your task as a leader to help them move on. Perhaps most importantly it is your task to keep the vision burning brightly. For good work will always require a great vision to inspire it.

Notes

1   Knell, J. and Reeves, R. (2009) *The 80 Minute MBA*, Headline Publishing Group, London.
2   Oberlechner, T. and Mayer-Schoenberger, V. (2002) *Through Their Own Words, Towards a New Understanding of Leadership Through Metaphors*, John F. Kennedy School of Government Faculty Research Working Paper Series, Harvard University, Cambridge, MA.
3   www.boeing.com
4   Mintzberg, H. and Gosling, J. (2003) 'The five minds of a manager', in *Harvard Business Review*, November.
5   Alinsky, S. (1989) *Rules for Radicals*, Knopf Doubleday, New York.
6   Katzenbach, J. and Smith, D. (1993) *The Wisdom of Teams: Creating the High Performance Organisation*, Harvard Business School Press, Boston, MA.
7   Northouse, P. G. (2004) *Leadership: Theory and Practice*, 3rd edn, Sage Publications, London.

8   Bolden, R. (2004) *What is Leadership?*, Centre for Leadership Studies Research Report, Exeter.

9   Collins, J. and Porras, J. (1994) *Built to Last: Successful Habits of Visionary Companies*, Random House, London, p23.

10 Keep, E. and Westwood, A. (2003) *Can the UK Learn to Manage?*, The Work Foundation, London.

11 See Beevor, A. (1998) *Stalingrad*, Allen Lane, London.

12 See Beevor, A. (2008) *D-Day: The Battle for Normandy*, Allen Lane, London.

13 'Leadership literature review 2003–2006 ground data', unpublished paper, The Work Foundation, London.

14 Porter, M. et al (2003) *Competitiveness: Moving to the Next Stage*, Department for Business Innovation and Skills (formerly DTI) and Economic and Social Research Council, London.

15 According to OECD data.

16 Keep, E. and Westwood, A. (2003) *Can the UK Learn to Manage?*, The Work Foundation, London.

17 www.statistics.gov.uk/hub/index.html

18 See: Haynes, P. and Allen, M. (2001) 'Partnership as union strategy: A preliminary evaluation', in *Employee Relations*, 23(2), pp164–193.

19 See: *Framework for Company Law in Europe*, European Commission, 4 November 2002.

20 Gemmill, G. and Oakley, J. (1992) 'Leadership: An alienating social myth?', in *Human Relations*, 45(2) reproduced in Grint K. (1997) *Leadership: Classical, Contemporary and Critical Approaches*, Oxford University Press, Oxford.

21 See: www.timesonline.co.uk/tol/news/politics/the_blair_years/article2886547.ece

22 Bolden, R. (2004) *What is Leadership?*, Centre for Leadership Studies Research Report, Exeter.

23 Kets de Vries, M. (2004) 'Organisations on the couch: A clinical perspective on organisational dynamics', in *European Management Journal*, 22(2) and Maccoby, M. (2000) 'Narcissistic leaders: The incredible pros, the inevitable cons', in *Harvard Business Review*, 78(1).

24 www.guardian.co.uk/politics/2003/sep/26/uk.libdems20032

25 Castells, M. (2000 and after) *The Rise of the Network Society: The Information Age*, John Wiley, New York.

26 Hutton, W. (2004) 'Old wine in new bottles – why leadership has never mattered more', article for The Work Foundation Leadership Week 2004.

27 See: www.frankfuredi.com/articles/unreason-20051118.shtml

28 Think of how today's public view institutions such as Parliament, the Police, bankers, journalists, etc.

29 Smith, E. and Reeves, R. (2006) *Papering Over the Cracks, Rules, Regulations and Real Trust*, The Work Foundation, London.

30 Bolden, R. and Gosling, J. (2003) *Leadership, Society and the Next Ten Years*, Report for the Windsor Leadership Trust, Centre for Leadership Studies, University of Exeter, July.

31 Jenkins, R. (2001) *Churchill: A Biography*, Farrar, Straus and Giroux, New York.

32 Smith, E. and Reeves, R. (2006) *Papering Over the Cracks, Rules, Regulations and Real Trust*, The Work Foundation, London.

33 Ciulla, J. B. (ed) (1998) *Ethics: The Heart of Leadership*, Quorum, Westport, CT.

34 Goffee, R. and Jones, G. (2006) *Why Should Anyone be Led by You?*, Harvard Business Press, Cambridge, MA, pp18–19.

35 As described by Goffee, R. and Jones, G. (2006) *Why Should Anyone be Led by You?*, Harvard Business Press, Cambridge, MA, p21.

36 Goffee, R. and Jones, J. (2006) *Why Should Anyone be Led by You?*, Harvard Business Press, Cambridge, MA, p193.

37 The director was Michael Taylor who led Christian Aid from 1985–1998.

38 See http://forewordcommunications.wordpress.com/living-in-a-global-world/biological-altruism-are-we-hard-wired-to-behave-in-a-socially-caring-manner-or-to-maximize-personal-gain/

39 See the works of Emile Durkheim, Karl Marx, Georg Simmel and Max Weber for example.

40 Goffee, R. and Jones, G. (2006) *Why Should Anyone be Led by You?*, Harvard Business Press, Cambridge, MA, pp112–117.

Chapter 7

The 10 Steps to Good Work

Good work is an ideal. It is a set of concepts, approaches and practices developed from enlightenment thinking and the principles that underpin functioning citizenship and applied to the workplace. It takes a holistic view of work, performance and effectiveness and puts the individual and the group at its heart. It draws on the recent insights from behavioural economics, from psychology and sociology. In application it will always be situation specific and contextual. Most of the elements that support good work operate at the level of the intangible and require institutional expression to enable fulfilment. Good work operates at a systemic level. It cannot act as a sticking plaster to alleviate problems in product, price or place. It is a way of thinking about, and acting upon, the world that will lead to better outcomes for all involved in an enterprise.

Perhaps most of all, good work can never be a solution to a poor firm selling the wrong things to the wrong people. If the basic idea is dud, then no matter how well you organize, motivate and deliver ownership to your human capital, the organization is likely to fail. This is not to say that a good work environment won't enable better processes of innovation to occur. It will. Indeed, helping to increase innovation and increase the release of so-called discretionary effort may well help any organization move from being out-competed to finding a new market with new products.

In short, good work is often a set of contingent strategies and practices that necessarily support the organization's overall goals, business operations and markets. As Massachusetts Institute of Technology (MIT) professor of political science, Susan Berger's work has shown there are a myriad different ways in which firms can operate and choose to compete in a globalized world economy. Berger's 5-year study into the way 500-plus firms were coping with globalization, in what she describes as both fast-tech sectors such as electronics, and slow-tech sectors such as textiles, included more than 700 interviews with corporate leaders.[1] In all those interviews, nobody could have been said to have described their competitive strategies as being based on a 'good work' approach, focused on job quality. This may well have been a mistake, but the research made clear that the way companies approached the question was more to ask what were the capabilities required of any individual to do well in a world of disaggregated production? Who has the coordination capabilities in a disaggregated production chain?

Berger felt that it was a particular set of skills that companies were looking for. Skills that would enable key individuals to coordinate the functions of these often disaggregated supply chains. In a world where brands have more power than manufactured goods, coordination power will be a locus of control over other parts of the system and will provide the best examples of good work. The really satisfying jobs are the ones that have coordination at the heart of their role. These jobs would combine for the individual greater levels of ownership including task, time and place sovereignty. Rather than just needing to coordinate matters inside a single company, individuals need to be able to coordinate activity across many different companies – all part of the same supply chain – and, as importantly, across different cultures.[2]

However, in terms of production process, her conclusions are very clear. There is no single approach. In both types of business – fast- and slow-tech – different companies adopted different approaches to the manufacturing process. Where new phone models, for example, come out every six months it has made more sense for some companies to locate the production facility next door to the development facility. For others it has been about the cheapest labour supply. The most important part of intrinsic job quality in her studies has illustrated the importance of being in control.

Thomas Kochan, the George M. Bunker professor of management, again from MIT, believes that good work requires a lot more policy leverage and that that leverage lies in global supply chains. He argues that what happens is that companies very willingly and earnestly set out to improve terms and conditions but on the way usually hit a plateau where work practices settle around an often lowish median. Pressure on the government to continue to improve standards and processes is required to get those organizations to continue to improve and the leverage is in the supply chain.[3]

Howard Gardner, John H. and Elizabeth A. Hobbs professor of cognition and education, and his team at Harvard focuses on the ethical side of good work, which he defines as having three characteristics – excellence, engagement and ethics. He described to me three different deprived communities in Los Angeles, Detroit and the Heartlands. He argued that each of these systems has a 'lack'. The first area lacks ethics, the second an approach to excellence and the third lacks engagement.

He believes that good work is a bottom-up phenomenon but that the market makes professionals cut corners. He feels that alignment of values with the values of the organization is the most important element of good work.[4]

What these researchers and their work show is that good work has many facets and that those facets in great organizations interlock and complement each other. The strategic fit is tight.

So how does any organization and any operational manager start the process of establishing a good work environment in their workplace? What are the steps to good work? To make things more easily digestible, I have set out the 10 key steps to building and establishing a good work culture in any organization. Each step locks with the other to make a coherent whole. No one element on its own will deliver the desired results.

Step 1: Find your vision

Every good work organization requires a good vision. People who dismiss vision as a distraction are themselves distracted. As Collins and Porras discovered in researching their work among visionary companies, they were recommended as visionary companies by the Fortune 500 CEOs they asked for their opinions because they had strong visions.[5] If you already have a vision in your organization, that's great. Test it to see if it still has the same impact on employees, management and customers. Ask these stakeholders if they believe you when you tell them the vision is the organization's reason to be. The vision is the organization's DNA written down. Only visions that are true will work. From visions flow the values that underpin them. And values need to be lived to have any meaning. Leaders must walk the talk of the values they claim to adhere to. Charlatans and shamans will be found out.

Here is an example. One small UK charity working with the hardest-to-help long-term unemployed was growing and developing fast. The staff were led by an inspirational CEO who found it hard to delegate authority because she cared too much to risk anything going wrong. Her way of working needed to change as did that of her top team. In fact, the top team did not recognize they were a top team. They saw themselves as individual project managers. Instead of simply redescribing everyone's job profiles and saying get on with it, the CEO recognized she needed a different process to engage them and move the organization forward. She asked a consultant for help and that consultant suggested starting with developing a vision and values for the organization. The process would start with the top team whose members would then delegate some of their number to repeat the process with the rest of the staff. Maybe not surprisingly, given the work the organization did, they already had a vision. They just hadn't articulated it to each other or the wider world. There was also an astonishing degree of agreement among everyone involved in the enterprise about the values that underpinned the organization and by which they worked. The process of describing their vision and values unlocked hidden potential and made explicit the promise these people made to each other every day they went to work.

Vision and values matter. Ethics underpin all that we do as human beings. Expressing the values that drive you to do what you do allows people to articulate their inner motivations. You don't have to be engaged in explicitly ethical work (work such as healthcare or charitable activities, for example) to believe in the ethics of what you are doing. Even people who work for tobacco companies or oil companies have at some level an ethical dimension to what they do. For the employee of Rothmans it may be a feeling that they are producing a product that allows people to relax and choose their own way of living their lives. Smoking their product makes people feel better about themselves. For the employees of Shell they are providing energy that fuels growth and also developing new technologies that will be carbon neutral. Visions move people to act.

Step 2: Don't change what isn't broken

Organizational leaders love change. When a new CEO, department head, or even section leader starts their new job they want to make their mark upon the world. This is natural. After all, they usually haven't been appointed because everything was fine and dandy. Often they are replacing a person whose time was up or who has moved onto higher and better things. The key point is that it is human nature to want to prove oneself in any role. People want to do well, impress their boss and release their potential. There will always be one or two individuals in any group who do not conform to this view, but those individuals should not be allowed to corrupt the culture of the group or organization.

Given that a degree of change is inevitable, it is important that what you change actually does need changing. This requires an audit of people and processes. There are a number of tools on the market that are designed to help organizational decision makers improve their operations and businesses. Six Sigma is one such tool and worth looking at in more detail.

It offers a data-driven applied methodology for improving business and organizational performance. It utilizes a specific problem-solving approach and Six Sigma tools to improve processes and products. The point is to reduce unacceptable mistakes, because every mistake an organization makes ultimately incurs a cost. Indeed, on some estimates, mistakes cost organizations as much as 20–30 per cent of their potential bottom line.

So Six Sigma focuses on two levels, managerial and technical. At a managerial level, a Six Sigma initiative includes the people, technologies, projects and schedules being managed and coordinated. And for the technical elements of Six Sigma to be effective, management orientation is also examined. The approach looks at:

- customer satisfaction;
- work processes;
- profitability;

- speed;
- efficiency.

The first step in calculating the Six Sigma or understanding its significance is to grasp what customers expect. The customer requirements or expectations are called CTQs (critical to quality).

To better explain the calculation of the Six Sigma, let's consider an example of a pizza business. We could define the four CTQs of the business as: hot, correct ingredients, on-time delivery and undamaged. We would collect that data on, say, 500 deliveries and let's say we find that: 10 were cold, 16 had wrong ingredients, 25 were late and seven were damaged. To calculate Six Sigma, we take the total defects divided by the total number of deliveries multiplied by the number of defect opportunities (number of CTQs):

10 + 16 + 25 + 7 / 500 x 4 = 58 / 2000 = 0.029 (defect per opportunity [DPO])

Usually this is expressed as a count in a million opportunities so that would be 29,000 DPOs. That is quite a cost to the pizza business.[6]

For the Six Sigma process to be implemented, a team has to be trained and roles assigned to each member of the team. All the team members work closely together. However, each one has a specific role and task to deliver. Generally, the Six Sigma team is constituted of different hierarchical levels and sometimes martial arts grades are used when referring to these, e.g. project team members could be referred to as Yellow Belt, Green Belt, Black Belt, Master Black Belt, etc. There is also an implementation leader.[7]

A good case study is that of General Electric (GE). GE first began using Six Sigma in 1995. In 1996, Six Sigma cost GE US$200 million with a return on investment (ROI) of US$150 million. The following year it cost it US$400 million with returns of US$600 million. And then in 1998 it hit the jackpot; the programme cost US$400 million with returns of more than US$1 billion. GE went on to estimated benefits in the order of US$10 billion during the first 5 years of Six Sigma implementation.

This all sounds very impressive but so was 'total quality management' when it was introduced in the 1980s.[8] The problem with all such approaches is that they offer a silver bullet approach to efficiency. Moreover, it may well be that the disruption caused by implementing the changes uncovered by these approaches causes more hidden costs and more damage to morale.

So audit is important, but it should focus on three things: the people, the customers, the products and, as well as the obvious metrics, look at the sometimes hidden value-adding areas (see Post Office story below). Too often organizations become obsessed with the customer and not much else in developing their audit tools – 'Let's see what the customer thinks first and last'. But customers are but one group of stakeholders. They may respond telling you what they think now but too often their future intentions are not fully examined and the data do not capture the intangible networks of reciprocity between employee and customer that often exist and which are easily disrupted.

So a good work audit would examine culture, systems, customers and people. It would seek to see how embedded were the principles of fairness and ownership in the organization and how they flowed through to customers and other stakeholders. Be rigorous in the approach but use qualitative mechanisms as much as quantitative ones. Approaches such as Six Sigma can miss as much as they find. So when tempted to change things, always, always at first listen more than you act.

Step 3: Find your voice

If you have collective voice mechanisms such as a trade union or works council in your workplace that is a good first step. Review how this is working. Are the mechanisms truly collective or do a large number of people shun them? If so, would something (but not union derecognition) else be required? Or is it simply a case of enabling the mechanism to do a better job of getting people to engage? All of these questions need to be answered because the collective is as important as the unitarist in a good work organization, as David Coats has eloquently argued in his writing.[9]

If on the other hand no such mechanisms exist then you will need to implement them. To do so requires a process of consultation between official bodies such as a trade union and stakeholders, such as management, and staff. Each environment is unique. The institution needs to fit the culture. Of course, such processes can be time-consuming and sometimes costly but they should not be ignored. The mechanisms set up must not be tokenistic. They need to be able to punch their weight and in their deliberations add a genuine contribution to the objectives and strategies of the organization. Voice without any power is tokenism.

An additional option would be to put a representative, or representatives, from the voice institution on the main board as part of the governance arrangements for the organization. Those companies that have stakeholder boards tend to make better long-term decisions because there is a balance of interests around the board table.

Much of the management literature describes stakeholder boards in either over-affirmative or overly negative terms. The point is that a better-balanced board means more voice for the different stakeholders, a genuine commitment to more shared ownership and better business outcomes. Adding extra stakeholders increases the range of interests by adding employee or community interests to the financial interests of shareholders and business interests of managers. New perspectives on the business or organization are thus added. Nor should all stakeholder board representatives be the same – individual differences matter.

Of course, many senior managers are wary of stakeholder boards not just because it means, to a certain extent, the dilution of power from shareholders and managers but also because non-business educated board members are felt not to be capable of making tough business decisions. Companies like Citigroup give management training in the local communities in which they work. Such expertise could be used in the boardroom as well. The UK Institute of Directors offers many types of board-level training programmes. Neither option is very expensive.[10]

To go about designing a stakeholder board, the starting point would be for the company to clearly define the importance of shareholder interests in its profits, decide on a number of stakeholder members, conduct triage based on particular individuals' strengths and weaknesses, and then make sure everyone signs up to the same high standards of performance and governance. This will not lead to employee representatives 'going native' as some more adversarially minded trade unionists may argue. It means aligning everyone's interests in the same direction and then going for it.

To illustrate the potential advantages of stakeholder boards consider this story of corporate failure. A wholesale distribution company working in fast-moving consumer goods (FMCG) and supplying to big retailers such as Tesco and Asda went bust – a victim of the credit crunch. The loans it had acquired to expand quickly and build its own warehouse capability came due for renegotiation. The banks would not lend it any more money or extend the terms of its loan agreements. Its principal suppliers would not extend credit terms. More than 100 people lost their jobs and the company owners lost a lot of their personal wealth. Now it might not have made a difference, but given that there was considerable concern from members of the senior management team and other staff about the lack of 'speed limits' being imposed by the owners of the company on the expansion plans, and the degree of leverage the company was exposed to, a stakeholder board might just have counselled more caution. It is just possible that that company would still be a going concern if the hunger for growth of the owners had been tempered by the knowledge, insight and wisdom of other stakeholders, drawn from the ranks of their own top team.

Step 4: To own or not to own – give employees a stake

Give employees a share in the enterprise. If they do not have shares then set up a trust to hold shares for the employees along the lines discussed for John Lewis in Chapter 5. The Employee Ownership Association website www.employeeownership.co.uk has all the information required. If giving people a financial stake is not possible (which it cannot be for voluntary and public sector organizations) then look at your remuneration and reward strategy. Ask yourself the following six questions:

- How does my reward strategy align with my business strategy?
- How does my reward strategy promote fairness?
- How does my reward strategy reward effort?
- How does my reward strategy promote effectiveness?
- How is my reward strategy performance managed?
- How well does my reward strategy motivate employees?

When you have considered your responses, do not then go out and place all your eggs in the performance pay basket. As the evidence argued above shows, performance-related pay for individuals may motivate some but demotivate others. It requires godlike objectivity from hard-pressed and highly subjective managers and above all it too often acts as a distortion to fairness.

Keep any system of pay simple and make the processes of annual adjustments (or not) and pay progression transparent. Performance metrics need to be as objective as possible and include both hard, technical measures and so-called softer behavioural measures. How someone does their job is usually as important as what skills they bring to doing their job.

Recognize that teams matter. People are collective animals. Team rewards therefore are more important than individual rewards. Repressing the selfish gene will help pay and reward function better in most organizations.

Remember that innovation comes from the processes of interaction between individuals and ideas that require mutual reciprocity and respect. High levels of bonding social capital are required to get people working together well.[11] Make sure the reward system does not militate against that objective.

Make sure that any performance pay is based on the hardest of objectives such as an increase in profits, performance targets being met and customer satisfaction ratings going up. Use bonuses that do not consolidate performance pay into increased base levels for salary. This can lead to the incremental creep upwards of pay differentials, or create new differentials. Make performance pay proportional and group based. Nobody achieves anything on their own – even when they think they do. We all stand on the shoulders of giants to achieve our successes.[12] Even doing something as solitary as writing a book cannot be achieved without the support of many people – those who have gone before you and have done research that you draw on, or support the writing process such as your editor, or support the angst-ridden author through the creative process, such as friends and family.

Think of non-pecuniary measures as part of the reward process. Create a menu of options from which people can choose. Increasingly, people want their employer to develop them beyond just the narrow skills required for their specific job at this moment in time. Helping with that broader development could be part of your reward strategy.

Finally, look at the differentials you have in the organization; make them fair. What sort of message does it send to everyone else if the team at the top are paid 80 times more than those on average earnings? It creates an ocean of space between them. It says, 'Here are the heroes leading the average.' It demonstrates a gulf in equity that destroys any attempt to create shared optimism about the future. Why not convert some of that reward into long-term stakes in the business? Often myths perpetuate about why someone should be paid as much as they are. Highly intelligent, motivated and ambitious people are always very good at using arguments to support high levels of personal greed. The higher the flyer, the more narcissistic and self-absorbed they tend to be. All organizations operate in markets and those markets do indeed create arguments for and against relative levels of pay. Rare skill sets will attract a high pay premium. Not everyone can be a Jonny Wilkinson, Cristiano Ronaldo or Roger Federer; but place the pay at the top within an overall structure. Top football clubs do this (Manchester United does not pay its stars as much as Manchester City or Real Madrid for example); rugby clubs in England operate a salary cap and many organizations have similar mechanisms in place too.

In my previous writings, I have described the way top pay in the private sector in the US and UK has become distorted with those who run the top companies taking a larger and larger share of the profit compared with previous eras. These reward strategies are based on false arguments about the market for top talent now being truly international (it isn't), bearing more risk (they don't) and the people being more talented (they may be, but it may also be the case that they are more ruthless, dedicated, self-obsessed and lucky).[13] Buck the market and do what is right for your organization. By doing so you will build the type of organization that reflects the values and vision you own. But be proportional. It is always good to be a pathfinder but often it comes at great personal and professional cost.

Step 5: Release the craftsman

People go to work to earn a living, express themselves and act upon the world. They generally want to do well. Human beings respond to praise usually better than criticism. The Royal Mail in the UK decided to do something to speed up deliveries. It introduced a new computer system called Pegasus that worked out the postman or woman's best route for their round and set a time limit for that round (usually to deliver to around 400 or 500 addresses in a 3.5 hour timeslot). To achieve this result requires an average speed of around 4 miles an hour. This would mean going at quite a pace especially carrying a bag filled with paper. The trade unions were up in arms.[14] Apart from claims by the trade unions that most of the country's 66,500 rounds could not be negotiated physically that quickly, the management of the Royal Mail had also forgotten to factor in one very important element in their thinking. Did it matter how quickly the average postman delivered the post to the average receiver of that post? On a very surface level probably most people's immediate response would be that they would like to receive their post as quickly as possible. But on another level for many people it would not. For postmen and women are quite unique deliverers of not just a service but also of public value.[15] They are one of the very few groups of people who visit houses each day. They may strike up relationships with the owners of those houses. Some people may look forward to seeing their postman each day. It may be that some of the *customers* actually slow down the postman on his or her round by talking to them.

The management of the Royal Mail had not programmed that into their computer. The very people they were trying to deliver a better service to, were also the people who would undermine their attempts to do so. The value the good postman delivers is more than just letters through doors. He or she is a community figure. Releasing postmen's and women's ability to do that part of their job is part of the Post Office delivering to their customers.

Or examine call centres. The London School of Economics has done considerable research into what makes call centres good, bad or indifferent.[16] The good ones deliver huge amounts of training and discretion to their staff. Moreover, they see the workforce as an investment, not a cost to be minimized. The huge flood of call centre jobs to India has yet to materialize.[17] The reason being that people want people like themselves to speak to when calling for help, advice or to buy something. The call centre worker who actually likes talking to people and has the discretion to decide how she or he does so, will use their inner abilities to deliver a good job. The smarter organizations have realized this and are making a virtue of it in their advertising.[18]

Craft underpins innovation and creativity. And without these outputs, nothing improves. Moreover, letting people identify with their achievements is critical. Patents are the most obvious expression of innovation but daily, innovative acts go un-noticed and unrecognized. Start recognizing them. Recognize the green team who help improve recycling; praise the office administrator who improves the booking system for business travel and accommodation; hail the receptionist who welcomes people to the office with a smile; give time to the slightly autistic maverick who can't conform but is capable of the most beautiful work; develop the promising young intern and ask her to come back when she has finished her course. And do get some coaching for yourself. It isn't an indulgence unless you treat it as such.

Step 6: Time to work

I discussed time sovereignty in some detail in Chapters 4 and 5. Time sovereignty is enabling people to choose as far as is practicable when they work. The next generation of digital and mobile technology will enable faster, easier access to shared knowledge and communication systems. Work and life are becoming, and will become, far more integrated. When people work should increasingly be more up to them and less up to you. What matters is what they produce, not when they produce it. Create a menu of flexible working options and allow people to choose what works best for them. Clearly most organizations because of geography, sector and type of work will require limits to flexibility for some, or all, of their staff. A night security guard has to guard something at night. They need to be physically present and at a specific time. If this doesn't appeal don't choose to do that type of work.

By creating more time sovereignty you will create overall increases in productivity. Just ask senior managers at BT, Yorkshire Water, Lloyds TSB and elsewhere. Make people time-lords and they will repay you with productivity and performance. If you do not believe me, try this little experiment. Take your team and ask them to complete a set of tasks that will prove difficult to complete in a single working day of 8 hours. Split the team in two and get half to do the tasks when they want during that 24-hour period, but tell them they must only work for a maximum of 8 hours. Ask the other half to do the tasks between 9am and 5pm. Then measure the difference in productivity and output between the two groups.

Beware presenteeism. It is still the case that most managers measure output by the input of time. Just because someone is sitting there in front of you seeming to work does not mean either that they are or that it is very productive work. There is logic to this. The longer you spend on a skill or task the better you usually become at that skill or task and the more work you can get through.[19] But in a knowledge economy where quality is even more important than quantity, high productivity per hour worked is what is required. Help people to work smarter rather than just longer. Some people like to work long hours. It makes them feel valued and needed. Let them. Just don't pander to the tendency by judging everyone else's efforts in a negative light. The best workers are those who know when to work to maximum effect.

The types of flexible working arrangements can be up to you. They can range from work anytime you like, to start and finish times being flexible. They may include self-managed teams deciding on shift patterns in a collective manner. They may also mean splitting jobs up into different time patterns. There could be more part-time jobs, or term-time working for parents or project-based working with time off at completion of a given project. Unpaid leave may be utilized as part of the offer alongside paid vacations. Whatever the mix of options, the combination of choices should be aimed at freeing up as much time sovereignty as possible for each and every worker.

Step 7: Enabling craft and task

Task sovereignty is one of the three sovereignties that help create ownership and it is ownership that is the essential ingredient that enables good work to flourish. US academic Mihaly Csíkszentmihályi (pronounced chick-sent-mi-hi) describes how, when people are utterly immersed in an act such that they can block out all other stimuli and concentrate on the task at hand, they are in a state of flow. Flow is the state where the best work is done, when people are so absorbed that they innovate, create, write, process and do tasks to their highest ability.[20]

Csíkszentmihályi identified the following nine factors that can stimulate flow:

- clear goals;
- concentrating and focusing all of the time not just some of the time;
- a loss of the feeling of self-consciousness;
- distorted sense of time – as in time flies by when in such a state;
- direct and immediate feedback;

- balance between ability level and challenge;
- a sense of personal control over the situation or activity;
- the activity is intrinsically rewarding;
- people become absorbed in their activity, and focus of awareness is narrowed down to the activity itself, action awareness merges.

Csíkszentmihályi also had some suggestions for how groups could achieve flow:

- creative spatial arrangements so that work is done standing and moving;
- organize a playground design;
- parallel, organized working;
- target group focus;
- advancement of existing one (prototyping);
- increase in efficiency through visualization;
- existence of differences among participants represents an opportunity, rather than an obstacle.

The point about flow is that it is the state that most employers will want their employees to be in most of the time. A state of flow will usually lead to the best work being done whatever field of work you are in. However, as Csíkszentmihályi's criteria illustrate, this requires levels of skills and experience that stretch and develop each and every worker.

By conducting a skills audit of the workforce and developing some scenario-mapping of future business opportunities and market opportunities, it should prove possible to develop a future skills plan for each and every worker. This will allow development spend to be budgeted for each employee, in consultation with others, and provide each employee with the skills they require to maximize flow when it occurs. Other areas to consider are the physical working environment and whether that requires attention, ways of group working, and where and how people sit together or apart. Office and workplace design take on a new dimension when considering how to equip employees with task sovereignty. Complement organizational investment in skills with any government grants (such as the Train to Gain allowances in the UK) that may be available, and encourage individuals to invest in a learning fund from which they can draw for investment in their own development that potentially the employer can match, up to a given limit.[21]

It is still the case, as government report after government report has recorded, that too many workers do not have the skills required to do great work.[22] Without a more highly skilled workforce, productivity will not go up. Supply-side measures have got us so far, but it is the demand-side from individuals and employers that will deliver the big gains in performance and productivity that countries and organizations require. So, in the words of one of my former colleagues, 'Don't skill them softly, train them hard.'

Step 8: Places to work

Invest in enabling each worker to work where they work best for any given task. Freedom is as necessary for human expression as food and water. Freeing people to make their own decisions about how they work and where they work, wherever feasible, will reap a triple dividend of more output, greater intrinsic job satisfaction and higher overall levels of well-being.

For most organizations this will mean equipping people with digital tools such as mobile phones and Skype-enabled laptop computers. It may mean helping to equip an office at home. It may mean setting up drop-in centres in which colleagues can gather, or organizing awaydays for specific group planning or engagement activities. It may mean being more generous with travel allowances so that individuals can actually complete tasks while they travel, rather than resemble a cow in an over-crowded cattle truck. Indeed, a hot summer's day on a rush hour train on one of London's busier underground lines would be deemed too cruel an environment in which to transport livestock.

Think carefully about where to site the new corporate headquarters. Make it accessible for current workers where possible or look to recruit people locally as the major retailers do when siting new stores in urban areas. Part of the drive to be green involves better designed and thought-through home/work accommodation in city centres. Encouraging people to commute is not a very sensible option. Commuting saps the will and weakens the ability to give of one's best at work. Just ask most commuters. Hell is a crowded commuter train, delayed by signal failure somewhere outside Clapham Junction station in south London.

Step 9: Be authentic

As I described in Chapter 6, you can only be you. You can't be George Clooney even if some foolish ex-girlfriend flattered you by saying you looked like him. And if you are female you can't be Penelope Cruz, even if you can speak some Spanish. GE's Jack Welch was unique as was Walmart's Lee Scott and all the other great CEOs of academic and popular acclaim. To lead in a good work organization you need to offer an authentic version of yourself that builds on your strengths and is open and honest about your weaknesses. If you are not very good at process management, then make sure someone else on the team is. If you are not that creative, find people to work with who are. Be honest and open enough of the time to be trusted. You cannot be everyone's friend, so do not try. Reciprocate, praise and encourage more than you take, criticize and blame. When a mistake happens, blame yourself first for not having established good enough systems of control and audit. Support people and understand them as a whole person and not just as an engineer, draughtsman, plasterer, brickie, analyst or whatever other label work gives them. Treat people as fully human, not as a function of production.

Communicate all the time, not some of the time. Answer emails promptly, even if you have nothing concrete yet to tell people because you have not made any material decision on the subject matter under discussion. Being courteous is not a failing. Make yourself available enough of the time to appear not remote, but do not be afraid to stop people approaching you if you need to be alone for a given business reason. Understand you are part of a team. Indeed, you are probably part of many teams.

Invest in your own development, and work continuously on improving your skills, especially the skills that have made you a leader in the first place. As Malcolm Gladwell reports in his book, *Outliers*, research shows it takes around 10,000 hours of practice to get good at something.[23] That goes for your leadership abilities too.

Too often people think they have to focus exclusively on their weaknesses but have you ever heard anyone say, 'Hey, you know Bob, he got promoted to senior vice-president because of his poor planning abilities.' What you will have heard are comments like, 'Janice is such a great communicator' or 'Alex is very smart' or perhaps more commonly, 'Steve works so hard. He deserves that promotion, the bastard.'

Trust people and be courageous. Do not judge everyone by the one or two poor performers that every organization seems to have. Too often, performance management systems and disciplinary procedures are designed and applied as though every member of staff is a potential criminal. Don't apply rigid start and finish times for example because someone once 'swung the lead'. Deal with the lead swinger. Their colleagues will thank you for it. Moreover, every leader must take difficult decisions from time-to-time, the most difficult being to make people compulsorily redundant. The only course of action in these circumstances is to acknowledge the painfulness of the situation and be honest about why that person's role is going.

Finally, recognize your inner narcissist and deal with him or her. Make sure you have people around you that can talk to you straight and whose opinions you value. Remember thou art mortal.

Step 10: Good work is never achieved

Good work is not a state of grace. It is an ideal to be striven for and a set of practices and behaviours to be practised and applied. Combining effectiveness, equity and voice in some kind of equilibrium is a very hard thing to do. Never be satisfied that the balance has been struck, for as soon as you do, complacency will take over and the culture will become corrupted. Apply audit tools rigorously. Staff and customer surveys can never be done too often. Feedback loops, team briefings, intranets, wikis, social networking, socializing are all necessary ways to judge the temperature and gauge how much or how little your organization is achieving good work outcomes. As soon as the scores are not rising, re-strategize and adapt. Remember complacency is the enemy of progress.

Last word

This book has said little about the wider public policy environment that will help embed good work practices more deeply, but it is vitally important to good work. Governments have four roles to play. As an employer, they can practise good work themselves. As a procurer of goods and services, they can ask their suppliers to demonstrate a commitment to good work practices in their procurement processes. And as a regulator, they can regulate for good work by, for example, demanding that companies report on their human capital management practices against a range of metrics and other non-financial reporting requirements. They can establish bodies such as a High Pay Commission to help set new norms for top pay.[24] They can offer fiscal stimuli to organizations demonstrably doing things that lead to good work like develop their employees to certificated higher levels of skill. Finally they can exhort, encourage and help tell the stories about the good practice of good work through business organizations and their devolved networks.

Good work is work for this century. A more educated, demanding, fearful and aspirational workforce wants good work. It is an answer to many of the burning existential and physical challenges of our times. Good work will help bring green work which will help lead to a better future for our children's children. Let us all make sure that we rise to the challenge and build a better working future than our parents enjoyed.

Notes

1   Berger, S. et al (2005) *How We Compete*, Currency/Doubleday, New York.
2   Interview with Susan Berger, September 2007.
3   Interview with Thomas Kochan, September 2007.
4   Interview with Howard Gardner, September 2007 and see: http://pzweb.harvard.edu/Research/GoodWork.htm
5   Collins, J. and Porras, J. (1994) *Built to Last: Successful Habits of Visionary Companies*, Random House, London.
6   www.ameinfo.com/108562.html
7   www.scribd.com/doc/16689924/What-is-Six-Sigma-by-PETE-PANDE
8   www.ameinfo.com/108562.html
9   Coats, D. (2005) *An Agenda for Work*, The Work Foundation, London.
10 Stakeholder boards: Berman, S. L., Wicks, A. C., Kotha, S. and Jones, T. M. (1999) 'Does stakeholder orientation matter? The relationship between stakeholder management models and firm financial performance', *Academy of Management Journal*, vol 42, no 5, pp488–506.

11   For a good discussion on social capital see Puttnam, R. (2000) *Bowling Alone: The Collapse and Revival of American Community*, Simon and Schuster, New York.

12   In a letter to fellow scientist Robert Hooke, dated 16 February 1676; from Isaac Newton who modestly described his findings as achieved by 'standing on the shoulders of giants'.

13   Isles, N. (2004) *Life at the Top*, The Work Foundation, London, and Isles, N. (2007) *The Risk Myth*, The Work Foundation, London.

14   www.dailymail.co.uk/news/article-1093767/The-great-postie-debate-Just-fast-postmen-walk.html

15   For a good discussion of public value see: www.theworkfoundation.com/research/publicvalue.aspx and www.nationalschool.gov.uk/news_events/stories/Mark_Moore_Interview.asp

16   Fernie, S. (2004) 'Call centre HRM and performance outcomes', in S. Deery and N. Kinnie (eds) *Call Centres and Human Resource Management: A Cross-national Perspective*, Palgrave Macmillan, Basingstoke, pp54–74.

17   See: Rudiger, K. (2007) *Offshoring a Threat to UK's Knowledge Jobs?*, The Work Foundation, London.

18   www.visit4info.com/advert/NatWest-Overseas-Call-Centres-Natwest-Personal-Accounts/41637

19   Gladwell, M. (2008) *Outliers: The Story of Success*, Little Brown and Co, New York.

20   Csíkszentmihályi, M. and Csíkszentmihályi, I. S. (eds) (1988) *Optimal Experience: Psychological Studies of Flow in Consciousness*, Cambridge University Press, New York.

21   www.traintogain.gov.uk/

22   See for example the latest report: www.hm-treasury.gov.uk/leitch_review_index.htm

23   Gladwell, M. (2008) *Outliers: The Story of Success*, Little Brown and Co, New York.

24   Isles, N. (2007) *The Risk Myth*, The Work Foundation, London.

Index

LIBRARY
NSCC, KINGST
238 BE
KENT... NS B4N 0A8 CANADA

WITHDRAWN